The Sources of Democratic Responsiveness in Mexico

RECENT TITLES FROM THE HELEN KELLOGG INSTITUTE FOR INTERNATIONAL STUDIES

Scott Mainwaring, *series editor*

The University of Notre Dame Press gratefully thanks the Helen Kellogg Institute for International Studies for its support in the publication of titles in this series.

Guillermo O'Donnell, Jorge Vargas Cullell, and Osvaldo M. Iazzetta, eds.
The Quality of Democracy: Theory and Applications (2004)

Arie M. Kacowicz
The Impact of Norms in International Society: The Latin American Experience, 1881–2001 (2005)

Roberto DaMatta and Elena Soárez
Eagles, Donkeys, and Butterflies: An Anthropological Study of Brazil's "Animal Game" (2006)

Kenneth P. Serbin
Needs of the Heart: A Social and Cultural History of Brazil's Clergy and Seminaries (2006)

Christopher Welna and Gustavo Gallón, eds.
Peace, Democracy, and Human Rights in Colombia (2007)

Guillermo O'Donnell
Dissonances: Democratic Critiques of Democracy (2007)

Marifeli Pérez-Stable, ed.
Looking Forward: Comparative Perspectives on Cuba's Transition (2007)

Jodi S. Finkel
Judicial Reform as Political Insurance: Argentina, Peru, and Mexico in the 1990s (2008)

Robert H. Wilson, Peter M. Ward, Peter K. Spink, and Victoria E. Rodríguez
Governance in the Americas: Decentralization, Democracy, and Subnational Government in Brazil, Mexico, and the USA (2008)

Brian S. McBeth
Dictatorship and Politics: Intrigue, Betrayal, and Survival in Venezuela, 1908–1935 (2008)

Pablo Policzer
The Rise and Fall of Repression in Chile (2009)

Frances Hagopian, ed.
Religious Pluralism, Democracy and the Catholic Church in Latin America (2009)

Marcelo Bergman and Laurence Whitehead, eds.
Criminality, Public Security, and the Challenge to Democracy in Latin America (2009)

For a complete list of titles from the Helen Kellogg Institute for International Studies, see http: //www.undpress.nd.edu

THE Sources OF Democratic Responsiveness IN Mexico

MATTHEW R. CLEARY

UNIVERSITY OF NOTRE DAME PRESS
NOTRE DAME, INDIANA

Notre Dame, Indiana 46556
www.undpress.nd.edu

Manufactured in the United States of America

Library of Congress Cataloging-in-Publication Data

Cleary, Matthew R.
The sources of democratic responsiveness in Mexico / Matthew R. Cleary.
p. cm. — (From the Helen Kellogg Institute for International Studies)
Includes bibliographical references and index.
ISBN-13: 978-0-268-02301-0 (pbk. : alk. paper)
ISBN-10: 0-268-02301-8 (pbk. : alk. paper)
1. Political participation—Mexico. 2. Democracy—Mexico. 3. Government accountability—Mexico. 4. Elections—Mexico. 5. Mexico—Politics and government—2000- I. Title.
JL1281.C59 2010
324.973—dc22

2010004292

∞ *The paper in this book meets the guidelines for permanence and durability of the Committee on Production Guidelines for Book Longevity of the Council on Library Resources.*

CONTENTS

PREFACE

This book is the product of my attempt to broaden my own understanding of how democracy works. I hope that it will broaden the reader's understanding too. When democracy works well, it produces outcomes—in the form of policies, services, public goods, protections, or some other output—that are beneficial to, and desired by, the citizenry. I refer to the process of generating these outcomes as *democratic responsiveness,* and my overarching goal is to discover why some governments are better at it than others. Most people who have thought about the problem at all assume that electoral contestation is the primary motor of responsiveness. Politicians care about their future electoral prospects, so subjecting them to the periodic approval of voters forces them to behave as voters would want. That is what I always believed too until I started to take a closer look at the Mexican case. I was quickly confronted with reasons to be suspicious of this electoral worldview, and eventually my skepticism led me to generate a body of evidence that contradicts electoral explanations of responsiveness at the most basic level. In short, in this book I use evidence from Mexico to call into question common assumptions about the ability of elections to generate fair democratic outcomes. This does *not* mean that Mexicans are "bad democrats" or that the country is somehow unsuited for democracy, although its institutional structure clearly does limit the effectiveness of some democratic practices. Rather, it suggests that Mexicans must be making good use of other, nonelectoral types of influence over government. I offer evidence to suggest that various types of political participation and engagement, which are equally important to democratic practice, can have the effect that is usually attributed to elections. And in spite of contradictory evidence, I leave open the enticing possibility that electoral competition and political participation work in tandem in Mexico, producing better outcomes when used together than either strategy would produce on its own. I have not been able to satisfactorily answer all of the questions that I have posed. But I do believe that I have demonstrated the utility of thinking more broadly about the sources of democratic responsiveness in Mexico and beyond.

From the beginning, the research culminating in this book has exhibited a tension: Is it about Mexico, or is it about institutions and democratic responsiveness? Sometimes I feel pressured to insist that the country and the theme are equally important and foundational. But the truth is that the theoretical ideas came first. At a certain point in graduate school at the University of Chicago I became interested in what I thought were some ambiguities in our ideas about democratization, electoral competition, and institutional performance. My thoughts may not have been quite ripe, but they revolved around a fascination with subnational variation in democratic transitions, democratic performance, electoral competition, and accountability. Even within countries that were comfortably labeled democratic, why were there so many regions in which government displayed authoritarian tendencies and remained unresponsive to the public interest? And why was there so much variation from one town, city, or state, to the next? Obviously this was similar to Robert Putnam's puzzle; but the types of variation that I noticed encompassed much more than institutional performance and could be observed just about anywhere one turned.

Now, I do not disavow the logic of case selection that I describe in chapter 1. But I see no harm in acknowledging what is usually kept quiet, which is that my focus on Mexico owes as much to chance and good fortune as it does to a rigorous search for an ideal and uniquely suitable case. During the years in which I was developing an interest in these puzzles and a theoretical framework that might help to explain them, I had only a diffuse interest in Latin America and no particular expertise in Mexico. As I began to consider an appropriate case (or cases) for my emerging research agenda, I considered everything from Brazil, Argentina, or Venezuela to countries outside the region, including Indonesia and India. As I argue in chapter 7, I think the general approach I have employed here can help us to understand subnational politics in many other countries as well. But one has to start somewhere, and I was at an impasse. In a chance conversation on the fifth floor of Pick Hall, my good friend and fellow student Eduardo Guerrero settled the issue for me: "You should go to Mexico. I will help you."

Indeed he did. Eduardo put me in touch with his friends and colleagues at the Centro de Investigación y Docencia Económicas (CIDE) in Mexico City, where I spent a good deal of time in the early stages of my research effort. Francisco Abundis, Alain de Remes, Joy Langston, Susan Minushkin, Benito Nacif, Allison Rowland, Guillermo Trejo, and many others welcomed me enthusiastically and with a good deal of patience. Each of them, as well as Jorge Buendía, Rodolfo García del Castillo, Fabrice Lehoucq, Jeff Staton, and Steve Wuhs, provided valuable advice and assistance during my various research trips. I would especially like to thank Alain de Remes for freely sharing the fruits of his own diligent labor, in addition to his ideas, enthusiasm, and encouragement. Now, years later, I still recall his generosity when others approach me to ask for my advice, my data, or my opinions.

I would also like to recognize the influence of the large community of social scientists at the University of Chicago, with which I was proudly affiliated for (too) many years. Most obviously, I owe a great debt to the members of my dissertation committee, which included Susan Stokes, Carles Boix, and Delia Boylan. Each of them challenged me intellectually and offered sound advice over a period of years. John Brehm came off the bench on more than one occasion to help with committee duties and was always generous with his time even outside such official capacities. I also benefited tremendously from presentations and conversations in Chicago's workshops, including the Comparative Politics Workshop, the Political Economy Workshop, and the American Politics Workshop. In these forums and in between them, my thoughts and research were influenced by a great many people. This list should doubtless be longer, but in addition to those named above I would at least like to recognize the help of Matteo Colombi, Sven Feldmann,

Sujatha Fernandes, Sean Gailmard, Jake Gersen, Jeff Grynaviski, Gabor Gyori, Mark Hansen, Gretchen Helmke, Alfonso Hernández-Valdez, Stathis Kalyvas, Matt Kocher, David Laitin, Adria Lawrence, Luis Fernando Medina, Isaac Murphy, Susie (Pratt) Rosato, Sebastian Rosato, Gill Steel, Nathan Tarcov, Lisa Wedeen, and Pete Wolfe. The university took good financial care of me while I was there. I am particularly grateful for a four-year fellowship from the university's John M. Olin Center for Inquiry into the Theory and Practice of Democracy. I would also like to thank the Russell Sage Foundation for a grant awarded to Susan Stokes and me while I was still at Chicago. The main product of that grant is a book that Susan and I published in 2006, called *Democracy and the Culture of Skepticism*. But the funding for travel and survey research also contributed mightily to the present study.

Parts of this book project have appeared as conference papers or presentations at CIDE, the University of Notre Dame, and the annual meetings of the American Political Science Association, the Midwest Political Science Association, and the Latin American Studies Association, and Princeton's Center for the Study of Democratic Politics (CSDP), where I was lucky enough to spend the 2004–5 academic year as a visiting fellow. In such venues, I received excellent comments and suggestions from Michael Coppedge, Alberto Diaz-Cayeros, Michelle Dion, Todd Eisenstadt, Federico Estévez, Jonathan Hiskey, Sharon Lean, Scott Mainwaring, and William Reisinger, in addition to some of those already named above. The community at the CSDP was especially welcoming and challenging. All of my fellow fellows—Becky Morton, Andy Rudalevige, Boris Shor, and Rick Vallely—offered sage advice and support, as did many of the CSDP regulars, including Larry Bartels, Brandice Canes-Wrone, Tom Romer, and Jessica Trounstine.

Upon graduating from Chicago, and with a one-year layover at the CSDP, I began work as an assistant professor of political science in Syracuse University's Maxwell School for Citizenship and Public Affairs. As my work continued I benefited from extensive comments and conversations with Pablo Beramendi, Suzanne Mettler, and Brian Taylor, each of whom has read this entire manuscript, and from the companionship and support of many other colleagues here. I would also like to thank Barry Ames and Beatriz Magaloni for coming to Syracuse in October

2006 specifically to comment on the manuscript in a review workshop sponsored by my department. I am not sure that I have been able to answer all of their challenges, but I remain very grateful for their willingness to invest such an effort in my project. Most recently, I have benefited from a detailed and insightful anonymous review that forced me to clarify many aspects of my argument. And I would like to thank Barbara Hanrahan and Scott Mainwaring for shepherding the project at the University of Notre Dame Press, Elisabeth Magnus for skillfully editing the entire manuscript, and Eric Rittinger for additional assistance with the final product.

This book is a much-revised descendant of my doctoral dissertation (Cleary 2004). Earlier versions of some parts of the research contained here were published in *Política y Gobierno* and in the *American Journal of Political Science* (see Cleary 2003, 2007). I would also like to acknowledge that much of the data used in this book were given to me by Miguel Basáñez, Alain de Remes, Michelle Dion, Todd Eisenstadt, Doug Hecock, Jonathan Hiskey, and Guillermo Trejo. Although most of the data are in the public domain, collection can be difficult. And since it is not always easy to offer up one's hard-earned data for another's ready use, I think it is important to acknowledge the generosity of those who do.

Finally, I wish to record that my greatest debt during the years of research that ultimately produced this book is owed to my family. My wife, Heather, has been a constant source of love, hope, and encouragement, even when I have spent long hours in the office—not to mention my many research trips to Mexico. Those who know her need no convincing on this point—Heather is an inspiration. Her parents (Frank and Nancy Tetlow), my parents (Kevin and Louise Cleary), and both of our extended families have provided *all* manner of support throughout these years. It is no exaggeration to say that I would not have been able to finish this book without them. In particular, my three sons—Jacob, Adam, and Christopher—are so much fun, and such good kids, that they never fail to provide inspiration and welcome diversion just when I need it. Jacob does not understand why Notre Dame failed to offer *him* a contract for his comic books; Adam does not understand why he cannot find my books at Barnes and Noble; and I suppose that none of them fully understands what I do or why I am always going to Mexico. But I hope that one day each of them understands how profoundly they have contributed to my work and my vocation, of which this book represents a part.

There are many pleasures involved in spending several years on a dissertation and several more on revising the dissertation into a book. And while thinking back on all of those who have offered help and encouragement along the way is certainly one of them, fearing that someone has been inadvertently omitted is not. For any such oversight, and for any other errors contained in this book, only I am responsible.

CHAPTER ONE

What Good Are Elections in Mexico?

MOST SCHOLARS BELIEVE THAT ELECTIONS MAKE DEMOCRACY possible by providing mechanisms for popular control, policy responsiveness, or government accountability. Some argue that elections are the *only* reliable means to these ends and that, accordingly, competitive elections are a sufficient condition for political democracy.[1] But recent research has begun to cast doubt on the ability of elections to produce what most of us think of as "democratic" outcomes in all cases and at all times.[2] Biased electoral rules, principal-agent problems, pervasive clientelism, and authoritarian political cultures have all been identified as factors that might limit or impede the ability of elections—even free and fair elections—to produce responsive, accountable, or participatory regimes.[3] These problems are almost certainly more severe in unconsolidated and new democracies, where electoral rules and other democratic institutions are less firmly established and where the commitment to democratic procedures is weaker among both citizens and elites.[4]

There is no doubt that elections are a useful tool, and often the best tool, for producing democratic responsiveness. But their usefulness varies across institutional, social, and political settings. In addition, elections are far from the only "instrument of democracy" that most citizens have at their disposal.[5] Responsive government may depend on a citizenry's ability to articulate demands and pressure government through a wide range of political action beyond voting, such as protest, public speech, lobbying, collective action, or direct contact with government officials.[6] While some scholars view these participatory strategies as complementary to electoral accountability, others imply that participation influences responsiveness directly, even in the absence of competitive elections (Hirschman 1970; Mueller 1992, 1999; Putnam 1993; Verba, Schlozman, and Brady 1995).

Considerations like these have given rise to an immense amount of scholarship in political science. One line of research studies how electoral competition alters the behavior of representatives and influences political outcomes (Fiorina 1981; Key 1966; Mayhew 1974; Powell 2000; Stimson, Mackuen, and Erikson 1995). Another focuses on alternative strategies for democratic influence, such as protest, petitioning, and civic participation (Hirschman 1970; Putnam 1993; Tarrow 1994; Verba, Schlozman, and Brady 1995). Yet each instrument of democracy is typically studied in isolation. We still lack an integrated approach to democratic responsiveness, which simultaneously evaluates several instruments of democracy and attempts to determine the conditions under which one or more of them can help to increase responsiveness, in the sense of making government actions more congruent with public preferences. Thus a voluminous literature has not yet offered complete answers to the following series of questions, questions that are central to contemporary democratic theory and practice:

- Under what conditions should we expect elections to contribute to democratic governance? That is, when will elections enhance the correspondence between public preferences and government output? When will they fail in this regard?
- Do nonelectoral forms of political participation help to produce good government, even when elections fail?
- When should we expect these two forms of democratic influence to interact? Are they more powerful tools when used in combination?

In this book I provide answers to these questions by studying the causes of government responsiveness during Mexico's protracted transition to democracy (roughly from 1980 to 2000). The evidence indicates that, at least in Mexico, electoral competition has had no measurable effect on democratic responsiveness. But responsiveness does improve in the parts of the country where citizens make greater use of nonelectoral strategies of political participation to influence, inform, and pressure those who govern. I argue that the roots of Mexico's participatory transformation can be located in the late 1970s, when independent social movements became more powerful and Mexico's corporatist system of interest representation began to weaken. In turn, this participatory transformation gave rise to the increased level of electoral competition that is now common in most of Mexico. In sum, this book suggests that the sources of democratic responsiveness in Mexico are to be found largely outside the electoral realm and that even though elections are severely constrained as mechanisms of accountability Mexican citizens can and do make use of other strategies of political influence that force their government to be more responsive to public interests.

The Dominance of Electoral Approaches to the Study of Democracy

From 1929 to 2000, Mexico was governed by a single political party whose candidates won thirteen consecutive presidential elections. During the first five decades of this dominant-party regime, the Partido Revolucionario Institucional (Institutional Revolutionary Party, or PRI) controlled virtually every important political office in the country, to such an extent that it was difficult to distinguish between the party and the state.[7] In contrast to most authoritarian regimes of the time, Mexico had a well-established electoral system that played an important role in legitimizing the regime and the party's place within it. Elections were always held on time and were formally free and fair (though often fraudulent in practice). The principle of no reelection was firmly established and was not violated. Opposition parties always existed and competed, at least where they could field candidates. But election outcomes were invariably lopsided toward the PRI, and the party ruled virtually unchecked.

Scholars typically think about Mexican democratization against this backdrop, and we measure its progress by the extent to which the electoral scene differs from this depiction of PRI dominance. Seen in this way, the process of democratization began in the early 1980s, when some elections became more competitive. Opposition parties won a few mayoral races in important cities in 1983, and throughout the 1980s they gradually increased their representation in the federal legislature. In 1988 Cuauhtémoc Cárdenas, a leading figure in the PRI, split from the party and ran for president under the banner of an opposition party. The following year Cárdenas helped to establish the Partido de la Revolución Democrática (Party of the Democratic Revolution, PRD), which has been the main political force on the electoral left ever since. Opposition parties went on to win several governorships, majorities in many state legislatures, and the mayorship of Mexico City's federal district in the 1990s. Finally, in the year 2000, Vicente Fox won the presidential election as a member of the Partido Acción Nacional (National Action Party, PAN), ending the PRI's seventy-year hold on the office. Thus, in the eyes of most scholars, did Mexico become a democracy (see chapter 2 for a more detailed discussion).

This account of democratization in Mexico parallels the way we identify and evaluate democratization across the globe. Free and fair elections are the primary, and sometimes the only, indicator that scholars use to determine whether a given regime deserves to be called democratic. This conception is also common in policy and political circles. Adherence to electoral norms has been an important facet of "good governance" programs advocated by international development organizations since the early 1990s, particularly at U.S.-based agencies (Carothers 1995). And the Bush administration repeatedly placed elections at the forefront of its efforts to promote "the expansion of freedom in all the world," as the former president stated in his Second Inaugural.

The equation of electoral competition and democracy is one reason for the focus on elections. Another important reason is that scholars and politicians have a habit of attributing any positive social outcome in a democracy to the workings of electoral institutions. In this view, electoral competition is desirable not only because it is evidence of democracy but also because it solves all kinds of social and political problems.

Table 1.1 offers a representative (though partial) list of such claims. According to this body of research, competitive elections give citizens influence over government policy; improve economic performance; provide an alternative to violent rebellion or civil war; contribute to interstate peace; promote respect for human rights; protect the environment; control population growth; and the list goes on.[8] As we will see, students of Mexican politics frequently draw on arguments like these when explaining changes in political outcomes over the past twenty or thirty years.

Table 1.1. Selected Social Science Hypotheses about the Effects of Elections

Effect	*Literature / Citation*
1. Improve government performance/ policy responsiveness	Accountability theory
2. Improve representation	"Seats and votes" literature
3. Increase social spending	Brown and Hunter (1999) Ames (1987)
4. Reduce clientelism	Kitschelt et al. (1999)
5. Improve economic performance	Przeworski and Limongi (1993)
6. Increase wages	Rodrik (1999)
7. Foster environmental stewardship	Diamond (1999)
8. Control population growth	Diamond (1999)
9. Decrease infant mortality/ improve health care	Zweifel and Navia (2000) Baum and Lake (2001)
10. Promote respect for human/ minority rights	Beetham (1999) Beer and Mitchell (2001)
11. Alleviate pressure for rebellion/ civil war/ethnic conflict	Diamond (1999) Cleary (2000)
12. Prevent interstate war	Democratic peace theory

I suspect that many claims like the ones listed in table 1.1 have not yet been held to the proper level of theoretical and empirical scrutiny and that scholars have not sufficiently explored the ways in which competition can produce perverse outcomes such as electoral fraud, clientelist mobilization, logrolling among legislators, or other behavior that cuts against democratic responsiveness. Still, this new focus on elections as instruments of democracy—as mechanisms for democratic change, rather than as the end point of a transition to democracy—represents an important advance in the study of democratization. Putting electoral competition on the other side of the causal arrow, so to speak, allows us to ask questions about the types of effects elections can generate (see Powell 2000). Given how frequently elections are used, it makes sense to ask how well they work and what they can achieve. These are exactly the types of questions I pursue in this book.

Thus this book represents a new approach to studying the links between electoral competition and democracy by critically evaluating elections as a source of democratic responsiveness in Mexico. But the study of elections as a factor influencing the quality of government is hampered by three major difficulties that this book aspires to overcome. The first is empirical complexity. It is often exceedingly difficult to measure government output in such a way that governments can be ranked according to their "level of responsiveness" or some other performance index. Most studies focus on just one issue at a time: democracies are found to have stronger economies, or cleaner environments. But given that governments are charged with many tasks, and often with contradictory ones, even simple rank orderings can be difficult. We might easily agree that a government that fosters a strong economy and a clean environment is a good government. But is it better to have a strong economy and a weak environmental record, or the reverse? Even without the problem of multiple issues, quantification can be daunting. Is a city government performing well by raising taxes and investing millions of dollars in a sports stadium, or is it wasting money on a special-interest boondoggle? Given that economic analyses have not arrived at a consensus on such issues (see Noll and Zimbalist 1997), we might be tempted to conclude that government responsiveness in certain cases is just not measurable in practice.[9]

The second weakness of the current literature on electoral competition as an independent variable is that most studies do not adequately address alternative explanations. Since our normative priors favor elections so strongly, it is understandable that some scholars are tempted to attribute all favorable outcomes in democracies to electoral institutions. But we also know that the existence of competitive elections closely correlates with several other factors, including wealth, education, urbanization, trade openness, and so on. Too often, we attribute political outcomes to elections (or worse, to "democracy," which is broadly or ambiguously defined), without considering the possibility that some other factor is the true cause. The potential for confounds and spurious findings is enormous. Is it really true that elections improve human rights records, under the theory that abusive regimes would lose electoral support? Or might it be that wealth improves human rights records, by easing the economic tensions that are likely to trigger subversive challenges to state authority? Or might an educated citizenry be better able to prevent human rights abuses through the dissemination of information, more effective lobbying against such practices, inculcation of norms, or some other means? Given that wealth, education, and electoral competition are closely correlated across countries, we should be suspicious of any study that attributes human rights protections to any one of these factors unless it also evaluates the causal impact of the other two.

This discussion suggests a third problem with the study of elections as independent variables, which is a failure to develop theoretical explanations that have clear causal mechanisms. We must have a concise causal story to distinguish between correlations and true causal factors; development of these mechanisms also helps us adjudicate among competing explanations, as discussed above. As I show in great detail in chapter 2, clear causal mechanisms are especially critical in applying electoral theories of control to the Mexican case. The basic proposition derived from electoral approaches to democratic theory, and used to explain so many of the empirical findings related to elections, is that electoral competition affects the calculations and actions of self-interested politicians. This basic idea is beyond dispute. But knowing whether, when, and how they will react is far more difficult. So, for the theory to develop from a plausible idea to an empirically supported explanation, we need to know how voters, politicians, and parties perceive the electoral threat; when politicians and parties might have incentives to react to electoral pressures in ways that obstruct accountability or weaken government responsiveness; whether electoral institutions are designed in ways that make them effective tools of control for voters; and much more.

The research strategies I employ are designed to address all three of these potential weaknesses, though I encourage readers to decide for themselves whether I have done so successfully. To ameliorate the problems caused by empirical complexity, I use large-*N* comparisons, multiple measures of the key concepts, and careful specification of econometric models. These strategies help to resolve inferential problems such as multicollinearity (by distinguishing the independent effect of closely related factors) and the direction of causality (when used to test temporally specific models). Large-*N* methods are particularly useful for pitting alternative explanations against each other, which is a central aim of the analysis. In addition, by carefully treating the theoretical mechanisms through which elections and other means of political influence are thought to have an effect on government performance, I specify the extent to which we can be confident that statistical relationships support our causal conjectures. Qualitative and case-based evidence informs this effort by helping to illustrate the plausibility of the causal mechanisms I propose in chapters 2 and 3 and by speaking directly to my evaluation of the central hypotheses, primarily in chapter 6.

The research reported here draws on a large body of empirical evidence that I have generated and compiled via multiple methods, measures, and techniques of comparison. The sum total of this evidence suggests unequivocally that electoral competition in Mexican municipalities does not function to improve government responsiveness. I argue, and present evidence to suggest, that institutional features—some specific to Mexico (like term limits) but also some that are inherent in any electoral system (like informational asymmetries)—are the primary obstacles to democratic responsiveness in Mexican municipalities. At the same time, much of the evidence suggests that nonelectoral forms of participation can have a positive impact on responsiveness. The evidence on this point is less decisive and may be open to interpretation, but it supports my conclusion that participation can improve the responsiveness of local governments because it provides citizens with meaningful ways to communicate their preferences and to exert pressure for a response on those who govern.

The Importance of the Mexican Case

Mexico has long been an object of public and scholarly interest in the United States and elsewhere. The country's close economic and demographic links to the United States serve to keep it in the headlines and on the minds of many Americans. Among political scientists, Mexico has generated large bodies of scholarship devoted to examining its tumultuous presidential elections, its frequent and intense economic crises, its rebellions and their occasionally violent repression, its massive out-migration, and much more. But neither the inherent importance of the country nor the allure of recent events serves as the central motivation for this book's focus on Mexico. The underlying goal of my research is to improve our understanding of how democracy works and how electoral competition, nonelectoral participation, and other types of democratic political behavior affect the quality of democracy.[10] The Mexican case offers several pragmatic and methodological advantages that, in combination, constitute an excellent opportunity to pursue this goal and to rigorously test alternative explanations of democratic responsiveness. For current purposes, then, the Mexican case is important because it can teach us things about democracy that we would not be likely to learn elsewhere.

I employ a subnational comparative research design, which provides a novel way to test causal explanations of democratic responsiveness by increasing the number of observations while controlling for many factors that vary in unknown ways cross-nationally.[11] Specifically, while holding constant (with minor exceptions) the institutional structure, electoral rules, and national-level political and economic conditions, I am able to track changes in electoral competition, political participation, and government responsiveness across almost two thousand Mexican municipalities.[12] Mexico is not the only country in which such a design is possible—indeed, in the concluding chapter I suggest that my approach can and should be attempted elsewhere—but the contours of the Mexican case confer several advantages.

For example, there is a good deal of cross-sectional and temporal variation, across municipalities, in the level of electoral competition and other indicators related to democracy and democratic responsiveness. This should be no news to scholars of Mexico, who have long recognized that democracy seems to vary subnationally. Wayne Cornelius (1999, 3) reported that "subnational authoritarian enclaves" remained strong in several Mexican states, "even in an era of much-intensified interparty competition." Jonathan Fox (1994a, 157) found subnational variation in modes of interest representation and reported that "persistent authoritarian clientelism can coexist with new enclaves of pluralist tolerance." Caroline Beer (2001, 2003) investigated variation in the level of legislative influence and independence among three state legislatures in Mexico. Alfonso Hernández-Valdez (2000) found state-level differences in electoral competitiveness and civil liberties. And Alain de Remes (2000b) documented wide variation in the competitiveness of municipal elections across Mexico from 1980 to 1998. Variation is just as strong on other important dimensions, like political engagement, wealth, education and other socioeconomic resources, and government responsiveness.

Importantly, all of this variation exists in the context of a protracted transition to democracy, which allows us to analyze the potential causal impact of electoral competition and participation in ways that cannot readily be done in studies of the advanced industrial democracies. In established democracies low levels of electoral competition are often best interpreted as high levels of satisfaction with the incumbent government, thus making competition endogenous to performance. But in Mexico's transitional atmosphere this interpretation can be dismissed on its face, since subnational units with low levels of competition have typically never evinced multiparty competition. The proposition that good performance is responsible for the lack of competition in these places is implausible. The data presented in chapters 4 and 5 clearly indicate that, even if the relationship between competition and performance is weak overall, noncompetitive municipalities are invariably among the worst-performing municipalities in the country. This allows us to clearly separate areas where elections have been liberalized from those in which elections remain effectively closed affairs that do not really determine who rules.

The usefulness of subnational variation across several important dimensions in Mexico is enhanced by the fact that it is relatively well documented. Compilations of electoral data such as de Remes (2000a) and Banamex (2001) offer the official electoral returns for virtually every election in Mexico, at federal, state, and municipal levels, over the past twenty to thirty years. The Instituto Nacional de Estadísticas, Geografía e Informática (INEGI), Mexico's census and statistics bureau, collects and publicizes comprehensive demographic, economic, and social indicators. Most importantly, INEGI has collected data on public service provision and municipal financial characteristics that are direct indicators of municipal government performance and that I use as concrete measures of government responsiveness. In addition, recent trends in decentralization have led to a burgeoning Mexican literature on municipal governance and local public policy. The result is that this book can draw on a rich case-study literature that addresses the successes and failures of municipal policies and local governments, as well as an increasingly sophisticated literature on the effects of electoral competition and political participation in the Mexican political arena.

The advantages of the subnational comparative design discussed here help in a number of ways to address the three difficulties common to studies of elections as causal variables (empirical complexity, adjudication among alternative explanations, and identification of causal mechanisms). In comparison to cross-national studies, empirical complexity is rendered manageable because the key variables are more easily and accurately measured.[13] For example, government responsiveness is comparatively easy to measure in Mexico because "clarity of responsibility" (Powell 2000) is relatively high in municipal governments, where policy responsibilities are well known and power is concentrated in the office of the municipal president.[14] The federal government has collected data on these municipal services and responsibilities for several decades.

In addition, the Mexican case is almost uniquely positioned for evaluation of hypotheses about nonelectoral means of influence. The rise of electoral competition was caused, at least in part, by underlying socioeconomic changes such as a growing middle class, improved levels of education, and the turn toward a more urban, industrial economy

(Hernández-Valdez 2000; Chand 2001). These same factors are often thought to be closely linked to nonelectoral forms of political participation, such as protest, direct contacting of government officials (or what Cornelius [1974] calls "political demand making"), social movement formation, and so on. So this book investigates the relationship between changes in development and electoral competition over time. The goal is to determine, among other things, whether elections directly improve government performance or whether elections and improved performance are both products of exogenous socioeconomic changes. In chapter 6 I offer evidence in favor of the latter interpretation.

Finally, the established literatures on electoral competition, party behavior, and municipal public policy provide an excellent starting point for the development of clear causal arguments that generate testable implications. Arguably, causal mechanisms with respect to government performance are easier to identify at the local level, where the functioning of street-level bureaucracy and the political behavior of individual citizens are more directly observable, suggesting relatively clear, transparent, and testable causal explanations. We can check, for example, whether the observed behavior of voters, politicians, and parties conforms to the assumptions of accountability theories. Subjecting these assumptions to direct examination will help us determine whether any statistical link between electoral competition and government performance is a mere *correlation* or whether it supports *causal* claims.

Government Performance in Mexico: Electoral Competition or Voice?

The evidence presented throughout this book demonstrates that good government in Mexico is most often found in areas that also seem to be the most democratic. On this point, my research supports the conventional wisdom about democracy. But I also depart radically from the conventional approach to studying democracy by critically assessing the underlying causal logic according to which democracy is supposed to have the effect that so many scholars have observed. Instead of being satisfied that improved government performance is the result of "democracy," broadly understood, I examine the different means by which democratic regimes are purported to produce good government, and I test these causal hypotheses simultaneously, to determine which among them are the actual sources of the observed democratic responsiveness. (For a similar approach, see Fox 2007, especially chapter 1.)

Several theories claim to explain this democratic effect. Most scholars favor the theory of *electoral accountability,* according to which democracy promotes good government because voters can use electoral rewards and punishments to influence the behavior of politicians (Key 1966; Fiorina 1981). Others argue that good government can result from an *electoral selection* mechanism, according to which democratic government is better because (or insofar as) citizens are able to select leaders according to their platform proposals, personal qualities such as competence or integrity, or some other useful criteria (Downs 1957; A. Campbell et al. 1960). Both of these ideas, but especially the first, are common explanations of improved governance in Mexico over the past twenty-five years. But less attention has been paid to a third explanation, which posits that democracy produces good government because it allows citizens broader opportunities to participate: to protest, to petition, to assemble, and to complain. To use Albert Hirschman's (1970) term, we might argue that democracy improves government performance because it gives citizens the opportunity to use *voice* .

To understand how these theories might account for variation in the quality of government, and to put the Mexican case in a broader context, let us examine some basic data on the quality of service provision in Latin America. Measuring government responsiveness can be contentious and complicated, and I offer a detailed justification of the measures I use in chapters 4 and 5. But for now, let me simply equate responsiveness with public utility services. The provision of water and sanitation are among the central responsibilities of municipal governments in Mexico, and access to these utilities (or the lack thereof) is a common source of local contestation.

Figures 1.1 and 1.2 show the rates of coverage for water and sanitation in Mexico, compared to the average of twenty-one Latin American countries. Figure 1.1 shows that Mexico has made significant improvements in water provision, even while many of its Latin American counterparts have stagnated or had only modest gains. According to data from the World Bank, 95 percent of Mexicans had access to potable water in 1995, up from fewer than two-thirds of the population twenty years earlier. Figure 1.2, which shows improvements in sanitation coverage between 1985 and 1995, tells a similar story. The average improvement for these twenty-one countries, over the course of a decade, was just over 7 percent. Mexico increased its coverage by 19 percent, moving from about two points below the average to ten points above it. During the same time period, Mexican GDP growth and federal government revenue were both generally consistent with regional averages, meaning that improved coverage cannot be attributed to any sort of economic boom or funding windfall. While this is a crude comparison, the data do give the impression that local government in Mexico has become more attentive to the public interest, at least with regard to utility services.

But the situation becomes even more interesting when we observe variation in public service provision *within* Mexico. The general picture

Figure 1.1. Changes in Water Provision, Mexico and Latin America, 1975–95

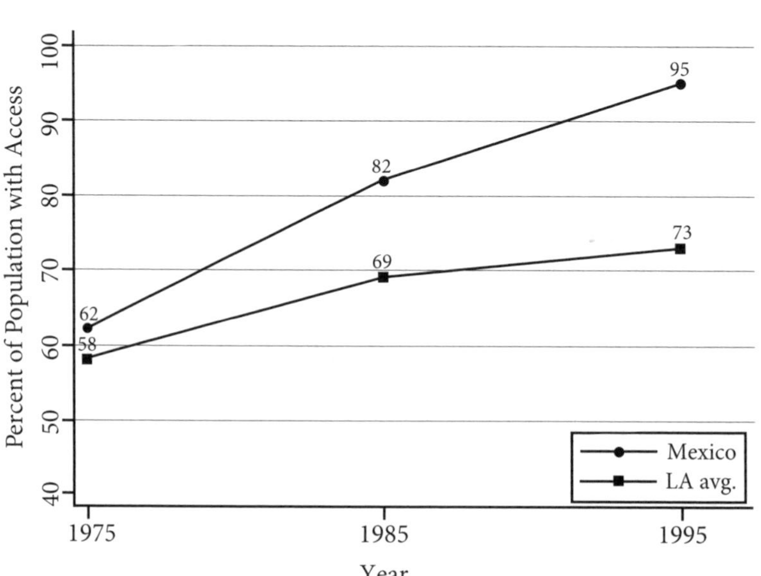

Source: World Bank (1999).

Figure 1.2. Changes in Sanitation Provision, Mexico and Latin America, 1985–95

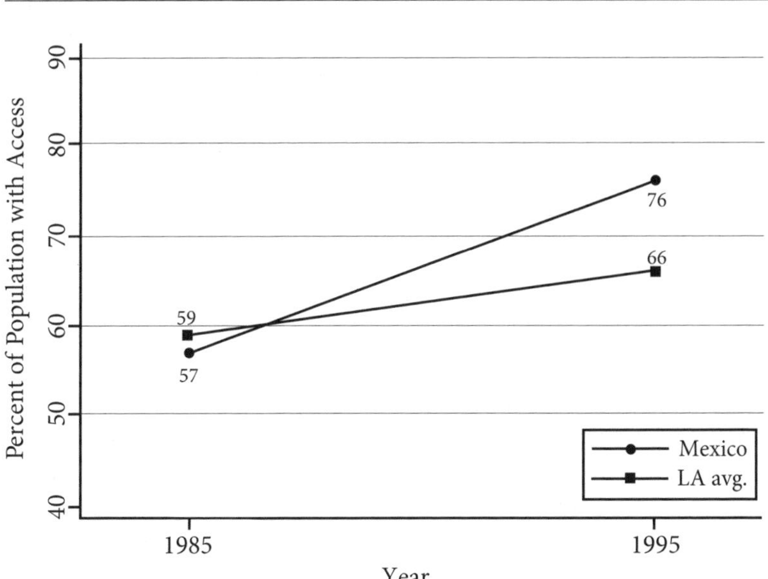

Source: World Bank (1999).

of municipal water and sewer provision resembles the trends shown in figures 1.1 and 1.2, with most municipalities steadily increasing their rates of coverage over time.[15] But there is wide variation among municipalities. By 1990, the top quartile of municipalities already had water coverage rates of 87 percent or better. But the bottom quartile all covered fewer than half of the households within their jurisdictions. These wide disparities coincide with widely different trajectories over time. Among the low-scoring quartile in 1990, just under half showed no real improvement in coverage rates between 1990 and 2000; but many improved significantly, with almost a quarter of the group improving their coverage by twenty percentage points or more. The municipal profiles for sanitation reveal the same trend. The bottom line is that some Mexican municipalities showed great improvements over the course of the 1990s, whereas others improved very little.[16]

It is well known that electoral competition was on the rise during this period. Furthermore, we know that the process was uneven, with elections in some municipalities becoming very competitive and others remaining noncompetitive. Thus the improvements relative to other Latin American countries, as well as the patterns of subnational variation, both give a certain prima facie plausibility to the argument that electoral mechanisms explain improvements in government performance. But other changes were taking place in Mexico as well. Social movements arose and became more assertive in many areas of the country. Unions and other popular organizations gained increasing independence from the PRI's corporatist structures, fundamentally altering the relationship between labor and the state. Industrial enterprises flourished in many parts of the country, particularly in the *maquila* sector concentrated along the northern border. Relatedly, Mexicans continued to leave the countryside in massive numbers, migrating either to Mexican cities or to the United States in search of work. By 1995, Mexico was a far more urban, industrial, and literate country than it had been in 1985 or 1975. The data presented in later chapters allow us to disentangle the possible effects of economic development, political democratization, and other competing explanations of local service provision in Mexico.

Most importantly, I develop and test a theory according to which government performance in Mexico is a function of political participation. Citizens can make government responsive, I argue, not only by threatening to remove incumbents from power when they perform badly but also by petitioning, pressuring, or cajoling incumbents while they are in office. Mexican citizens exhibit a number of behaviors that seem to favor this explanation, and local governments even encourage participatory behaviors on occasion as a way of gaining information about public needs and demands.[17] For example, contact between citizens and public officials has become more common in many municipalities. It has also changed qualitatively—the image of the poor *campesino* approaching the beneficent *señor* with his hat in his hand has been replaced in many parts of the country by a more assertive style of contact, in which citizens remind officials that they are public servants with obligations toward the public.[18] At the same time, many local governments have begun to make their officials more accessible to the public, and some have taken to forming citizen governance groups, in which public committees are given formal authority for deciding spending priorities or development plans within their localities. I argue that these forms of citizen engagement and participation are more effective causes of improved government performance in Mexico. The data strongly favor this interpretation, thus casting doubt on the widely held belief that electoral competition is the single most important political change in Mexico's ongoing democratic transition.

In fact, some of the evidence presented in the coming chapters suggests that voice can influence government performance even when elections are not competitive and where the incumbent party does not perceive any significant electoral threat to its continued tenure. In other words, voice may influence government performance even in authoritarian regimes. Thus my findings may expand on and qualify those of Brown and Hunter (1999), who note that authoritarian regimes in Latin America *are* responsive to the needs of their citizens in many ways, even if they are less responsive than democratic governments and more tightly constrained by economic downturns.

What Can We Learn from Mexican Democratization?

The available evidence indicates that the commitment to democracy in Latin America and most of the developing world, among both elites and publics, is often instrumental at best. If democratic governments in these countries do not deliver, they will stagnate and maybe even perish. Therefore it is critical to understand the components of a well-functioning democracy, especially in countries like Mexico that (arguably) have not fully consolidated their democratic institutions and practices. I address this question head-on by rejecting the simplistic conflation of democracy and electoral competition. Instead, I critically assess how competition and other modes of contestation may (or may not) interact to produce democratic outcomes. In the process, this research suggests that democratic practice, and the consolidation of democratic institutions, may depend on factors other than the repetition of free and fair elections. Most importantly, I argue that democratic tendencies are most apparent in Mexico when and where citizens are able to make use of nonelectoral means of political influence, such as participation in local councils or assemblies, personal lobbying of local officials, and the free expression of political opinions.

But the ability to understand democratic responsiveness in Mexico is not the only justification for the current endeavor. Mexico also presents students of democracy with a rare set of problems and conditions that can help answer questions not answered by studies of the advanced industrial democracies. For example, Powell (2000, 238) concludes his study of "elections as instruments of democracy," based on a comparison of twenty established democracies, by telling us that all is well in the electoral world: because of electoral competition, he writes, "democracies generally, if imperfectly, deliver the goods they promise." Would Powell have been able to offer such a sanguine appraisal of electoral politics if he had been studying Mexico, Venezuela, and Indonesia?

The Mexican case allows studies like Powell's to be challenged by situations that cannot be found in Europe and the United States. For all of its progress toward meaningful democracy, Mexico has a long (and continuing) history of authoritarianism, clientelism, severe poverty, illiteracy, biased electoral rules, and weak electoral institutions. Fortunately, it also has a decades-long, well-documented experience with elections, as well as high-quality data relevant to the quality of government output. Mexico thus provides an opportunity to study the effects of elections in the context of a developing, transitional democracy. Furthermore, it provides a chance to pit theories of electoral accountability against other explanations of the quality of government performance. The remainder of this book takes full advantage of the analytical opportunities provided by the case to explore hypotheses about the sources of improved, responsive, democratic government.

Plan of the Book

The next two chapters review and develop the two main theoretical arguments under consideration in this book. Chapter 2 offers a critical assessment of electoral accountability theory, both in general and with respect to the Mexican case. It also shows preliminary evidence that casts doubt on the effectiveness of accountability mechanisms in Mexico. Chapter 3 presents an alternative theoretical explanation of democratic responsiveness, based on the employment of nonelectoral strategies for democratic influence. Chapters 4 and 5 offer statistical tests of hypotheses that I derive from the electoral and participatory theories. Chapter 6 expands the empirical reach of the book on several fronts, most notably by analyzing the interplay between changes in participation, competition, and government responsiveness over time. In the concluding chapter 7, I offer a general evaluation of how electoral competition and participation have influenced the quality of government in Mexico, and I suggest a framework for the analysis of democratic responsiveness in other countries.

CHAPTER TWO

Elections and Democratic Responsiveness

THERE CAN BE NO QUESTION THAT THE RISE OF COMPETITION in Mexican elections has produced real changes. The PRI has now lost two consecutive presidential elections. Federal and state legislatures are far more plural than they used to be and are more assertive because of it (Beer 2003). And in contrast to the era of PRI dominance, party alternation in power is now a real possibility in most states and municipalities, given sufficient dissatisfaction among citizens. Alternation has already occurred in some seventeen states, the federal district, and several hundred municipalities, often multiple times. At least in this sense, then, one can say that Mexican elections work: voters have the ability to replace politicians with whom they are dissatisfied.

However, citizens and academics in developing democracies such as Mexico have much higher expectations for electoral institutions. It is not sufficient that the ruling party respects electoral results, in the sense that opposition candidates are actually allowed to take office when they win elections. Those who advocate competitive elections believe that new officials, having been forced to compete for office, and being under the threat of future electoral punishment, will typically *perform* better than they would have in the absence of competitive elections. This is certainly the hope and belief of many observers of Mexican politics. Accordingly, this chapter critically evaluates a family of claims within democratic theory, all of which share a contention about the effect of electoral contestation: elections make government work better. I aim to understand how and under what circumstances we should reasonably expect elections to have such an effect.

I proceed by offering a narrative description of the rise of electoral competition in Mexico, reconstructing the debate over the effects of this transformation. I show much of this debate to be misguided, resting as it does on an application of U.S.-based accountability theory to Mexican politics, without regard to the distinctive electoral institutions that make accountability so difficult in the Mexican setting. I develop a more precise theoretical argument for electoral accountability in Mexico, offering two general mechanisms through which electoral control is possible, given the Mexican institutional context.[1] Under the logic of a *party-sanctioning* mechanism, voters can control politicians by holding parties retrospectively accountable for their partisans' performance in office. According to a *candidate selection* mechanism, voters can control politicians by successfully selecting those who are most competent and likely to serve the interests of constituents. I offer some preliminary empirical evidence that casts doubt on the plausibility of the first explanation but that seems compatible with the second.

The Centrality of Elections in Mexican Politics

The Rise of Electoral Competition in Mexico

On July 2, 2000, the PRI conceded the Mexican presidency for the first time in its history. The country was quickly and ceremoniously proclaimed to be a democracy by world leaders, by the press, and by academics (see Domínguez and Lawson 2004; Tulchin and Selee 2003). Certainly, July 2 was a watershed and will prove to be one of the most important dates in Mexican political history. But the truth is that Mexico's electoral transformation had been under way for at least the prior two decades. Vicente Fox's victory was only one prominent episode in a long, complicated, and continuing process.

Mexico's turn toward multiparty electoral competition began in the late 1970s.[2] In earlier decades the PRI had completely dominated the government at all levels. The PRI and its predecessor parties had won every presidential election since the 1920s, and through the 1970s the party also held 100 percent of the governorships and senate seats and all but a handful of congressional seats and municipal presidencies. Fraud was common but not ubiquitous: while the PRI appears to have had rigged elections when necessary, it would be a mistake to argue that the party had no real support among the citizenry. In fact, it enjoyed a relatively high level of genuine popularity throughout most of its seventy-one-year reign, and it remains the single most popular party today.[3] But the PRI's continued electoral dominance seemed to damage the regime's legitimacy as a democracy.[4] In the 1970s, opposition parties withdrew from several electoral contests in protest. Most notably, the PAN withdrew its presidential candidate from the 1976 presidential election, forcing the PRI's candidate, José López Portillo, to run unopposed.

In response to this perceived crisis of legitimacy, the government approved a constitutional reform in 1977 that allowed for a greater opposition presence in the Chamber of Deputies (the lower house). The reform increased the total number of deputies from 237 to 400, and it increased from 41 to 100 the number that was assigned by proportional representation (PR).[5] This reform was symbolically important, but its authors also carefully calibrated the effect it would have on the composition of the Chamber. Opposition parties were not able to challenge the PRI's dominance in single-member districts, which still composed most of the legislature. And they did not do much better competing for the PR seats. In spite of the reform, the number of seats controlled by the PRI only fell from 82 percent in 1976 to 75 percent in 1979, and the PRI's delegation continued to hold 70 to 75 percent of congressional seats until 1988 (Lujambio 2000, 33–41). Also until that year, the PRI maintained its hold on all state governorships and most municipal presidencies. Still, the 1977 concession marked the beginning of a trend: in the years to come, the PRI would become increasingly accepting of electoral defeats and would make several other constitutional changes that favored electoral competition.[6]

In the early 1980s, opposition parties began to take advantage of these slight openings in the electoral arena. One of the more interesting characteristics of the Mexican case is the zeal with which opposition parties pursued electoral victories in relatively unimportant local contests. Since they would not be allowed to compete fairly for the presidency (as demonstrated by electoral fraud in the 1988 presidential race), the opposition, especially the PAN, turned its energy toward municipal, state legislative, and gubernatorial elections (Mizrahi 2003, 26–27). Over time, opposition victories became more frequent. But in the early 1980s, an opposition victory in any municipality, no matter how small or marginal, carried political significance that was far out of proportion to the power of the office at stake. Opposition parties had two largely symbolic goals: first, to defeat the PRI in open competition, and second, to demonstrate to voters that municipalities or states run by opposition governments would not collapse into chaos.[7] The ability to pursue alternative public policies was, at least in the short term, of secondary importance.

As the 1980s progressed, the PRI faced an increasing number of challenges to its hegemony. Social and labor movements began to challenge the sectoral nature of political representation, and the PRI's long-standing (though constantly evolving) pact with labor became increasingly strained by the government's pursuit of neoliberal economic policies. Collier (1992, 111) notes that "during the de la Madrid *sexenio* [1982–88] the political position of labor . . . deteriorated substantially and the state-labor coalition and the social pact upon which it was based [was] severely undermined."

At the same time, several new political parties had formed in the late 1970s and 1980s (Craig and Cornelius 1995). Other parties that had been part of the "loyal opposition" began to assert their independence. Demands for democratization were also coming from within the PRI. In 1986 several prominent *priístas,* including Cuauhtémoc Cárdenas and Porfirio Muñoz Ledo, formed the Corriente Democrática (Democratic Current), which pressed for a return to the PRI's populist and nationalist roots, as well as for democratizing reforms within the party (Bruhn 1997; Garrido 1993; Laso de la Vega 1987). The importance of this challenge to the PRI's hegemony became obvious when several members of the Corriente, including Cárdenas and Muñoz Ledo, left the PRI. After failing to secure the *dedazo,* or the PRI's nomination for the presidency, Cárdenas quit the party and announced his candidacy under the banner of the Partido Auténtico de la Revolución Mexicana (Authentic Party of the Mexican Revolution, PARM). Several opposition parties, including the PARM, the Partido Popular Socialista (Popular Socialist Party, PPS), and the Partido Socialista de los Trabajadores (Socialist Workers Party, PST), endorsed Cárdenas's bid for the presidency, and after the 1988 election the core of this coalition evolved into the Partido de la Revolución Democrática (PRD).

The split between the PRI and Cárdenas, who was the son of a popular former president and a rising political star in his own right, proved to be a major blow to the party's unity and dominance. Although the PRI candidate (Carlos Salinas) won the presidency, the election was in many ways a Pyrrhic victory for the PRI. It was widely believed that Salinas had won only through electoral fraud and that Cárdenas had actually won the popular vote. The PRI also lost its supermajority in congress for the first time. Although it still held a bare majority, the party was no longer able to pass constitutional changes without opposition support.

The deterioration of PRI dominance continued in subsequent years. The party lost its first governorship in 1989, and several more went to opposition parties in the 1990s.[8] Throughout the 1990s, opposition victories at the municipal level also increased dramatically. Even before the 2000 elections, the opposition parties collectively had managed to capture executive office in almost six hundred municipalities, nine states, and the Federal District. And of course on July 2, 2000, Vicente Fox of the PAN won the federal presidency, by far the most important elective office in the country. Thus, starting with the constitutional reforms of 1977, increasing after the tumultuous elections in 1988, and continuing up to the present time, Mexican politics has been characterized by a steadily increasing but spatially uneven level of electoral competition.

Electoral Competition as Democratization

In one sense, this electoral transformation displays many of the characteristics that are consistent with a "bottom-up" process of democratization. In this view, democratization began primarily at the municipal level, in the geographic periphery of the Mexican system. Prior to 1980 the vast majority of municipalities were held by the PRI. Opposition parties won only 135 municipal elections between 1979 and 1987 (out of over 5,000 local elections held during those years). But opposition parties became more competitive throughout the 1980s, and by the 1990s opposition victories were commonplace. The PAN has been especially effective in urban areas. As of 1999, it held just under three hundred mayoralties, which, because of their urban concentration, contained about one-third of the total population of the country. The PRD controls a similar number of municipalities, but they are typically smaller and more rural. Minor parties control only a handful of municipalities (see Lujambio 2000, 77–83).

The increase in opposition control of municipal governments was accompanied by an increase in municipal authority. The federal government undertook decentralizing reforms in the 1980s (T. Campbell 2003), and in 1983 it passed a constitutional reform that gave municipal governments authority for policy formation and implementation in eight specific areas, including some public utilities, local policing, and the maintenance of public spaces.[9] For the first time, municipal presidencies became offices where real political power, however minimal, could be exercised by an opposition government with some level of autonomy.[10] The conventional wisdom among Mexicanists was that these small political openings served as "schools of democracy" that taught the opposition how to organize, campaign, and rule.[11] And to the extent that opposition parties could use municipal victories to demonstrate their ability to compete for office and govern effectively, these local contests provided a starting point for the broader democratizing trend in Mexican elections.

At the same time, Mexico's electoral transformation provides considerable evidence of a "top-down" process of democratization. One arena in which these elite-level characteristics are evident is the ideological and organizational split between the PRI and the Corriente Democrática in the late 1980s. Cárdenas's behavior cannot be attributed merely to the ambition of one man to become president, even though Cárdenas clearly harbored such an ambition. His strategic move was also the result of an increasingly difficult accommodation between organized labor and the neoliberal (or technocratic) elite within the governing party. While the dominant element within the PRI preferred to constrain political contestation and expand neoliberal economic policies, Cárdenas's faction was substantially motivated by a preference for more democracy (at least within the party) and a return to the PRI's populist tradition of state-led social welfare policies. These strategic and political differences became increasingly difficult to reconcile, to the point at which Cárdenas and many other *priístas* opted to leave the party in which they had served for their entire political careers.

A second arena in which the top-down nature of the Mexican transition is evident is the federal Chamber of Deputies. As I mentioned above, the first critical event in opening the federal legislature to competition was the constitutional reform of 1977, which increased to 25 percent the number of seats awarded by proportional representation.[12] Another reform just prior to the 1988 elections further increased this proportion to 40 percent. These institutional changes clearly contributed to the steady increase in opposition representation in the legislature, which culminated in the PRI's loss of a supermajority in 1988 and its loss of even a simple majority in 1997. In both cases, the PRI held majorities in the legislatures that enacted the reforms, suggesting that the reforms were an elite-level response to a perceived legitimacy problem rather than a compromise agreement among competing legislative factions.

These reforms at the federal level had far-reaching symbolic and material implications. Lujambio (2000) notes that among other effects legislative pluralization led to "the cohabitation *(convivencia)* among the several political groups," which produced "contact, understanding, and personal relations between members of distinct political parties." This contact increased the level of trust to the extent that (at least some members of) the PRI became less fearful of an opposition with real political power. After the PRI lost its supermajority in 1988, interparty bargaining became even more salient, given the continued efforts to amend the constitution by both the PRI and the opposition (Lujambio 2000, 33–34).

Thus, over the course of more than two decades, Mexico underwent a long-term transformation, encompassing both elite-level competition at the center of the political system and a broader political conflict in the periphery. But for all of this, few Mexicanists were willing to call Mexico a democracy unless and until there was *alternation* in the presidency.

Given the PRI's historical willingness to use any means necessary to ensure its own electoral victories, and given the overwhelming power of the presidency in the (pre-2000) Mexican political system, this view has merit. Consider that even though there were no significant allegations of fraud in the 1994 presidential election, few observers changed their assessment of the Mexican regime on the basis of this election. Further, if the PRI candidate had won in 2000, even in a free, fair, and clean election, most scholars would have continued to view Mexico as an authoritarian regime. Whether these verdicts are justified or not, it is clear that most Mexicanists agree with the criteria set forth by Przeworski and his collaborators: democracy requires alternation in high office pursuant to an election (see Alvarez et al. 1996; Przeworski et al. 2000). The fact that few observers were willing to believe that the PRI would have stepped down before they actually witnessed the event in 2000 suggests the degree to which democratization in Mexico has been construed as an *electoral* process.

The Perceived Effects of Electoral Competition in Mexico

As we have seen, most of the scholarship on Mexico views this electoral transformation as an obvious step forward for Mexican democracy, and rightly so. But it would be a mistake to interpret this transformation as clear evidence that Mexico has completed some type of transition to a fully consolidated democracy. Indeed, the recent literature on democratization shows the fallacy of assuming, on the basis of the type of electoral transformation witnessed in Mexico and many other countries, that competitive elections are necessary and sufficient conditions for democracy, or even that elections automatically produce representative, responsive, or "democratic" outcomes (O'Donnell 1994; Levitsky and Way 2002; Carothers 2002).

The early literature on Mexico was optimistic. In comparing the Mexican and Venezuelan experiences up to the mid-1980s, Michael Coppedge (1993, 253) identifies electoral competition as the factor responsible for the latter country's closer approximation of democratic ideals: "In rural and urban communities, party competition makes local bosses *(caciques)* less abusive, intimidating, and violent toward their clients, and therefore more respectful of citizens' property, persons, and opinions. In national politics as well, a competitive party system encourages governmental responsiveness, moderate opposition, and peaceful evolution of the political system." Like Coppedge, most scholars of electoral competition in Mexico evoke theories of electoral accountability. Victoria Rodríguez (1998, 164) writes that elections "have already begun to deliver on their promise to have a more lasting effect by forcing all parties in government to perform better if they aspire to win the next election." Ibarra, Somuano, and Ortega (2006, 488–89) conclude a study on municipal financial capacity by arguing that "political competition produces *[se traduce en]* in this case a strong incentive for local political actors who want to keep their positions, to obligate them to better perform the functions for which they were elected" because politicians are "under the constant threat of losing power." Yemile Mizrahi (1999, 2) expresses a similar sentiment: "Faced with a competitive political environment in which the parties actually win and lose elections, it is to be hoped that governments would strive to achieve better levels of governmental performance and that they would promote their achievements to the citizenry. When there is electoral competition, the electors use their vote to reward or punish the party that is in power."[13] In addition to summarizing common expectations about elections, this argument also shows the close theoretical link between accountability and responsiveness. The basic argument can be summarized as follows: for whatever reason, Mexican politicians have not performed well in the past. But now that they are faced with a credible electoral threat, they must be more responsive to public interests so that their parties stay in power.

Still, some Mexican scholars recognize that electoral competition may not be the panacea that many expected. A minority goes even further, questioning whether party alternation is the proper basis on which to judge the advance of democracy in Mexico. Juan Manuel Ramírez Sáiz (1998, 28–29) writes that "the alternation of elites and parties in power is one of the expressions of formal democracy. From this viewpoint, the first is evidence of the existence of the second. But, by itself, alternation does not imply an advance in the democratic transition. That is, there could be a change of the party in power without necessarily changing the quality of democratic life in a country or in a city or, in other words, in the system of government, of the existing relations between authorities and citizens and of their public life." Tonatiuh Guillén-López, a scholar of municipal government in Mexico, makes a similar point with regard to subnational politics. According to him, the most pressing problems with municipal governance include an ineffective bureaucracy, financial centralization, and biased electoral laws. Alternation in the mayor's office may make the municipality appear more democratic, but it has little or no effect on the problems that Guillén identifies, which he attributes to federal and state laws. To democratize at the municipal level, he suggests, institutional reform is much more important than alternation (Guillén-López 1994).

The concerns of scholars like Ramírez and Guillén call into question the dominant way of thinking about democratization in Mexico, which focuses on clean elections and periodic alternation. The turn to multiparty electoral competition in Mexico has clearly been a positive development. But the belief that this change will result in an unambiguous improvement in political outcomes rests on the assumption that the new governments will, in some way, be *better* than the governments they replaced. Rather than assuming this to be the case, in the remainder of this chapter I identify a series of theoretical difficulties with the link between electoral competition and democratic responsiveness, and I develop a theoretical explanation for responsiveness that, in principle, could surmount these difficulties in the Mexican institutional context.

Elections as Mechanisms of Control

Representative democracy is a noteworthy form of government only to the extent that its institutions induce rulers to act differently than would rulers under other regimes. It is widely expected that elected officials will heed the public interest, or at least public opinion, more than will a dictator. Nothing prevents a benevolent dictator from pursuing the public interest if he so desires. But proponents of electoral regimes believe that elections can, more reliably than other forms of government, empower public-minded rulers or induce knaves to act public-mindedly. As Madison summarized the argument in Federalist No. 52, "As it is essential to liberty that the government in general, should have a common interest with the people; so it is particularly essential that the branch of it under consideration [the House of Representatives], should have an immediate dependence on, & an intimate sympathy with the people. Frequent elections are unquestionably the only policy by which this dependence and sympathy can be effectually secured" (Hamilton, Madison, and Jay 1787–88/1992, 267). While an authoritarian regime may occasionally (perhaps by chance) come under the rule of a dictator who is truly interested in the public welfare, electoral regimes can empower such people on a regular basis. Elections make responsiveness *routine*. And while responsiveness may depend on any number of additional factors, elections are a basic necessity, without which citizens cannot reliably control rulers or induce them to pursue constituents' interests.

In one form or another, all theories of electoral accountability frame the relationship between citizens and representatives as a principal-agent problem. Like all agents, representatives often have incentives to act contrary to the interests of their principals, so citizens need to devise some strategy for controlling their behavior. There are two general explanations for how elections solve this strategic problem. Elections may help voters *select* competent representatives who will attend to their constituents' interests either out of a sense of duty or because they happen to share their constituents' preferences. Or elections may help voters *sanction* representatives who are not sufficiently responsive (Fearon 1999; Manin, Przeworski, and Stokes 1999a; Stimson, Mackuen, and Erikson 1995).

These two theoretical approaches have long pedigrees in American political science. Downs (1957) and A. Campbell et al. (1960) both conceived of elections as opportunities for voters to select parties whose platforms were most appealing. V. O. Key (1966) proposed a retrospective approach to voting behavior, according to which voters opted for parties that had performed well in the past. Other scholars challenged the focus on parties, arguing that both selection processes (McKelvey 1975) and retrospective evaluations of performance (Fenno 1978) could be more usefully applied to individual candidates rather than parties.[14] Fiorina (1981) synthesized many of these ideas by arguing that voters think primarily in prospective, candidate-centered terms but that they can use their knowledge of candidates' party affiliation and past performance to form judgments about how these candidates are likely to act in the future. Fiorina's simultaneous appeal to both selection and sanctioning mechanisms is evident in this summary passage: "Like Downs we should view the voter as looking ahead and choosing between alternative futures. Past trends are not ignored, to be sure; they are incorporated into future projections. But the latter incorporate other things as well. Good past performance, which creates favorable future expectations, is a helpful thing for an incumbent candidate to have. But there is still an opponent who may succeed in stimulating even more favorable future expectations. And he may win" (Fiorina 1981, 197). The literature since Fiorina has tended to adopt a similar synthetic approach. While formal studies often model the vote as exclusively prospective or retrospective (Downs 1957; Ferejohn 1986), most recent work shows that both past performance and future expectations influence voters' judgment at the polls to some extent.[15] This may be because, as in Fiorina's argument, past performance is a good indicator of future performance, and information about it is easy to acquire. Or it may be that voters employ mixed rationales: some are concerned to punish incumbents, and others to find good leaders for the future.

As I argued in chapter 1, the (largely American) literature on electoral accountability has been extremely influential for at least a half-century. Few scholars of democracy doubt the basic premise that elections make government more responsive to citizens, and this idea has permeated thinking in academic, political, diplomatic, and policy circles. This is surprising because, for all of its promise and intuitive appeal, the literature rests on shaky theoretical ground. One potential problem is that these theories require voters to have far more information (and to use it more rationally) than most real voters actually have. Another problem is that theories of electoral control typically require strong assumptions about the structure and functionality of electoral institutions. Finally, even if these theories succeed as accounts of voting behavior, it is difficult to establish that government policies or outcomes actually improve as a result of elections, as the theory would predict.[16] I discuss each problem in turn.

Information

The ability of voters to separate good representatives from bad ones hinges on the quality of information that they have about representatives and their activities. Exactly how much information voters need to have is an open question; but all theories of electoral control assume that some threshold level of knowledge is necessary. Here I focus on two types of information that are widely considered to be essential: knowledge about who is responsible for outcomes and knowledge about outcomes themselves.[17]

Voters need to know whom to praise or blame. They cannot effectively sanction a politician for poor performance unless they know which politician(s) is responsible for the poor performance. As G. Bingham Powell argues (2000, 51), "If citizens in a democracy cannot identify responsibility for policy, they cannot use elections precisely to hold policymakers retrospectively accountable for their actions. When policy responsibility is unclear, the incentive for policymakers to anticipate what citizens want and work to achieve it is also lessened. Clarity of responsibility, then, is an important condition if elections are to serve as instruments for citizen control in a democracy." In some early versions of accountability theory, the amount of information that voters needed to have was unrealistically high. More recent approaches have attempted to minimize the informational requirements, since it is well known that most voters have very little information regarding representatives and their policy positions. Scholars have also argued that voters use any number of informational shortcuts, such as party identification, to make inferences about a candidate's position or performance. Finally, information about who is responsible for political outcomes can be easier to acquire, and less ambiguous, under favorable institutional arrangements. Writing in a comparative context, Powell (2000) argues that minority governments in parliamentary systems offer little clarity of responsibility, while single-party majorities (in a parliamentary regime), or presidents with congressional majorities (in a presidential regime), provide much greater clarity. All else equal, then, we should expect voter control to be more effective when voters have more information and when those responsible for policy and outcomes are more easily identifiable.

Voters also need to know how their rulers have performed, or at least how they are likely to perform in the future. Obviously, the information that voters must have depends on the criteria that are thought to be relevant to government performance. For example, early policy-based studies found accountability wanting. They described an electorate that was overwhelmingly ignorant of the details of policy and of the corresponding positions of politicians or parties (see, among others, A. Campbell et al. 1960). But Key (1966) challenged this pessimism in part by changing the informational requirements for accountability.[18] Expecting voters to have information only on general outcomes such as the state of the economy, Key was able to offer a more optimistic assessment of voter control. Achen and Bartels (2004) have recently argued that even Key's informational assumptions are not met by the American public, who are thus susceptible to last-minute pandering that thwarts performance-based accountability. Other recent work is more optimistic; but all researchers are forced to reconcile accountability mechanisms with low levels of information. No theory can dispense of informational assumptions entirely, and thus we know that (1) electoral control is impossible in the absence of information and (2) if elections serve as mechanisms of control, responsiveness is likely to improve as the amount of relevant information increases.

Electoral Institutions

Most electoral theories require that elections themselves be basically transparent. There is no fraud, and votes are counted honestly, according to well-known rules. Candidates are generally well behaved, too. They may eventually break their campaign promises, but they do not buy votes illegally or subvert electoral institutions. These assumptions seem appropriate, as they are implied by the definition of an electoral regime. In other words, a regime in which ballot boxes are routinely stuffed in favor of the ruling party is not really an electoral democracy.

At a minimum, then, we can say that electoral mechanisms of control require well-functioning electoral institutions. If elections are not conducted fairly, or if the aggregation of votes is biased toward a particular party or set of candidates, then the prospects for electoral accountability are grim. In a certain sense, this requirement usefully separates those electoral systems that our intuitions tell us are truly democratic, such as the American and British systems, from those that do not seem to meet the requirements of an electoral democracy, such as Zimbabwe's or Cuba's. But at the same time, even the definitive examples of electoral democracy are subject to a potentially devastating critique from social choice theory.

For example, the early work of Black (1958), Arrow (1963), Plott (1967), and many others reintroduced to social science the aggregation problem that was originally observed by Condorcet. According to the most basic version of the problem, in any social choice with three or more alternatives, the pairwise comparisons may fail to produce a stable winner, even under conditions of perfect information. This implies that in a large number of real-world social choice situations, including elections, results are dependent on the (arbitrary) method of preference aggregation. William Riker (1982, 236) summarizes the point by concluding that, since no method of vote aggregation is demonstrably superior to all others, "the claim that voting produces a fair and accurate outcome simply cannot be sustained when the method of counting partially determines the outcome of counting. . . . Outcomes of voting cannot, in general, be regarded as accurate amalgamations of voters' values." Furthermore, since it is always possible that those in power chose or imposed a given counting method because of the particular amalgamating effect it would have, "Outcomes of any particular method of voting lack meaning because often they are manipulated amalgamations rather than fair and true amalgamations of voters' judgments and because we can never know for certain whether an amalgamation has in fact been manipulated" (238). Riker claims to salvage some utility for electoral regimes by appealing to the "liberal" view of elections, according to which they are useful so long as they can remove, even occasionally, officeholders who have "offended enough voters" (243). But under no circumstances should we expect that elections could play the positive "populist" role of consistently empowering officials whose policy preferences are shared by clear majorities among the public.[19]

My own view is that social choice critiques of electoral institutions can sometimes be alarmist. Although it is difficult to argue with the results of social choice analysis on mathematical grounds, the gloomy predictions of Riker and others run up against several hard facts. For example, most Americans believe that the government does in fact pursue popular policies most of the time. Policies do not cycle wildly and endlessly, as social choice theory predicts. And recent studies have found that the advanced industrial democracies do in fact govern in close relation to the policy preferences of the median citizen (Stimson, Mackuen, and Erikson 1995; Powell 2000). Riker's gloomy predictions simply fail to match the intuitions of most scholars who study elections in established democracies.

What, then, is the value of the social choice critique of electoral mechanisms? First, recent work in formal theory has offered more specific claims about how accountability mechanisms might fail. Thus Ferejohn's (1986) claim that electoral control requires sociotropic voting and Myerson's (1993) demonstration of how politicians have incentives to serve only a minority of the electorate (which minority they may create in the first place) offer suggestions about where exactly an empirical investigation of accountability should focus. For example, if Ferejohn is right, effective electoral control should be found only in conjunction with survey evidence of sociotropic voting.

Additionally, social choice research has made clear that electoral rules matter. The most obvious example in the Mexican context is the effect of the strict term limit rule, which I discuss below. Holding representatives directly accountable for their actions in office is not possible when reelection is forbidden; selection mechanisms may still function but become more complicated in such an institutional context. Another relevant example of the impact of electoral rules is the use of plurality decision rules in Mexican municipalities, which primarily benefits the PRI. By holding the center, the PRI has often been able to split the opposition between parties of the Left, like the PRD, and more conservative parties, such as the PAN, thus maintaining itself in power even when its commands only minority support among the electorate. Following Riker, we cannot claim that this somehow makes municipal elections illegitimate—Riker's point is that *all* particular voting mechanisms have characteristics that may produce "undemocratic" results in certain cases. But we are certainly free to wonder whether the plurality rule in Mexico has sustained the ruling party in power in municipalities it otherwise would have lost some time ago. Manipulation of the electoral rules is even more evident in legislative elections, where the PRI regularly tinkered with electoral formulas to increase its electoral advantage (Balinski and Ramírez González 1999; Lujambio 2000; Méndez de Hoyos 2006).

Finally, and more generally, the social choice critique exposes the "electoralist fallacy," or the misguided assumption that any electoral regime, just by virtue of its holding elections, will necessarily have a government that serves the public interest and is responsive to the will of the voters (Booth 1995). In fact, electoral regimes vary widely in this respect. It is simply not true that elections always fail to produce accurate or "democratic" results. But neither do elections always produce equally fair results or empower equally responsive governments. Social choice theory exposes a class of potential problems with electoral control that, properly viewed, should help us to evaluate the ability of elections to deliver what they promise.

Electoral Control and Government Performance

Assuming for the sake of argument that a given accountability mechanism functions properly, why would government work better as a result? Some might argue that this question is tautological: if the government is being punished for poor performance, it is accountable by definition. But the logic of this argument is incomplete. Accountability implies that citizens have the power to "throw the bums out" when they need to (Riker 1982). But the problem of government performance requires an additional step: that the ability to "throw the bums out" actually improves the way politicians behave while they are in office. There are good theoretical reasons to believe that the former power does lead to the latter outcome; but the relationship should not be assumed. (Fox [2007] offers a similar conceptual distinction between elections and accountability.)

The issue is most easily illustrated with respect to retrospective sanctioning. If voters judge based on past performance, and if incumbents care about retaining office, then the possibility of losing a periodic election may cause incumbents to make sure that their performance is good enough to merit their reelection.[20] There are two ways that this process could work: as a *dynamic process,* in which politicians occasionally fail to perform well and voters replace them when they do fail (Lott and Reed 1989); or as an *equilibrium condition,* in which the voters' credible threat to remove a poor performer and the politician's decision to perform well are mutual best replies. In other words, "The anticipation of not being elected in the future leads elected officials not to shirk their obligations to the voters in the present" (Fearon 1999, 56).

Both of these explanations have their weaknesses. If retrospective accountability works as a dynamic process, then something must be said about the challengers who occasionally win office when an incumbent has been ousted. Most retrospective models are silent on the characteristics of the challengers in any given election. If the incumbent is removed, his replacement has no experience in office (by assumption) and therefore no record that could be used to evaluate him. For accountability to lead to improved responsiveness, then, there must be some nontrivial probability that a politician drawn from the pool of challengers is more susceptible to the electoral threat (or more committed to the public interest) than was the ousted incumbent. If all challengers are likely to be just as bad, the voters have no real incentive to oust a poorly performing incumbent. In fact, this logic is often used to explain why voters do not remove poorly performing incumbents in single-party-dominant regimes, such as Mexico, Japan, or Taiwan (see Magaloni 1999). The logic is captured in the familiar Mexican expression, "Better the devil you know than the devil you don't."[21]

If, on the other hand, retrospective accountability is seen as an equilibrium condition, it becomes extremely reliant on the assumption that politicians desire to remain in office. This assumption is fair enough, except for the fact that all politicians eventually leave office. When they do so of their own volition, as in a choice to retire, or when their departure is a foregone conclusion, as happens under term limits (Michelle Taylor 1992; Carey 1996), the accountability mechanism is subject to failure because of the *last-term problem.* As the label suggests, politicians who know themselves to be in their last term no longer have an incentive to garner voter approval. They are therefore free to ignore the wishes of their constituents and pursue their own policy preferences, or even personal financial gain.[22]

When the last term is common knowledge (that is, when voters know beforehand whether a candidate would be entering his last term), accountability mechanisms can "unravel" (Fearon 1999). If voters know that politicians will not faithfully represent them in their last term, they should not empower them for a final term. But if the representatives foresee their own ouster, they have an incentive to shirk during their penultimate term. The strategic analysis unravels to the first interaction between the voters and the politicians, and the voters cannot be assured that any politicians will represent them well, even in their very first term of office (Barro 1973; Ferejohn 1986; Carey 1996). Without some method of policing representatives during their last term, retrospective accountability may not last as an equilibrium condition, again frustrating hopes of electorally induced "good government."

It is also difficult to establish a firm theoretical link between improved government performance and prospective selection mechanisms. In all selection models, voters are charged with selecting candidates who are committed to acting in their constituents' interests. But politicians, once in office, may not have a clear incentive to keep their campaign promises or to forego rent-seeking activity. Knowing this, voters have reason to doubt campaign promises or discount other signals that candidates may send during a campaign. Therefore, at least within a rationalist framework, purely prospective models cannot explain why a politician would work toward the public interest (Ferejohn 1986). And even if we allow for nonrational candidates who would forego rent seeking, selection mechanisms cannot explain how electorates could reliably identify and empower such candidates, since rent seekers have incentives to obfuscate during campaigns (Fearon 1999).

Many scholars suspect that a mixed mechanism, or a synthesis along the lines of Fiorina's (1981) formulation, would provide a more suitable explanation of the relationship between electoral competition and improved responsiveness. Surely, even if sanctioning and selection mechanisms have their theoretical limitations, an electorate that combines the two can produce a greater degree of electoral control. Yet recent work suggests that electorates can "strive for one goal only at the expense of the other" (Manin, Przeworski, and Stokes 1999a, 46). For example, Fearon (1999) shows that an interaction between selection and sanctioning mechanisms can be effective under certain conditions (like high levels of information) but that in general they work at cross-purposes, so that under most conditions the rational option for the electorate is to drop one goal in order to focus completely on the other.

Finally, proponents of electoral theory must consider the possibility that mechanisms of electoral control produce perverse incentives, according to which politicians do adjust their behavior, but in ways that damage (or have no effect on) responsiveness. This is especially likely with sanctioning mechanisms. For example, rather than forcing representatives to become responsive to the public interest, the electoral threat may lead representatives to cultivate a strongly supportive minority following (Myerson 1993) or a minimum winning coalition at the expense of the broader constituency. They may also embrace elite preferences, since elites have disproportionate influence in the electoral process. Politicians are often known to pander to voters according to the electoral cycle, offering short-term benefits at election time to make up for a full term's worth of neglect; this is especially effective if voters have low levels of information (Achen and Bartels 2004). Finally, representatives may respond to electoral pressures by constructing clientelist or patronage networks, again using the resources of office to distort the preferences of an important segment of the electorate. These are just a few examples of the ways in which electoral mechanisms may produce nonresponsive outcomes.

The issues I have outlined in the past two sections do not prove that electoral control is a hopeless endeavor. Rather, in pointing out the theoretical limitations of electoral control mechanisms, the discussion gives us the information that we need to develop a logical explanation of how elections might contribute to more responsive government in Mexico. The previous section established that functional electoral control requires voters to have adequate information regarding who is responsible for political outcomes and regarding the outcomes themselves. This section has elaborated several institutional problems; as we will see, the most critical problem in the Mexican context is the strict term limit rule, which introduces the last-term problem into the Mexican system. Finally, underlying the entire discussion of selection, sanctioning, and combined mechanisms of electoral control is the requirement that elections provide challengers who are real alternatives to the status quo. This implies that *both accountability and selection mechanisms require electoral competition if they are to be the cause of improved government performance.*

How Does It Work In Mexico?

Most social scientists hold elections in high regard because they view elections as a critical instrument for producing responsive governance. But here is the conclusion of two prominent scholars of Mexico regarding the possibility of electoral accountability under the hegemonic PRI:

> Elections are usually thought to be the most legitimate and effective way of guaranteeing accountability. . . . Electoral defeat . . . is viewed as the ultimate (and often the only) general sanction on leaders who do not so markedly violate community standards as to land in jail. But there is a multiple irony in the concept of electoral accountability as applied to Mexico. In the first place, . . . where apathy, ignorance, unequal distribution of resources, complicated policy issues, secrecy, and bureaucracy define the common condition, elections can make little difference. Political elites are already assured almost complete autonomy from the rank and file in their decision-making, and the threat of an election some years hence . . . is hardly a real check on authoritarianism and unresponsiveness in office. In the second place, the noncompetitive nature of Mexican elections and the no-reelection rule violate the basic premises on which the hope of electoral accountability rests. Where there is no real public competition for office and where a politician never has to face the people who elected him to answer for his sins in office, the hypothesized structure of institutionalized constraints crumbles. (Fagen and Touhy 1972, 165)

Obviously, much has changed in Mexico in the decades since Fagen and Touhy's pessimistic assessment. But it would be a mistake to assume, without investigation, that the conditions for electoral control in Mexico have improved. We need to know what characteristics of the Mexican system remain, thus inhibiting electoral control, and what characteristics may have changed in ways that improve the prospects for electoral control. Accordingly, this section derives a theoretical explanation for election-induced responsiveness in Mexico. Mirroring the theoretical discussion above, I begin by discussing informational limitations and then turn to institutions before generating a plausible explanation that has clear mechanisms and is faithful to the Mexican institutional context. In keeping with the overall theme of the book, I focus on local politics and municipal institutions.

Information

The Mexican political system under the PRI was characterized by centralization and the dominance of the executive branch at the federal, state, and municipal levels. Governors and mayors are extremely powerful within their own spheres; in the era of PRI dominance, there was little that state legislatures or municipal councils could do to block the actions of their executive counterparts (Guillén-López 1994).[23] This may not be appealing to those who favor the separation of powers, but it is a clear benefit in one respect: voters know whom to blame. Interestingly, mayors are just as prominent as governors and the president in this respect. For example, in a 2001 national sample survey, citizens were asked which political representatives "best represent their interests." They named their mayor more frequently than any other office except the president, and more than three times as often as their *diputados* (federal congressmen).[24]

Clarity of responsibility at the municipal level is also enhanced by the fact that the duties of municipal governments are clear and well known. The Mexican Constitution stipulates that municipal governments assume primary responsibility for eight issue areas, which include providing utility services such as water and sewers; caring for public parks and monuments; and ensuring public security (see table 4.1). In chapter 4, I show evidence to indicate that voters do in fact have a relatively clear idea of the sorts of issues on which municipal government performance should be evaluated.

Of course, as is true in many countries, the Mexican public often displays a lack of basic information regarding politics: they may not know the name of their representative, the responsibilities of the judicial branch, or the platforms of two competing candidates. But local issues in general are relatively easy for citizens to monitor. Judging a government's efforts toward combating inflation or trade imbalances may be difficult, but it is easy to know whether many of one's friends have been robbed recently or whether one's neighborhood (or one's own home) has water and sewer service. In addition, for reasons that I discuss in later chapters, many municipal governments became more transparent in the 1990s, publishing budget information and holding public assemblies to explain spending allocations. In general, and especially with respect to local elections, it seems reasonable to assume that the Mexican electorate usually has sufficient information on political outcomes and the actors responsible for those outcomes. Or, at a minimum, we can say that informational constraints cannot be seen as a general, categorical deficiency with respect to mechanisms of electoral control.

Electoral Institutions

Mexico's electoral institutions, on the other hand, present several serious obstacles to mechanisms of electoral control. The country's strict prohibition against reelection presents the most significant problem by far. Other potential deficiencies include the short (three-year) terms of most elected positions and the (informal) practice of allowing incoming mayors to replace entire levels of bureaucracy.[25] These institutional features present problems for both selection and sanctioning mechanisms of control, and thus any attempt to construct a coherent theory of electoral control in Mexico *must* address the limitations they introduce.

The easiest way to begin the analysis is to consider the effect of term limits. Mexico's prohibition of consecutive reelection is universal and strictly observed. In principle, politicians can return to a post after having vacated for a term, but in practice only a small proportion do so. Nacif (1996) reports that 82 percent of the deputies in the federal congress from 1982 to 1991 had no prior experience in that body. Fifteen percent had served one term previously, and 3 percent had served two or more terms. The proportions are similar for state legislators and mayors. By tradition, governors never return for a second term; presidents are expressly forbidden to do so by Article 83 of the Mexican Constitution.

To a much greater extent than electorates in most countries, then, Mexicans need to worry about the last-term problem, since every elected official is simultaneously serving his or her first and last (consecutive) term in a given office. Most elected officials aspire to other elected offices, so they may have an interest in building a good reputation (Michelle Taylor 1992). However, the constituency for the new office will by definition be different from the old one and thus less likely to be familiar with the politician and his or her activities in prior office. Career advancement also depends on pleasing party officials who can confer future nominations, rather than the constituents who are presumably being served. In fact, many scholars argue that the no-reelection clause of the constitution was drafted by the PRI precisely to create career dependency by preventing partisans from gaining independence through incumbency (Michael Taylor 1997; Langston 2003; Lujambio 1995, 174; Ugalde 2000, 97–120).

All politicians have some history behind them. But if we are to believe rationalist accounts of agent behavior, we have to worry that there is insufficient incentive for any Mexican politician to favor the public interest over his or her own, since there is no need to secure reelection. Sanctioning as a dynamic sorting process, as conceived by Lott and Reed (1989), breaks down because the electorate does not have the ability to keep good representatives in office; sanctioning as an equilibrium condition fails because the electoral threat is noncredible, even nonsensical, to representatives who cannot aspire to reelection. Therefore, candidate-sanctioning mechanisms, such as those offered by Fenno (1978) and Austen-Smith and Banks (1989), cannot possibly explain electoral accountability in Mexico.

The term limit law also presents a problem for candidate selection mechanisms, perhaps to a lesser degree. Like the sorting process mentioned above, term limits make it impossible to keep good representatives in office for more than one term. True, the electorate always has another opportunity to select a good representative. But if we believe that there are fewer skilled (and honest) representatives than there are positions to fill, then we must recognize that term limits complicate the voters' task by removing some good candidates from consideration. Thus Mexican-style term limits are a potential barrier to accountability under *any* reasonable set of theoretical assumptions.

A second institutional feature that limits electoral control in Mexico is the common use of three-year terms.[26] While three-year terms are not problematic on their own, their combination with term limits in Mexico is widely thought to hinder good government. As early as 1972, Fagen and Touhy wrote that "members of the *ayuntamiento* [the municipal government] seem to take their short tenure in office as a reason not to act in the realm of planning. It is a realm in which activity brings no immediate career rewards and is moreover almost certain to engender divisive conflicts, at least in the short run. . . . The short, three-year term of office also detracts from an *ayuntamiento*'s collective sense of responsibility, for officials are in office only briefly and cannot be held accountable in the next election" (63–65).

Contemporary scholars have identified several additional factors that exacerbate the institutional problems in Mexican municipalities. One additional effect of current institutions is that even politicians who are inclined to perform well have little time to learn the bureaucratic intricacies of the job or to gain policy expertise. They are also forced to spend much of their energy angling for their next job (occasionally a nomination for an elected position, but often an appointed position in the state or federal executive branch).[27] The result, potentially, is that at the beginning of their terms Mexican politicians are too inexperienced to serve their constituents well, while at the end of their terms they are too distracted. And with a three-year term, there may not be much room in the middle during which officeholders are both competent and public oriented (see Guillén-López 1995, 1996). These problems are particularly damaging to government performance, especially at the local level, because power is so heavily centralized in the office of the mayor and because mayors typically replace the entire top level of the municipal administration with their own partisans. Some civil servants remain, especially in larger municipalities with large service sectors. But the top level of administration usually turns over with each election, and personnel changes occasionally run deeper into the bureaucracy.

Considered in combination, these institutional features present significant obstacles to electoral control in Mexico. We have already seen that candidate-sanctioning mechanisms are incompatible with Mexico's term limit rule. Therefore, any explanation of electoral control in Mexico must either focus on selection mechanisms or devise a solution to the problem of sanctioning under term limits. In what follows I introduce two theoretical explanations that abide by these requirements, and I evaluate their plausibility as explanations for responsiveness in Mexico.

Potential Solutions: Electoral Control and Government Performance

Arguments in which Mexican voters hold individual candidates accountable by threatening to vote them out of office are logically inconsistent. But there are ways to reconcile electoral control with institutional contexts like Mexico's. Fearon (1999) suggests prospective selection mechanisms, specifically because of the difficulties involved in retrospective sanctioning: "Imagine, for instance, a system in which elected officials can serve only one term in office, so elections cannot serve as a sanctioning device to induce good performance by those elected. But if the voters think they are able to distinguish among types of candidates and that some types are more inclined to act of their own accord in the public interest, then they could still understand the elections as the fundamental mechanism of democratic governance" (Fearon 1999, 58). Although Fearon was not writing about Mexico, his theoretical description clearly applies here. And it reasonable to wonder, as he does, whether prospective *selection* plays a role in electoral control where retrospective *sanctioning* cannot.

To be effective, selection mechanisms must overcome at least two important obstacles. First, selection would require voters to be able to choose "good types" of politicians, who are "principled, competent, and share the electorate's ends, independent of reelection incentives" (Fearon 1999, 82). Although there are doubtless many principled and dedicated public servants among the ranks of politicians in Mexico, it would be risky to assume that they routinely present themselves for election. Much of Mexico is governed poorly from one term to the next, without significant improvement. This makes it difficult to argue that Mexican voters are consistently selecting public-interested politicians whom they can then trust to work in their interest without any need for monitoring. Further, given the degree of party control over both candidate selection and politicians' postelectoral futures (see below), it is hard to imagine that candidates who would put constituents' interests over their party's would ever make it onto the ballot. A second reason to doubt the possibility of purely prospective selection is that even Fearon's model does not favor this type of explanation. He drops the hypothetical case of single-termed politicians and allows voters to use past performance as a criterion on which to select good types for the subsequent term. In this mixed case, "bad types" have incentives to mimic good types, so responsive government can be achieved even when good types are not always selected. In the end, he concludes that sanctioning and selection are at work at the same time, and in this respect his argument is similar to Fiorina's (1981) synthetic explanation.

As a practical matter, the necessary conditions for any electoral selection mechanism are not met in those parts of Mexico that still lack competitive elections. But it remains possible that selection mechanisms can explain why government performance is improved in areas where elections present voters with real alternatives. Thus the candidate selection mechanism represents one potential solution to the puzzle of electoral control in Mexico and deserves to be tested empirically.

A second potential solution is to introduce parties into the sanctioning mechanism. Even if voters cannot punish (or reward) individual candidates, they may be able to target parties. Parties will then have an incentive to promote responsiveness among their office-holding partisans. Parties will also have the leverage needed to control their own partisans because they control appointments and nominations to future political positions. If parties play off their partisans' "progressive ambition," or their desire to obtain increasingly important or influential positions, elections may enforce accountability indirectly, through political parties (Carey 1996; Michelle Taylor 1992). For example, Carey (1996, 102) concludes his study of term limits in Costa Rica by writing that "the interest of parties is to win elections. To do so they need to build reputations for providing the goods and services that voters want. . . . But where politicians cannot be reelected, the question arises of what incentive they have to work hard maintaining their party's reputation. . . . The data presented here [in Carey's study] suggest that patronage [i.e., political appointments] is the solution to this problem. . . . The electoral connection is not gone in Costa Rica; it is just indirect." In many ways, this theoretical adaptation seems appropriate for the Mexican case as well. Mexican elections are usually thought to be heavily "party centered." Party labels figure prominently in political advertising. Ballots consist of large party insignias next to or above a candidate's name, and voters cast their vote by drawing an "X" over the insignia. Many Mexicans are known to vote according to party allegiance, especially when considering whether to vote for the PRI (Domínguez and McCann 1996).[28]

If elections can be seen as collective judgments on parties (rather than on individual candidates), then retrospective sanctioning would require two things. First, voters would have to conceive of elections as opportunities to hold parties accountable for the performance of their office-holding partisans. Second, parties would then have to use internal procedures or incentives to police the performance of their elected officials (Ferejohn 1986). For example, Barro (1973) insightfully suggests that parties may promise political appointments as a means of maintaining party discipline among their elected officials. Alesina and Spear (1988) offer an "overlapping generations" model of accountability, according to which politicians in their last term are persuaded not to shirk by younger members of their party, who are concerned to maintain the reputation of the party for the sake of their own political futures. In sum, "As long as individual legislators remained responsive to parties, which in turn are subject to electoral competition, then a collective electoral connection might remain" (Carey 1996, 176). If Carey's conjecture is accurate, then retrospective accountability is still possible, even in the absence of a direct threat against individual politicians.

My sense of the literature is that most country specialists favor this sort of party-sanctioning mechanism. However, the available survey evidence suggests that most Mexican voters conceive of elections as opportunities to select rather than sanction and that they typically focus on candidates rather than parties. For example, in a national survey after the 2000 presidential election, most respondents gave prospective responses to a question that asked for the "main reason" for their vote. The most frequent response to that question was "for a change" (43 percent of the sample), which might be interpreted in either prospective or retrospective terms. But the second most frequent response was "candidate's proposals," which clearly communicates a prospective thought process.[29] Additionally, the same sample shows strong approval of Zedillo's *priísta* administration (1994–2000). Sixty-six percent of the sample approved of President Zedillo (while 29 percent disapproved and 5 percent "didn't know"). Even more striking, those who voted for Fox were more likely to *approve* of Zedillo's presidency (25 percent) than to *disapprove* of it (17 percent). Surely, a retrospective public would have shown a stronger correlation between its evaluation of Zedillo's term and its vote in the 2000 election.[30]

My own survey data show similar evidence of prospective, candidate-focused attitudes among Mexicans. In 2001, I fielded surveys in four Mexican states (Baja California Norte, Chihuahua, Michoacán, and Puebla) and collected four hundred responses in each state.[31] Among other things, we asked respondents questions to probe whether they viewed elections in prospective or retrospective terms and whether they thought parties or candidates were the appropriate focus of their vote choice. The wording and response frequencies for three questions are listed in table 2.1. When asked to explain why the general public supported the "most important party in the area," respondents mentioned the party's plan for the future twice as frequently as they referenced past performance.[32] When we asked respondents to consider their own thought processes, they were far more likely to consider a party's plan for the future than its past performance and to consider candidates rather than parties.[33] In table 2.2, I cross-tabulate the responses to the questions about citizens' temporal frame and candidate/party focus. Doing so reveals that the orientation required by the party-sanctioning mechanism is the one held by *fewest* respondents (16.9 percent). The most common combination is for respondents to be focused on candidates and on the future (39.1 percent). With the important caveat that the sample was not national, these findings seem to challenge the conventional wisdom on voting behavior in Mexico. Rather than sanctioning or rewarding parties for their partisans' past performance, Mexican voters are oriented toward selecting candidates who they think are most likely to perform well in the future.

This chapter has applied theories of electoral control to the Mexican case in an attempt to develop a logically consistent explanation for how elections might contribute to responsive government in Mexico. My primary purpose was not to dismiss electoral explanations out of hand

Table 2.1. Response Frequencies to Questions about Voter Orientation in Mexico

Thinking about the most important political party in this area, would you say that people support it because . . .

	N	%
it has been accountable in the past, OR	379	32.4
it has a good plan for the future	791	67.6
it distributed things during the campaign, OR	429	36.4
it has a better proposal	749	63.6

When you decide for whom to vote in an election, do you think more about what that party did while it governed or do you imagine how that party will resolve problems in the future?

	N	%
What the party did	501	35.5
How the party will resolve problems in the future	827	58.6
Other	84	5.9

When you decided for whom to vote in the election for governor, what did you consider more, the party or the candidate?

	N	%
The party	462	31.0
The candidate	716	48.0
Neither	158	10.6
Both	155	10.4

Note: In the second question, respondents who spontaneously said "both" were pressed to choose one or the other in a follow-up question; those responses were aggregated into the responses reported here. The third question was also asked of the most recent mayoral election instead of the governor's race, with similar results.

Source: See Cleary and Stokes (2006).

Table 2.2. Voter Orientations in Mexico, 2001

	Voter Target		
Temporal Orientation	*Party*	*Candidate*	*Total*
Past	175 (16.9%)	227 (21.9%)	402
Future	230 (22.2%)	406 (39.1%)	636
Total	405	633	1038

Note: Number of valid responses in each cell; cell percentage (*not* column percentage) in parentheses. There is a substantively small but statistically significant association between future- and candidate-oriented responses (Pearson chi-square 5.62, Pr = 0.018).

Source: See Cleary and Stokes (2006).

but rather to show just how difficult it is to establish clear causal mechanisms between electoral competition and government responsiveness, especially in an institutional context like Mexico's. Two distinct mechanisms seem to offer some promise for electoral theory. According to the *party-sanctioning* model of electoral control, voters must conceive of parties, rather than candidates, as the main focus of electoral praise and blame. And parties must have the inclination and ability to induce their officeholders to work toward the public interest. Alternatively, control might be achieved through a *candidate selection* mechanism, according to which open competition among opposing candidates with real possibilities of winning allows the electorate to choose the candidates who are most willing and able to produce outcomes that are in their constituents' interests. Both mechanisms are logically possible, although evidence from public opinion surveys clearly favors the latter.

The discussion in this chapter suggests two avenues for research that will help to determine whether the theoretical explanations offered here are consistent with reality and thus whether electoral competition improves government responsiveness in Mexico. The first line of research aims to determine whether electoral competition is a cause of government responsiveness in Mexico. Electoral competition is a necessary condition for responsiveness according to both causal mechanisms outlined above. It is required by the party-sanctioning mechanism because competition ensures that the voters' threat to sanction poor performance is credible. It is required by selection mechanisms because voters can select good representatives (if they ever can) only when there is real choice among competing alternative candidates. Accordingly, in chapters 4 and 5 I test the hypothesis that *government is more responsive in municipalities that have competitive elections.*

A second line of research aims at a more direct implication of electoral theory, which is that electoral competition causes politicians to change their behavior in ways that actually improve responsiveness. It would be foolish to dispute that politicians in Mexico, like politicians everywhere, are interested in winning elections and that this desire drives much of their behavior. Yet I have argued in this chapter that politicians do not always respond to electoral pressures by changing their behavior for the better. Often they respond by mobilizing clientelist networks, by using patronage to curry favor, by pandering, or by any number of other strategies that may enhance their electoral support without serving the public interest. In chapter 6 I discuss evidence suggesting that Mexican politicians use such strategies frequently, so much so that it explains the lack of an association between electoral competition and government responsiveness in Mexico. But before turning to the empirical analysis, in chapter 3 I offer an alternative theory of government responsiveness in Mexico that focuses on the role of political demand making, engagement, and the prevalence of nonelectoral participation.

CHAPTER THREE

Political Participation and Democratic Responsiveness

ELECTORAL CONTESTATION HAS BEEN A PROMINENT CONCEPT in democratic theory at least since the publication of Schumpeter's *Capitalism, Socialism, and Democracy.*[1] For Schumpeter, democracy's distinguishing feature is the peaceful competition for power among elites, while the citizenry is relegated to the solitary, almost passive role of voting. As a positive theory of democracy, Schumpeter's formulation can be understood as an outgrowth of classical elite theory, which argued that in any social system politics is the result of the interactions among a small group of people with disproportionate amounts of power (Putnam 1976). As a normative idea about how democracy *should* work, Schumpeter's view can be understood as a reaction against the perception that mass participation in politics is destabilizing. The fear held by Schumpeter and many subsequent democratic theorists, that the unbridled participation of the masses was a recipe for the persecution of minorities, regime instability, and democratic breakdown, has since fallen out of favor. In fact, the dearth of citizen participation is commonly identified as a source or a symptom of democratic malaise.[2] But

Schumpeter's theoretical bias toward a purely electoral conception of democracy remains. Electoral definitions of democracy, such as Schumpeter's, Lipset's, and Przeworski's, dominate the comparative literature. American politicians and academics routinely use the existence of "free and fair" elections as the litmus test for democracy in other nations. Even studies whose founding motivation is the recognition that democracy means more than elections usually identify voting as the sine qua non of democratic governance (see Dahl 1956, 1971; Verba, Schlozman, and Brady 1995).

The dominance of the electoral conception is odd, given what we know about the limitations of elections as instruments of democracy and about the importance of nonelectoral forms of democratic participation.[3] Chapter 2 introduced several important criticisms of the link between electoral processes and democratic outcomes, including the inherent arbitrariness of electoral decision rules (Riker 1982), the impossibility of discerning a policy mandate (Manin, Przeworski, and Stokes 1999a), and the last-term problem (Ferejohn 1986; Carey 1996). To these theoretical problems we can add several practical limitations of elections, such as gerrymandered districts, malapportionment, and the influence of money in campaigns.[4] Perhaps we should not be unduly impressed with the gravity of these criticisms—elections do a better job of selecting public-spirited leaders and guiding policy formation than many of these criticisms would lead us to believe. But it also seems that the identification of serious flaws in the electoral process has not led scholars to rethink their conceptions of democracy. Electoral theory is the "Teflon" theory of democracy, to which criticisms simply do not stick.

This is not to deny, however, that most political scientists recognize the importance of participation. In fact, the Dahlian tradition of democratic theory emphasizes that the "free and fair" requirement for elections implies a full range of civic and political freedoms, to ensure that electoral decisions are subject to informed debate and free choices. Dahl (1971) gives equal standing to competition and participation, which he sees as conceptually distinct phenomena. Furthermore, numerous studies have shown that strategies of direct participation—contacting governing officials, joining community organizations, or even protesting and demonstrating—enhance democratic governance.[5] But several important questions remain unanswered. First, how exactly do engagement and participation induce changes in the behavior of governing officials? Second, is participation an integral part of the electoral process, as the Dahlian tradition would argue, and if so, how tightly connected are these two forms of democratic action? Third, could participation be a useful tool of democratic influence in its own right, even in the absence of a competitive electoral environment, as Mueller (1999) has argued?

To develop an answer to these questions, this chapter proceeds through three steps. First, I build on Hirschman's (1970) conceptual framework of exit and voice as a way to distinguish electoral contestation and voting from other, more direct forms of political action. Second, I offer several theoretical mechanisms that aim to explain why citizens might decide to utilize voice as a strategy of political influence. Third, I explain how participation might produce improved government responsiveness. The focus of the chapter is primarily theoretical, but in the conclusion I explain why the theory offered here is relevant to the Mexican case; in subsequent empirical chapters I offer greater detail on the nature of Mexico's participatory transformation and its effect on democratic responsiveness.

Exit and Voice as Strategies of Influence

Political scientists have long recognized the potential influence of civic and political participation on the quality of democracy. But none has framed the distinction between elections and other forms of political demand making as usefully as has Albert O. Hirschman in *Exit, Voice, and Loyalty* (1970). Hirschman's lasting contribution is to remind us that those who feel compelled to act because of dissatisfaction with a given state of affairs have two strategies available: exit and voice. For example, Hirschman asks us to consider the relationship between a firm and its customers. If, for some exogenous reason, the firm begins to produce goods that are of unacceptably low quality, the customers have two options. They can exit from the relationship, taking their business to a competitor or ceasing to buy that type of product altogether. The loss of customers serves as a signal to the company that if it does not improve its product its future is in jeopardy. But the customers can also use voice, by directly expressing their dissatisfaction to the firm without withdrawing from the economic relationship. The firm may then respond with improved quality, to placate its dissatisfied customers. Both strategies have the potential to ameliorate grievances. The conditions under which exit, voice, or a combination of the two strategies would be most successful is a complicated empirical question. But in theory, either of these strategies might get results.

In politics, electoral mechanisms of accountability and selection can be seen as exit strategies. Essentially, citizens are engaged in an exchange with politicians, in which they use their votes to "purchase" goods, services, and policies from a politician or political party. If citizens become dissatisfied with what politicians provide, they can sever their relationship, either by engaging a political competitor or by dropping out of the exchange relationship altogether. A poorly performing politician who is subject to periodic reelection is faced with a stark choice: perform well, or suffer a loss of business. Since the business of electoral politics is the business of choosing who will rule, the quality of government should improve either way, at least in theory.[6]

Most other forms of political activity, including public speech, direct contact with government officials, political protests, and anything else commonly referred to as political participation, are voice strategies. Their common feature is that they contain a substantive expression of preference or dissatisfaction, by one or more citizens, aimed at government officials or at the government in general.[7] In contrast to voting, political voice strategies do not imply that those who use them have severed their relationship with those at whom their voice is aimed. Indeed, it is often the strength of the relationship that citizens have with government that lends so much weight to their voice.

In fact, Hirschman argues that in politics voice tends to be more effective than exit. For voters, exit threats may not be credible or feasible: the withdrawal of support from a political party may go unnoticed, and in noncompetitive systems it is likely to be ineffectual. Modes of political and civic activity, though, may be well institutionalized: parties and regimes often have established patterns of behavior and formal organizations whose purpose is to foster communication between citizens and the party (or state). Political participation is often the most direct form of action available, so it is not surprising that in free societies citizens frequently employ strategies of voice, such as protest, public speech, or letter writing, to press their demands on government. But Hirschman does not offer a complete account of when and where voice mechanisms are most likely to be effective. Although he suggests several conditions under which voice might be a dissatisfied customer's best option, he does not offer a sufficient explanation for why a firm (or other organization) would *respond* to voice, absent a latent or potential threat of exit. Without such an explanation, voice remains dependent on the possibility of exit and cannot be considered an independent strategy for political influence. Accordingly, one aim of this chapter is to provide an explanation for how voice can be an effective tool of political influence even in the absence of an exit option.

Why Citizens Opt for Voice

There are several reasons that an aggrieved citizen would use a nonelectoral participatory strategy to press the government for a resolution. Strategies like letter writing, public speech, or visits to government offices are more direct than a periodic, anonymous vote. They can be used anytime, and they can be used multiple times. Citizens can vote against an incumbent only once every few years, but they can protest against government inaction every day (see Verba, Schlozman, and Brady 1995, 169). Voice is not costless and its supply is not limitless, especially given the resource constraints of many who use it. But resource-based constraints against repeated use of voice are certainly not as severe as formal constraints against repeated recourse to the ballot box. Furthermore, those who use voice can calibrate their level of participation according to the nature or intensity of their grievance in ways that those who vote simply cannot. Direct forms of participation also allow for more nuanced communication with government. Electoral mandates are notoriously hard to decipher, so (absent voice) even a successful effort to remove a poorly performing incumbent may leave the new government with little information about which issues and problems were responsible for the anti-incumbent vote. Voice, on the other hand, allows citizens to explain the exact source of their dissatisfaction, sometimes in great detail (see, among others, Ackerman 2004; Cornelius 1974; Smulovitz and Peruzzotti 2000).

These advantages seem to be particularly pertinent to the local political issues that are the primary focus of this book. For example, it seems more likely that a citizen would visit a municipal office to complain about potholes than that he would visit the national finance ministry to complain about the central bank's monetary policy. The reason is that participation at the local level is less dependent on large-scale collective action. A solitary citizen who has a grievance against local government may not have a good chance of forcing a response under any circumstances, no matter what the strategy. But a single visit to a government office is more likely to garner a response than a single anti-incumbent vote. Also, additional participants are likely to have a greater marginal effect at the local level than at the national level: all else equal, a group of ten protesters, or one hundred, has a greater chance of winning a concession from a local office, concerning a local issue, than it would have of winning a concession at the national level. The participatory strategies of political influence that I detail below typically have this local, small-scale characteristic. In contrast to studies of large social movements or national-level protests, I aim to understand a more common, quotidian style of small-scale engagement with governing officials. Because solutions to large-scale collective action problems are not required for citizens to take advantage of these strategies, we would expect to see a smaller, but more constant, level of protest or mobilization in local settings.

In the end, however, the true test for voice is its effectiveness. Voice is a viable strategy only if it works, or at least works better than exit. And while it may not be difficult to explain the advantages of voice, or to show empirically that it is a common strategy of influence in any reasonably free society, it turns out to be a bit more difficult to explain the *effectiveness* of voice. Some recent studies have focused on the periodic ability of high-profile protests or political movements to force a response from government (Smulovitz and Peruzzotti 2000). But this form of "societal accountability" is haphazard and rare: most political grievances do not trigger the widespread public anger and broad media coverage that make societal accountability effective. Beyond these cases, and thinking in terms of everyday forms of engagement and political demand making, why would governing officials ever respond? Why pay any attention at all?

Why Government Responds to Voice

The most obvious and one of the most commonly cited explanations for a link between voice and responsiveness is that voice greases the wheels of electoral accountability. Politically engaged citizens provide politicians with information they would not otherwise have about voter preferences and grievances. If elections loom as a future threat to the politician's self-interest, this information can be put to good use in formulating policy and prioritizing agendas. Participation may also enhance the efficiency of electoral mechanisms by providing politicians with a signal about the credibility of the latent electoral threat. In a quiescent constituency politicians should not perceive a large threat and may be more tempted to abuse the public trust or to ignore the public interest. But in a mobilized constituency it should not be difficult for a politician to imagine that one hundred protesters today could easily become one thousand anti-incumbent votes tomorrow or that a community group soliciting signatures on a petition today could solicit anti-incumbent votes tomorrow. Third, participation is thought to enhance the ability of voters to make informed decisions when they go to the polling booth. Thus political participation may make electoral selection mechanisms more efficient as well. This is the rationale for the inclusion of civic freedoms in many conceptions of democracy, such as Dahl's (1971). A poorly performing politician will be punished at the polls only if the voters know his record, and voters are more likely to have that knowledge when facts are freely reported by the press, discussed in public forums, and shared among members of social networks.

Below, I will return to the theoretical possibilities of an interaction between electoral and participatory mechanisms. But we need not limit ourselves to an interactive view, which relegates participation to a supplementary role in an essentially electoral story. In fact, one of Hirschman's boldest arguments in *Exit, Voice, and Loyalty* is that voice is a force of influence that can be largely independent of exit and in some cases may be more effective than exit. Although this is certainly not a common view among students of democracy, some recent work does argue that participation can be effective even in the absence of an electoral connection (among others, see Mueller 1999; Guidry and Sawyer 2003; Tsai 2007). But the theories offered by Hirschman, Mueller, and others do not provide a sufficiently sound theoretical account of voice as an independent means of influence. After critically assessing their contributions, I will discuss two mechanisms through which voice may have an independent effect on government responsiveness.

Voice as an Independent Influence

The participatory view of democracy has a long pedigree. In fact, Pateman (1970) argues that the participatory conception dominated early liberal thought, until Schumpeter's (1942/1950) influential work recast democracy in electoral terms. But the specific means by which participation may improve government performance are not always well defined. Pateman (1970, ch. 2), for example, drawing on the work of Mill, Tocqueville, and others, argues that participation produces better-informed citizens, educates them in the virtues of democracy, and creates a sense of solidarity among a citizenry. But it is not immediately apparent (nor was it Pateman's aim to make it so) how education and solidarity improve government performance. With regard specifically to government output, Verba and Nie (1972, 310–11) argue that participation works by giving politicians information about citizen demands (see also Verba, Schlozman, and Brady 1995). More recent work has argued that participation gets results when it is channeled through social movements. But the exact mechanism linking participation or mobilization to government responsiveness, and the relationship between participation and coexisting electoral mechanisms, are not always clearly articulated.

Hirschman's original essay repeatedly asserts that voice can be a viable alternative to exit under certain conditions. But his account makes sense only if the customers or voters have access to the exit option at the same time. So Hirschman repeatedly characterizes voice as a warning to the organization that further dissatisfaction may cause exit (and a loss of profits, customers, or members) at some later date. "If customers are sufficiently convinced that voice will be effective, they may well *postpone* exit. . . . In some situations, exit will therefore be a reaction of *last resort* after voice has failed" (Hirschman 1970, 37, emphasis in original). Or consider Hirschman's explanation for why the dissatisfied purchaser of an automobile might reasonably expect a response to his voice option: "His complaints will be of some concern to the firm or dealer whose product he has bought both because he remains a potential customer in one, three, or five years' time and because adverse word-of-mouth propaganda is powerful in the case of standardized goods" (41). Clearly, in this example, the efficacy of voice lies in its linkage to an implicit threat to exit in the future.

Hirschman may be right to argue that voice becomes more attractive as the possibility of exit decreases, to the point at which, in a pure monopoly situation, voice is the only possible alternative (33). But he does not sufficiently explain why firms or organizations would ever respond to voice in such situations. If a firm has a monopoly on a product for which demand is highly inelastic (which is equivalent to saying that the firm should have no fear of losing business in the future, even as the quality of its product declines), then why would it bother to correct its inefficiencies?

Hirschman speculates but does not provide a complete answer. At one point he writes, "The firm will tend to minimize the discontent of its customers, for the highly rational purpose of earning goodwill or reducing hostility in the community of which it is a part" (63). Elsewhere he suggests that dissatisfied individuals "can impress their unhappiness on a firm or a party and make their managers highly uncomfortable" and that discomfort may include "loss of sleep by the managers" (73–74). Finally, in an appendix, he posits that firms might respond to voice to minimize the costs incurred when their personnel have to deal with irate customers (131), but he insists that these types of direct costs are not necessary for voice to be effective. These propositions are suggestive of some of the voice mechanisms that I offer below; but given Hirschman's scant attention to these issues in his own essay, it seems fair to argue that the mechanisms through which voice asserts an independent influence deserve closer theoretical development.

More recently, Mueller's *Capitalism, Democracy, and Ralph's Pretty Good Grocery* (1999) has provided an important and thought-provoking attempt to recast democracy in participatory terms. Mueller points out, for example, that the two most important political developments in twentieth-century U.S. history, women's suffrage and civil rights, were achieved with little or no recourse to electoral institutions. Indeed, the suffragists were mobilized precisely because they did not have the right to vote, so it would be difficult to argue that they gained the franchise by threatening politicians at the polls. In more general terms, Mueller makes much of the ability of democratic citizens to strike, protest, write letters, voice opinions, and so on as a means of forcing government to be responsive.

But like Hirschman's, Mueller's account lacks a convincing explanation for why governing officials should pay any heed to such forms of voice. The reason he does give is that politicians fear for the loss of their office either as the result of an election or via some other "nonviolent methods for removing office-holders" (Mueller 1999, 140). But this justification reveals the same flaw that we identified in Hirschman's account. Namely, short of violence, and unsupported by a latent electoral threat, it is not clear how any of these forms of voice would force governing officials from power. Of course, in contemporary democracies officials are often driven to resign when they are criticized by colleagues, exposed as incompetent by the press, or targeted in public demonstrations. But such demonstrations or media campaigns are relatively rare and sporadic. Further, it is hard to know whether these types of pressures would carry the same weight if their targets did not face future elections. And even in a competitive electoral environment, when a politician is willing to be obstinate there is typically no (nonelectoral) formal means of recalling him from office. As a method of preserving political accountability, then, Mueller's participatory mechanisms are likely to fail without a corresponding electoral threat.

This weak and haphazard vision of participatory influence is especially troubling given that Mueller believes that democracy's main advantage is its ability to *routinize* responsiveness (Mueller 1999, 139–40). While all regimes respond to some public interests some of the time, democracies are more responsive, more often. But without an electoral mechanism to reinforce the pressure applied through voice, Mueller cannot explain why politicians would ever bow to public pressures on a consistent basis. Furthermore, his own appeal to the suffrage and civil rights movements as exemplars of responsiveness in the absence of elections gives the lie to the argument: these phenomenal social events are the exceptions, not the rule. These are not good examples of "routine responsiveness."

Mueller's instrumental defense of democracy—that citizens should prefer democracy only to the extent that its citizens are comparatively better off than they would be under a different regime—is persuasive. So is his idea that democracy's strongest claim to legitimacy is its ability to routinize responsiveness to the public interest. But Mueller has not successfully shown that participation can have a persistent, routine effect on government behavior over time, on minor issues as well as major ones. And like Hirschman he has not clearly separated participatory mechanisms from electoral ones: his argument still relies on career-oriented politicians fearful of losing office in the future, but it provides no mechanism, other than elections, through which such a loss could occur.

Although Hirschman's and Mueller's accounts—insofar as they aspire to provide an explanation for purely voice-induced responsiveness—are ultimately incomplete, there are several ways to fill in the gaps. Here I offer a simple theoretical account, based on two widely recognized effects of political participation. Participation provides useful *information* to governing bureaucrats and political leaders, and it subjects these actors to (positive and negative) *psychological pressures* that condition their behavior. Subsequently, I embed this explanation in the broader theoretical framework of social capital. I do *not* believe that the well-organized, collective civic activity engendered by social capital is the only means through which participation can be effective. Particularly in the local political settings on which this book focuses, participation often happens one individual at a time, or among small groups for whom collective action is not particularly problematic (Olson 1965, 22–36). But the discussion will suggest that the informational and psychological dynamics I introduce here are also the underlying causal mechanisms that do the "heavy lifting," so to speak, in most studies of social capital, social networks, civic engagement, and similar concepts.

One reason that participation improves government responsiveness is that it increases the quantity and quality of information that politicians have about citizen preferences and demands (Verba and Nie 1972; T. Campbell 2003, 67–68, 100). There is little question that empirically, at least in the United States, participation does increase the sheer size of information flows (Verba, Schlozman, and Brady 1995). But the "quality of the data" is no less important and in fact is one of the great advantages of participatory forms of political activity. Letter writing, protesting, speaking to government officials, attending public meetings—all of these strategies allow for nuanced communication that can give those who govern detailed information on the source of citizen grievances, their intensity, and the most promising means of alleviating them. Understanding the intensity of grievances can help bureaucrats know when they really need to respond. Understanding the reasons behind grievances gives them the ability to respond appropriately.

Brehm and Gates (1997) have formalized this argument in an information-based model of American bureaucratic performance. To the extent that direct citizen contact influences bureaucratic behavior, it functions as a "smoke detector," which gives the bureaucrats information about citizen demands before grievances ever reach the intensity at which a "fire alarm" would catch the attention of the elected officials who supervise the bureaucrats.[8] As I will argue in subsequent chapters, Brehm and Gates's arguments with respect to bureaucratic influence are equally applicable to the local elected officials who are responsible for government performance in Mexican municipalities.

However, Brehm and Gates's account also reveals a limitation common to information-based arguments, which is that they cannot easily explain why governing officials would respond differently to improved information about citizen preferences unless they feared that nonresponsiveness would threaten their careers. Government responsiveness still depends on an assumption about motivations that is linked (indirectly, in this case) to electoral accountability. Brehm and Gates recognize the potential for an indirect electoral connection in their model, since the reason for the bureaucrat to respond to direct contact is to avoid escalation to the point at which citizens go "over his head" to his elected superiors (in this case, Congress), who are subject to periodic voter approval. But they argue that the far more important influence on government performance lies in the bureaucracy's ability to recruit principled, dedicated staff. A pessimistic reading of the theory would suggest that better information only improves government performance under the happy circumstance in which governing officials are already predisposed to labor faithfully in the public interest. But if we are more charitable toward the informational mechanism, we might argue that information is always helpful to some extent: given any two representatives with identical (though small) inclinations to work toward the public interest, the representative with better information will produce better results.

Political participation can also improve government responsiveness by subjecting governing officials to social and psychological pressures to perform well.[9] As any moderately engaged citizen can affirm, public officials just hate having angry people in their office. They do not like to be harassed. Nor are they comfortable when citizens confront them about their own inaction or failure to provide goods and services that citizens expect from them. Whether these political actors are motivated to pursue the public interest or their own private ends, contact with citizens who have grievances can produce psychological stress, and responding to these grievances is often an efficient way to reduce it. Calling attention to an official's inadequate performance can also have more of a social character to it, with an emphasis on shame rather than guilt. For example, Cornelius (1974) describes citizen efforts to gain concessions from local bureaucrats in Mexico City under the hegemonic PRI. Relations had to be cordial and deferential, but citizens would routinely visit government offices in large groups to lodge their complaint or to present a petition. And if they felt that the official did not properly respond, they might turn to the mass media in an attempt to embarrass the official: "One major newspaper in Mexico City maintains a section for 'complaints and petitions' directed at government officials by residents of predominantly low-income neighborhoods," and citizens "frequently visit the newspaper's offices to . . . request news coverage of the situation in their community. The resulting stories may be highly embarrassing to unresponsive bureaucrats" (Cornelius 1974, 1142).

These types of psychological pressures can also be positively reinforcing. For example, Tsai (2007) argues that local officials in some Chinese villages are motivated to be responsive to the public interest because doing so confers "moral standing." High moral standing can have a material payoff in terms of "economic and social advancement," and thus officials may seek moral standing for purely instrumental reasons. But it is also valuable because it "makes people [i.e., governing officials] feel good about themselves" (356). Positive psychological rewards may be as useful as negative ones, and as valuable as material benefits.

Relatedly, public participation represents an opportunity cost for public officials, who are forced to spend time dealing with citizens and their complaints rather than pursuing other ends.[10] Public officials are often forced to satisfy petitioners, respond to written requests, and explain the presence of protesters to their superiors. If participation is costly to governors in terms of time, energy, and opportunity costs, then the official may use a decision rule according to which he becomes responsive to the public interest whenever the cost of neglecting the petitioners outweighs the cost of servicing their demand (see Hirschman 1970, 131). Since participation increases the costs of not responding, it makes government officials more likely to respond. The cost could represent a rational cost-benefit calculation, since the official's time is valuable, but it could also represent a psychological cost, such as being embarrassed in front of one's peers, having to suffer personal insults, or being made to feel that one is a bad person or a poor representative.

This seems to be a major motivation of government bureaucrats in Stokes's (1995) study of Peruvian social movements, and it is certainly the main strategy used by the activists she identifies as "radicals." These radicals target the officials who are directly responsible for the provision of whatever government service is lacking, with the express intention of occupying their time, making them feel uncomfortable, and embarrassing them in front of their superiors. In one of Stokes's most telling illustrations of this process, a neighborhood women's group visited the health ministry in Lima to demand a clinic in its neighborhood. They took over one of the offices, and with women both in the office and out on the street they began a loud chant of protest. The men working in the office, Stokes writes, "got scared" (4). Before long, an official from the ministry was obliged to go out onto the street to speak to the group of women, and he promised the protesters that the ministry would provide the materials for the construction of the clinic.[11]

This is a style of public appeasement that is common in the Mexican context as well. Classic studies of the Mexican system, such as Fagen and Touhy (1972), Cornelius (1974), and Smith (1979), always note the importance of public consultation—but usually for symbolic reasons.

During the period of PRI hegemony, it was important for officials to be seen among the people, listening to complaints and promising solutions. But typically, action was really taken only when the government feared an embarrassing public protest or the escalation of protest into a violent or uncontrolled movement. In fact, it is this sort of responsiveness to public protest that leads Mueller (1999) to cite Mexico as one of two examples of democratic governance in the absence of competitive elections.[12]

My own interactions with Mexican politicians have also suggested the plausibility of these mechanisms, at least for Mexican municipalities. Particularly at the local level, government functionaries whom I interviewed seemed to care what their constituents thought of them, and they tried to anticipate the public mood so that they could act before any public displays of discontent even started. These politicians might cultivate a good reputation or constantly gauge the public mood for instrumental reasons, such as a desire to run for higher office in the future, and it would be foolish to argue that this type of logic never explained their behavior. But information I gleaned from interviews suggests that this was not the whole explanation.[13] All of the mayors I interviewed declared, in one way or another, that their most important goal was to serve their constituents. As one mayor explained to me, doing a good job was important for him because "we are from there," implying both that he took some pride in his hometown and that he was sensitive to the view that his lifelong friends and neighbors would have of him.[14] Consider that the median municipality in the year 2000 had about 11,700 residents. Many municipalities—not all, but many—are the types of small towns where interpersonal connections run deep and news travels fast. Interviews (and other evidence) also revealed that most mayors put considerable effort into gathering information about the public mood and the likely source of discontent. Most mayors prefer to gather information on their own terms, in public assemblies and other venues where they have some degree of control, rather than having aggrieved citizens come directly to their office to lodge complaints. Even mayors with a reputation for poor performance perceive the need to assuage constituents with grievances. When I asked one mayor what happened if he did not "do a good job" in responding to a particular concern, he replied with some agitation, "They complain." His vice-mayor *(síndico),* seated next to him, immediately added: "Yeah. They complain."

Merilee Grindle (2007) reports similar exchanges with local public officials in Mexico. Speaking about visits from the leaders of a community group who were pressing a demand with the local government, one said, "It is impossible to escape from them. They always come to the town to investigate [what's happening] and demand attention for their projects" (132). Grindle notes that many community groups adopt a strategy of returning to the municipal offices "on a weekly basis" until a resolution is reached (131). Another interviewee credited a successful demand-making effort "to the capacity of a local group to go public with its demands or otherwise be obstreperous," and Grindle notes that "making waves sometimes paid off in terms of getting a speedier response from government officials eager to keep the political peace" (132). This is not the only successful mechanism that Grindle identifies in her study of local governance in Mexico, but these efforts to cause shame, discomfort, or embarrassment among recalcitrant public officials are clearly a common strategy.

The two mechanisms discussed here, information flows and psychological pressures, are not dependent on arguments about social capital or collective action. But the fact that social capital can stimulate increased levels of participation and political engagement suggests an affinity between the two theoretical approaches. In fact, the mechanisms I discuss here are consistent with—and may help to explain and qualify—the burgeoning amount of empirical data linking social capital to government responsiveness. Robert Putnam argues that social networks help to produce "collectively desirable behavior" by enforcing social norms. Social capital, which he defines as the "features of social organization . . . that can improve the efficiency of a society by facilitating coordinated actions" (1993, 167), also implies a level of interpersonal trust, which lowers the transaction costs of repeated interactions, thus "greas[ing] the wheels that allow communities to advance smoothly" (2000, 288). Further, Putnam argues that social networks increase the citizenry's "awareness of the many ways in which our fates are linked," "serve as conduits for the flow of helpful information," and even have salutary psychological and physiological effects (2000, 288–89).

Putnam's theoretical discussion identifies clear links between levels of civic engagement and the generation of social capital and offers a persuasive account of why we might expect social capital to help solve collective action problems. Indeed, his account seems most applicable to the sort of local, community-level settings with which this book is primarily concerned, and the theory offers a transparently true and insightful description of how many community problems are solved. But the majority of public problems in modern nation-states, even local community problems, are solved only when the state plays a leading role. A community may organize to demand the construction of sewers, the paving of roads, the construction of a health center or a school, vaccinations, or other public concerns. But the community does not rely only on its own members to resolve such demands; it turns to the state. And it is on this score that the collective action mechanism falls short, for it "leaves us without an explicit articulation of the mechanism by which the ability of people in society to co-operate affects the performance of the governmental institutions that sit on top of them" (Boix and Posner 1998, 689).

In other words, the state is oddly absent from the theoretical story that is meant to explain how to "make democracy work." Collective action may be aimed at a public end, but it need not be. Interpersonal trust is a clear social good, but it does not necessarily imply that the state also becomes more trustworthy. And communities cannot translate their social capital, organizational capacity, or solidarity into government responsiveness without engaging the state at some point in the process (see also Cleary and Stokes 2006). The link between social capital and community action is only half of the story. To understand how social capital may affect government output, we must identify the mechanism through which the former has a causal effect on the latter: How does community action make government *respond?*

One possibility is that, where social capital is abundant, social networks are both broader and stronger and thus are more likely to link governing officials to citizens and communities. According to Putnam (1993, 2000), strong social networks influence behavior by enforcing cooperative social norms. If public officials are not part of such networks, they will be far less susceptible to norm-enforcement pressure from the community (see also Tsai 2007). Historically, many (nondemocratic) governments appointed stewards and governors to geographical areas with which they were unfamiliar, precisely because such officials could more easily disregard local pressures. Most dioceses in the Catholic Church periodically rotate parish pastors for similar reasons. There is no plausible explanation for such practices, other than the organizations' desire to insulate their officials from public pressure while keeping them dependent on (and therefore responsive to) the central hierarchy.

Most democracies, in contrast, require that elected officials reside in the jurisdiction that they represent. This makes it more likely that governing officials will be enmeshed in their communities' social networks. Thus it is easier to understand how citizens could use these networks to induce representatives to behave responsively. Furthermore, there is good reason to believe that communities with strong social networks are more likely to have network members in positions of authority. Most methods of selecting officials, electoral or not, should favor individuals with "good connections." But even if there is no correlation between the depth of one's ties to social networks and the likelihood of one's election to a public post—even if positions were filled by drawing lots—we would still expect that public officials would be more likely to be members of social networks when those networks encompassed a larger proportion of the population.

The informational and psychological mechanisms I have discussed above are critical components of this theoretical story because the process of norm enforcement requires that citizens confront governors with information about community grievances or (poor) government output and that they use social pressure to force a response. Furthermore, these mechanisms help to fill in the gap in the social capital explanation identified by Boix and Posner (1998) and others, by showing how political participation can solve the principal-agent problem inherent in representational schemes. Strong social networks encourage participation (see Rosenstone and Hansen 1993; Verba, Schlozman, and Brady 1995). But they also make participation more routine and more effective. Thus the reason scholars find an empirical link between social capital and government responsiveness is that social capital makes political participation more common and routinized.

The Interaction of Elections and Participation

The discussion to this point has tended to portray electoral and non-electoral forms of participation as mutually exclusive strategies. This is clearly an incomplete representation of what participation in democratic regimes looks like. Indeed, many forms of participation, in addition to voting, are centered on the electoral process: citizens can discuss political issues during campaigns, encourage others to vote, contribute time, money, and energy to political campaigns, and so on. Furthermore, as we have seen, many scholars see a direct link between nonelectoral forms of participation and electoral processes: a politician may fear a public protest, not because of any worry about civil unrest or physical violence, but rather because it is a signal of how the vote may go in the next election.

There are two ways to conceive of a system in which both elections and other forms of participation have a causal influence on government responsiveness. In the first case, electoral and participatory mechanisms are independent but additive. In the discussion above, as in Hirschman's (1970) original formulation of the problem, citizens are confronted with a choice: exit *or* voice. But there is no reason that an aggrieved citizen could not do both. In the political context, this would be analogous to arguing that the aggrieved citizen could vote against the incumbent party at every opportunity, in the hopes of deposing the incumbent party in favor of a challenger, while also pressing his or her case with governing officials in the interim. Unless the incumbent party is aware of the individual's electoral defection, his or her participatory influence is likely to carry as much weight as anyone else's.[15]

The second possibility is that elections and participation have an interactive effect. Recourse to either strategy alone may be relatively ineffective, for reasons I have discussed. Without participation, electoral mechanisms may not be adequate to produce responsiveness because of the difficulty of discerning policy mandates, the dearth of information about citizen demands, and so on. Without elections, participation may lack credibility as a threat to the continued incumbency of governing officials. But when combined, each strategy could have an enhanced effect. The expectation would be that, in polities with competitive elections, participation has a relatively strong effect on government performance: elections give government the incentive to respond, and participation gives it the information it needs to respond well. Where there are no elections or where elections are not competitive, governing officials remain free to ignore the demands expressed through participatory channels. I explore both the independent and the interactive possibilities in the empirical analysis in chapters 4 through 6.

Hirschman conceived of exit and voice as alternative strategies and recognized that attempts to understand how they might work in conjunction with each other faced serious theoretical difficulties. He writes, "Once you have exited, you have lost the opportunity to use voice" (1970, 37). Voice works because firms care about the satisfaction of their customers, and organizations care about the satisfaction of their members. But if a customer or member withdraws from the relationship, Hirschman argues, it is no longer clear why the firm or organization should heed its voice. And it seems unlikely that the customer or member would continue to speak out: presumably, the customer has left an unsatisfying relationship with one firm only to enter into a satisfying relationship with another firm. There is no longer any reason for the customer to be concerned with the declining quality of the first firm's product, and therefore no reason for him to voice his displeasure.

When we consider who among consumers or voters is most likely to use these strategies, it seems plausible that those who exit would have been the most vocal critics had they not exited. Exit of the most dissatisfied then leaves the organization or customer group with its least vocal or least dissatisfied members, reducing the pressure for change (Hirschman 1970, 44–54). Consider a political example: suppose a political party contains two main factions, traditionalists and reformers. If the party's platform and policies lean too far toward the traditionalists' preferences, the reformist wing will become dissatisfied with the party. As always, they have two options, exit and voice. The reformers may leave the party if they feel that there are political gains to be made by forming a new party or joining a competitor. But if they do leave, change toward a reformist platform in the original party will become even less likely, since the reformers no longer have a say in the party's policy formation. In Hirschman's model, the party is "declining" for some exogenous reason, so we cannot assume that political market forces will be sufficient to bring the party back into line.[16] Given this assumption, the exit of the party's most vocal supporters of reform will leave the party more likely to resist such reform.

These are important theoretical considerations, but in the end their relevance in the political context is limited by two factors that Hirschman (1970) does not address. First, Hirschman's dictum that "once you have exited, you have lost the opportunity to use voice" (37) is not always true in the political context. One reason that exit does not foreclose the possibility of voice is that political parties or ruling governments do not always know when a supporter has exited. As long as ballots are secret and parties cannot accurately infer how people voted, there is not much risk in surreptitiously casting a vote against an incumbent while presenting oneself as a supporter when requesting government action. In addition, to an extent that is rarely true in the economic contexts that Hirschman has in mind, much of government output is a public good, to which supporters and nonsupporters can lay equal claim. So Hirschman's logic is most applicable to a case in which exit is detectable, or even publicly acknowledged, and in which benefits can be effectively limited to supporters. Such a situation characterizes only a small part of what most governments do.

Another distinctive characteristic of the political context is that the goals of political parties and incumbent governments are often different from those of firms and social organizations. A firm aims to maximize profits, which typically means that, all else equal, more customers are preferable to fewer customers. Many social and political organizations operate under the same logic. But political parties are often in the business of cultivating minority constituencies (Myerson 1993) or minimum-winning coalitions (Riker 1962). Even in a regime that respects the legitimate right of nonsupporters to access government goods and services, some of what government does is inevitably tied to constituency service. To the extent that this logic defines government activity, a party may actually prefer for its dissenters to exit, since this shrinks the size of the constituency whose voice must be heeded and whose demands must tended to. And, in contrast to the argument of the preceding paragraph, exit would actually preclude the use of voice (or more accurately, it would make voice ineffective).

In sum, there are three plausible expectations about the combined effect of electoral pressures and nonelectoral participation on government responsiveness. First, the two strategies may work independently of one another.[17] Second, there may be a positive interactive effect, such that participation is more effective when elections are competitive and less effective when there are no elections or when elections are uncompetitive. Third, a negative interactive effect is possible, in which citizens who can exit and vote a government out of office are less likely to use voice, whereas citizens in hegemonic systems resort to voice more often because exit strategies are not available. Each of these possibilities is addressed empirically in subsequent chapters.

Interactions over Time

In addition to the type of static complementarity just discussed, we know that electoral and participatory strategies interact over time. In some situations, one might give rise to the other, making their relationship more complicated than the previous discussion suggested. The possible combinations and temporal dynamics are open and fluid, but it will simplify the discussion to consider two main possibilities. First, electoral contestation may generate broader political movements that operate outside of the electoral arena. Second, a social movement or some other form of mass participation may arise during a political opening, and over time this political activity may generate an increased level of electoral contestation.

In established democracies, we do not typically conceive of voting as a catalyst for other types of political participation. Voting is usually a mundane affair, to the point that many scholars identify voter apathy as a major threat to the quality of democracy. If a causal link is drawn, scholars tend to view electoral participation as a consequence of preexisting levels of civic engagement or political mobilization. But in new and "hyphenated" democracies it is easier to see elections as a catalyst for mass participation. The reason is that elections in such settings are not only *contested,* in the sense that multiple candidates compete for votes, but also often *disputed,* in the sense that major social forces either disagree about the fairness of given electoral procedures or challenge the results of electoral contests as fraudulent or illegitimate. When one or more sides perceive inherent unfairness in the electoral arena, they are more likely to opt for nonelectoral forms of political participation.

Recent history has given us many examples of disputed elections that catalyze protest movements. But in most cases it would be odd to claim that participation in the electoral arena engendered some broader or more lasting form of mass political participation. Most postelectoral protests, after all, are organized and directed by the elites of the losing party, and they deploy participants who are already mobilized partisans (see Eisenstadt 2004). For example, López Obrador was able to organize massive demonstrations in Mexico City after he narrowly lost the 2006 presidential election. But the vast majority of the street protesters were PRD partisans and López Obrador supporters. While the extent and length of the protests were certainly impressive, it is far from clear that this electoral protest has led to any sort of broader shift in the general public's political engagement or participation. Even the iconic "Color Revolutions" in several East European and former Soviet states are suspect in this regard. In each case, disputes over electoral results led to massive street protests that seemed, at least for a time, to herald a significant transformation in mass political participation in these countries. But even if some of these protests were not fully under the control of the losing party's leadership, they were all short-term protests with specific aims, and whatever participatory spirit they engendered in thousands of citizens has not outlived the original issue on which they were mobilized. Several years after the fact, it is hard to argue that these "revolutions" have led to a real change in the quantity and quality of mass political participation in countries like Georgia and the Ukraine (Kalandadze 2006).

The second, and in my view more interesting, dynamic posits that electoral contestation results from a prior shift in participatory politics. Again and again, we witness complacent publics becoming energized and mobilized over a particular issue. The immediate response rarely involves the ballot box. Rather, citizens act more directly, by raising their voices, joining protests, visiting government agencies, or mobilizing neighbors to do the same. Only later (if at all) do these citizens turn to elections as a potential strategy for pursuing their grievances. One reason that this second dynamic may be more common is that, unlike social movements, protests, or direct contact with government officials, effective electoral contestation typically requires formal organization. These organizations can develop over time but rarely do so in the short term.

Furthermore, the formalization of mass participation over time gives us several clues as to why, or under what conditions, nonelectoral participation can generate increased electoral contestation. As mass political movements mature, they often develop formal organizations. When they do, there are at least three reasons that the organization's leadership may attempt to channel participatory energies toward the electoral arena. First, the existence of a formal organization enhances the leadership's ability to extract resources (mainly time and money) from their membership, and these resources can be quite valuable in electoral politics. Second, the turn to electoral politics can serve as a means for a mass organization to further routinize participation. Street protests are notoriously hard to sustain (again, witness the López Obrador demonstrations); but it is much easier to convince these partisans, once mobilized, to show a limited form of support by taking the time to vote once every so often or volunteering some time to a campaign. Thus a mass organization may turn to the electoral arena as a low-intensity but sustainable form of politics when high-intensity strategies become infeasible over time. Third, a mass organization's leadership may come to see value in elected office. Their motives may be selfish, or they may view office as a necessary means for pursuing the group's agenda. Either way, elected office can be a means of preserving political power that the leadership first gained at the head of the mass organization; poor results from years of mobilization may also facilitate the leadership's decision to enter electoral politics more directly.

In established democracies, this process may not be conspicuous because it happens repeatedly over time and because elections are usually already competitive. Where multiple mass movements constantly exist at different stages of organization, and occasionally alter patterns of voting behavior among significant portions of the population, the net effect may still be hard to recognize. But in transitional democracies or liberal authoritarian regimes (like the Mexico of the 1970s and 1980s), this dynamic process of mass participation leading to increased electoral competition over time can be particularly dramatic and interesting. This is because the rise of a social movement, protest movement, or even uncoordinated, amorphous mass mobilization is often the first sign of weakness in nondemocratic regimes, and the electoral competition it engenders (if any) is usually a novel occurrence.

For example, Van Cott's (2005) recent study of indigenous politics, tellingly titled *From Movements to Parties in Latin America,* documents the rise of social movements among Latin American indigenous groups and their eventual transition into the electoral arena. While the historical exclusion of indigenous people from the political process clearly contributed to indigenous grievances, most of these movements were not motivated by concerns about democratic representation or electoral fairness. Rather, indigenous movements formed around issues of land tenure and distribution, respect for cultural or language rights, and a variety of economic grievances. The early efforts of these movements to further their collective goals did not involve any substantial efforts in the electoral arena, even after some of the movements had formed national organizations. The shift to electoral politics happened years or even decades later, and usually occurred only after significant internal debate about the potential downside of electoral participation (Van Cott 2005, esp. 42–43, 107–8). In cases like Ecuador and Bolivia, the progression from social movement to political party is obvious and striking, as indigenous political parties are now among the most powerful electoral forces in their countries. But these are only the most extreme examples of a broader phenomenon, in which nonelectoral forms of political participation eventually give rise to significant changes in the electoral arena. As I will discuss in chapter 6, this was clearly the type of interaction between participation and electoral competition that occurred in Mexico, roughly in the 1980s.

Theoretical considerations and a cursory review of historical events both suggest that no single causal or temporal logic governs the interactions between participation and electoral competition. This should not be surprising, since participation and competition are merely different manifestations of the same underlying phenomenon—citizen discontent. Still, the differences in strategies are important because we need to know why certain actors adopt particular strategies and why their success varies across cases. The discussion here should merely prepare us to be able to recognize interactions among different strategies of citizen influence, however they happen to occur in combination and over time.

I have argued in this chapter that nonelectoral forms of participation can powerfully influence government performance. I discussed several advantages that participatory mechanisms have over electoral mechanisms, including that they can be used repeatedly (indeed, continuously) and that they convey much more information to governing officials. More importantly, I have outlined several reasons why government might actually respond to such citizen activity. Social networks may play a role in enforcing norms of public service among those who hold government posts. And whether stimulated by strong social networks or not, participation can also produce government responsiveness simply by conveying information about the public's concerns and demands and, through psychological mechanisms, inducing politicians to respond in order to alleviate stress, discomfort, or embarrassment. Of course, these mechanisms are not mutually exclusive, and it seems plausible that they would complement each other.

The argument I have outlined here is general and abstract and may be fruitfully applied to a wide variety of political settings or cases. But there is particular reason to suspect that this participatory theory of democratic responsiveness helps to explain government performance in the Mexican case. Social movements and civic organizations became more prevalent in the late 1970s (Foweraker 1993; Foweraker and Craig 1990). Nonelectoral forms of political participation have subsequently become more common, particularly at the local level. This type of political activity has the explicit aim of improving local government responsiveness to citizens' demands (Grindle 2007). In addition, the past two decades have witnessed a qualitative shift in participatory politics away from a cautious, obsequious approach to grievance making and toward a more assertive, rights-demanding orientation.[18] At the same time, the evidence suggests that municipal governments are increasingly concerned to receive this participatory information, and in many cases they have even constructed institutions like citizen governance groups to channel and encourage it. These changes coincide with (or precede) observed improvements in local government performance across much of Mexico, giving the participatory explanation for responsiveness the same sort of prima facie plausibility that I previously ascribed to the electoral explanation. The nature of participation in Mexico, and the way it has changed over time, call for a much more detailed discussion, which I offer in chapter 6. But the general observations noted here lend support to the idea that citizen participation has contributed to improved government performance in Mexico over the past two decades.

This chapter has offered a theory according to which government performance relies crucially on citizen participation. Yet even as I have focused on participatory explanations for government performance, electoral mechanisms have never been far from sight. Not only has the discussion in this chapter failed to rule out electoral mechanisms of accountability, but it has repeatedly suggested some sort of interactive effect between electoral competition and participatory mechanisms. It may be that competitive elections give politicians the incentive to respond, and direct engagement gives them the information they need to respond well. This would imply that they are not really concerned with the participatory pressures (like psychological discomfort) that I have described above; rather, they merely use the information that they receive from political participation to improve their own (or their party's) electoral chances. The fact that Mexican politicians increasingly solicit and manufacture participatory pressures does not make this any less reasonable—indeed, this is exactly the sort of behavior we would expect from enterprising and ambitious politicians who know that they need to deliver good performance in exchange for future electoral benefits. Neither the electoral hypothesis nor the interactive hypothesis can be dismissed on theoretical grounds; the ultimate adjudication among them will be empirical.

CHAPTER FOUR

Testing Hypotheses about Responsiveness

The Public Services Approach

IN PREVIOUS CHAPTERS I GENERATED TWO BASIC HYPOTHESES about the political causes of democratic responsiveness. According to the first, *government is more responsive where elections are more competitive.* According to the second, *government is more responsive where participation is more frequent.* I have also discussed several ways in which the two independent variables in question (electoral competition and participation) might have an interactive effect on responsiveness. In principle, these hypotheses are applicable to any level of government, in any country in the world.[1] But my specific concern in this book is to understand whether these hypotheses are true of Mexico, particularly at the local level. Thus I proceed as follows. First I generate more specific hypotheses about the determinants of variation in local government performance in Mexican municipalities. Next I introduce a data set including several measures of the main variables of interest, I discuss the advantages and limitations of the main measures, and I link them to testable implications of the hypotheses. Finally I present a series of statistical tests. The results support the contention that participation generates democratic responsiveness in Mexico; the data show rather convincingly that electoral competition does not.

Democratic Responsiveness and Municipal Government Performance in Mexico

As I mentioned above, these hypotheses about the political causes of democratic responsiveness might be applied to any number of situations. In principle we might test them by comparing the quality of community policing in Chicago and San Diego; by asking whether Russian government under Putin is more responsive to the public interest than it was under communism; or by asking whether efforts toward local development are more effective in Brazilian cities that use participatory budgeting. Here I choose to test these hypotheses by analyzing government performance in Mexican municipalities. I do so both because of an inherent desire to understand contemporary Mexican politics and because the Mexican case happens to offer an auspicious opportunity to get analytical leverage on the practical complications that bedevil most attempts to discover the sources of democratic responsiveness.

Mexico offers an ideal opportunity to study democratic responsiveness because its protracted transition to democracy has produced useful variation on several key dimensions. As I discussed in chapters 2 and 3, many municipalities in Mexico became increasingly democratic in the 1980s and 1990s. Multiparty elections replaced single-party dominance, ordinary citizens began to participate in politics more often (and with greater autonomy from the corporatist hierarchy), and local governments became more responsive and efficient. But these changes occurred haltingly, unevenly, and in some places not at all, so that by the late 1990s municipalities varied widely in terms of their level of electoral competition, political participation, and government responsiveness. In this chapter and the next, I exploit this variation to test several propositions regarding the sources of democratic responsiveness in Mexico. This method is best described as a subnational comparative research design, which compares cases within a country (see Menéndez-Carrión and Bustamante 1995; Snyder 2001b). Here the cases are municipalities, which are at the lowest level of Mexico's three-tiered federal system. Municipalities are useful for this analysis because there are many of them, good data exist on relevant municipal characteristics, and the nature of Mexico's federal arrangement makes responsiveness relatively easy to measure at the municipal level.

In many situations, responsiveness is exceedingly hard to define and operationalize because citizens (and analysts) disagree about what responsive policies would look like. Some disagreement is a result of empirical complexity: Will tax cuts really "pay for themselves" by spurring economic growth sufficiently to offset the effects of lower social spending, resulting in a net benefit for society? It is difficult to know, so even citizens who share preferences for economic expansion and social welfare may disagree on policy. One might take refuge in public opinion, defining responsive policies as those that match (or move toward) the median voter's position. But public preferences about policy are often incongruent with the public's own long-term interests, so in practice it is not always easy to condemn a politician for acting against public opinion (or to praise one for acting with it; see Stokes 2001). Responsiveness is further complicated by purely normative disagreements that create zero-sum outcomes, where one side or the other is certain to view policy as nonresponsive.

One reason for a focus on Mexican municipalities is that it helps us to simplify the task of quantifying responsiveness. In Mexican municipalities, we can conceive of democratic *responsiveness* in terms of government *performance* on a range of issues that are central to local politics in Mexico. Municipal government performance is relatively easy to measure in Mexico because the responsibilities of municipal governments are (1) explicitly stated in the Mexican Constitution (Article 115), (2) concrete and tangible, and (3) recognized as salient local issues among both politicians and local citizens. Thus the responsiveness of any municipal government in Mexico should be reflected in its performance on the explicit responsibilities assigned to it in the constitution. And if either electoral competition or participation is a cause of responsiveness in Mexico, we should be able to find empirical confirmation of one or more of the following three propositions, which clearly parallel the general hypotheses generated in chapters 2 and 3:

1. Municipalities with competitive electoral environments exhibit better government performance than municipalities lacking electoral competition.

2. Municipalities with high levels of political participation exhibit better government performance than municipalities with low levels of participation.
3. Municipalities with high levels of political participation exhibit better government performance, but only when participation coincides with a competitive electoral environment.[2]

To analyze these propositions I have assembled a data set that includes electoral, socioeconomic, public finance, and demographic data for virtually all of Mexico's 2,419 municipalities from 1980 to 2000.[3] The following sections explain how I employ the variables in the data set as indicators of the main theoretical constructs.

Measurement

Here I discuss measurement strategies for the three main variables of interest: government performance, electoral competitiveness, and political participation. Later I introduce measures for several control variables and alternative statistical tests.

Government Performance

There are any number of ways to measure government performance, depending on what level of government is being evaluated and what aspects of performance are of theoretical interest. Here I offer one strategy that is tailored to measure the performance of Mexican municipal governments.[4] I use data on public service provision to estimate directly the government's performance on two issues that are central to municipal politics in Mexico. The Mexican Constitution explicitly assigns responsibility to municipal governments for eight issue areas, which are listed in table 4.1. While state and federal governments often exert influence over these issues, both by providing funds and by coordinating supra-municipal public works, formally speaking, these issue areas are the exclusive responsibility of municipal governments (see García del Castillo 2003). A large case-study literature developed by scholars of Mexican public policy also attests to the importance of these issues for municipal politics (see, among others, Cabrero Mendoza and Nava Campos 1999; Ziccardi 1995; and Cabrero Mendoza 1996).

There is also broad agreement among citizens and municipal officials that certain of these constitutional responsibilities are among the most salient political issues in local politics. The available evidence suggests that citizens have a fairly good sense of what municipal governments are responsible for doing, since their most common complaints about municipal governments closely match the list of responsibilities presented in table 4.1. In open-ended survey questions in 1998, Yemile Mizrahi asked respondents in Chihuahua and Puebla to name "the most serious problem" first of their state and then of their neighborhood.[5] In both states, the three most common answers to the question about state-level problems (excluding nonresponse) were crime, unemployment, and the economy. The three most common answers to the local-level question were public security, pavement of roads, and lack of water service (see table 4.2). These results suggest that the respondents were generally able to differentiate state and municipal government responsibilities and that they viewed the provision of public services as an important local issue.

These surveys and several others consistently demonstrate the centrality of public utility services in local politics. In Mizrahi's surveys

Table 4.1. The Constitutional Responsibilities of Municipal Governments in Mexico

a. Potable water, drainage, sewage systems, treatment and disposal of residual water
b. Public lighting
c. Cleaning, collection, removal, treatment, and disposal of waste material
d. Markets and supply centers
e. Monuments
f. Slaughterhouses
g. Streets, parks, gardens, and their equipment
h. Public security (municipal and traffic policing)

Source: Mexican Constitution, Article 115 (author's translation).

Table 4.2. Ranked Survey Responses to Questions about Important Local Problems

Sample and Year of Survey	*Jalapa, Veracruz, 1966*	*Chihuahua State, 1998*	*Puebla State, 1998*	*Four States, 2001*	*National Sample, 2001*
Source	Fagen and Touhy (1972)	Mizrahi (1999)	Mizrahi (2000)	Cleary and Stokes (2006)	ENCUP (Secretería de Gobernación 2002)
1st	Pavement and Public Utilities (43%)	Security/ Crime (21%)	Public Utilities (23%)	Security/ Crime (37%)	Public Utilities (35%)
2nd	Economic Situation (39%)	Public Utilities (19%)	Roads and Pavement (18%)	Utilities/ Public Works (31%)	Roads and Pavement (23%)
3rd	Cost of Living (7%)	Roads and Pavement (9%)	Security/ Crime (13%)	Economy/ Employment (17%)	Security/ Crime (19%)
4th		Employment (6%)	Employment (7%)		Economy/ Employment (5%)
Valid *N*	1409	1002	994	1435	1692

Note: Question wording and categorization of responses varies among the surveys. All questions were open-ended. Fagen and Touhy (1972) asked, "What are the most serious problems of Jalapa?" and reported responses aggregated into categories (which I further aggregate here). Mizrahi (1999, 2000) asked, "What is the principal problem of your district, neighborhood, or locality?" (see note 5 in this chapter); I report responses aggregated by category. Cleary and Stokes (2006) asked, "In your opinion, what is the most serious problem of your locality?" The ENCUP survey asked, "Is there some problem in your community that you would be interested to help resolve?" and as a follow-up to those who responded affirmatively, it asked, "What is that problem?" (see Secretería de Gobernación 2002).

respondents frequently mentioned public utilities as the "most important" problem in their locality. Lack of water on its own was the third most common response; the sum total of responses indicating a concern with public utilities (water, sewers, public lighting, and "public services") was relatively high in both surveys. As table 4.2 shows, other recent surveys have produced similar findings. In a four-state survey that Susan Stokes and I conducted in 2001, responses related to public utilities were offered by 31 percent of respondents; in a national sample survey conducted by INEGI in the same year, 35 percent offered such responses (see Cleary and Stokes 2006; Secretaría de Gobernación 2002).[6] Interestingly, an old survey reported in Fagen and Touhy (1972, 72) gives similar results. In October 1966, the authors asked 399 citizens of Jalapa, Veracruz, "What are the most serious problems of Jalapa?" The most frequent responses (after weighting for their stratified sample) were complaints about road pavement and public utilities (not reported separately by the authors), followed by concerns about the economy and employment. These survey results clearly indicate that the provision of public utilities is one of the centrally important issues in local politics in Mexico.

Municipal officials agree that the provision of public services is the main political issue in local politics. While conducting fieldwork for this project in the state of Puebla in 2002, I asked a number of mayors and other local politicians about the responsibilities of municipal government. Unprompted by me, *every* local official I asked mentioned the provision of public utilities in general, and usually water specifically, as an important part of his or her job description. National surveys of municipal officials confirm what I learned from local officials in Puebla in that mayors themselves, nationwide, consistently identify the provision of water and other utility services as fundamental responsibilities. For example, García del Castillo (2003) reports the results of two national surveys of municipal officials, cosponsored by INEGI and conducted in 1995 and 2000. The 1995 survey forced respondent mayors to choose the most problematic issue. "Potable water" was the most common response (36 percent) and was offered almost three times as frequently as the second-place answer (public security, 14 percent). Sewerage was the third most common answer at 10 percent. In the 2000 survey, mayors were free to offer as many answers as they wanted. Potable water and sewerage were the most common answers, and a full 60 percent of respondents mentioned water provision as one of the most problematic issues (García del Castillo 2003, 242).

Together, the official responsibilities of municipal governments, survey responses about the most serious problems in municipalities, and evidence from interviews and case studies all suggest that data reflecting municipal efforts to address road pavement, public security, and the provision of public utilities would be excellent indicators of municipal government performance. Yet reliable data do not exist for the first two categories. Data on road maintenance, construction, or pavement are simply nonexistent across any large number of cases. Some crime statistics do exist, but they are problematic. The Mexican government has reported the number and classification of alleged crimes, arrests, and convictions since 1987. However, the data are collected according to judicial districts, which do not always correspond to municipal boundaries. Scholars and legal experts also suggest that these data are inaccurate because most crimes are never reported. Finally, more than with other potential measures of municipal performance, it is not clear that the municipality has effective control over crime rates. Municipal governments are not sufficiently empowered with police who have the ability to investigate crimes and make arrests; and crime rates are primarily shaped by a host of socioeconomic factors exogenous to the level of policing. Given these problems, any measure of municipal government performance based on the available crime statistics would not be reliable.[7]

In contrast, the data on public service provision are relatively good. The Mexican Census (which is taken every ten years) reports the number of households in each municipality that have access to water and sewerage, two of the municipal government's main responsibilities.[8] Coverage on these variables is virtually complete, although they are only reported every ten years. Temporal coverage would improve somewhat if we accepted the 1995 *Conteo* as sufficiently accurate, but it is still not possible to construct an annual indicator of government performance without making unrealistic assumptions about the rate of change of each variable in the intervening years.[9] For this reason, the best way to use public utility data as a measure of municipal government performance is to analyze changes in service coverage between 1990 and 2000.

Obviously, the decade-long interval between measurements of the dependent variable has certain disadvantages. I cannot tie this measure of performance to particular administrations, as might be possible with an annual (or even triennial) measure. It is also impossible to measure short-term fluctuations in performance. There is no question that an annual measure would be useful (and in fact, I devise such a measure in the next chapter). However, it is also worth noting that the longer-term view of government performance provided by the decennial census measures does capture many of the salient features of the process of government responsiveness. For example, most public work projects are multiyear efforts; even a well-executed plan can take several years to get from the planning stage to the final implementation. So an annual indicator of changes in coverage rates might not be an accurate reflection of the efforts that a particular administration undertook to improve government performance. Furthermore, even if an annual indicator were accurate, we would not necessarily expect a tight linear relationship between our periodic indicators of competition and participation on the one hand and the annual change in coverage rates on the other. Rather, we should be concerned to know what the general electoral and participatory environments of municipalities are, on the belief that political factors such as the propensity to participate and the competitiveness of the electoral environment are underlying conditions, of which a particular electoral return or public protest are manifestations. This suggests that a longer-term view, such as that provided in this chapter, not only is useful but also has certain advantages over an annual time-series analysis.

One might also object that public utility coverage is only a partial indicator of municipal government performance. Table 4.1 listed many responsibilities in addition to utility services, and we know that mayors are often burdened (formally or informally) with additional charges, such as attracting business investment and jobs (especially in larger municipalities), constructing schools or other community buildings, managing social programs, bargaining with state and federal bureaucracies, and so on (see Rodríguez 1997, 116–27). Data that accurately reflected some of these other responsibilities would certainly improve our ability to measure government performance if such data existed.

But there are good reasons to believe that the indicators of public utility coverage are sufficiently accurate measures of performance. As I have demonstrated above, the provision of public utilities is a central and fundamental aspect of municipal government performance. And in contrast to other potential measures, public utilities are relatively important in virtually *all* municipalities. The salience of most issues varies from one municipality to the next—for example, public security is a major concern in the urban centers of Chihuahua but is less important in Puebla (Mizrahi 1999, 2000). Because of the centrality of utility provision to municipal agendas, there should be less variability in issue salience than there is with other municipal responsibilities that might be measurable. This is true even where coverage is high, since the provision of utility services is a valence issue in municipal politics. Politicians never publicly argue that utilities are not important or that partial coverage is acceptable. The only legitimate area for debate is the means and cost of securing full coverage. Thus, even where coverage is already high, municipal administrations are pressured to extend coverage to the remaining population that still lacks it (see García del Castillo 2003, 235).

The simplification involved in representing a broad concept (like government performance) with a concise indicator (like utility coverage rates) is not problematic in itself. All measurement requires simplification; indeed, the very goal of measurement in the social sciences is to categorize complex realities into simpler schemes so as to facilitate the search for patterns and trends. The relevant question for any measure is whether the indicator is a *useful* simplification of the concept. In this case, the usefulness of public utility coverage as an indicator of government performance is suggested by the weight given to utility service provision by both constituents and local politicians; by the centrality of the issue across virtually all municipalities; and by the good quality of the available data from which measures can be constructed.

Electoral Competitiveness

All of the measures of competition I use in this chapter are based on official electoral returns, which are reported in de Remes (2000a) and Banamex (2001). These data can be used to generate any number of specific indicators of competitiveness, and the best choice of indicator depends on the way in which we conceptualize elections as instruments of democracy, as well as the nature of the statistical task at hand. Both of these factors vary slightly throughout this chapter and the next. In the context of accountability theory, for example, we conceive of electoral competitiveness as the perceived level of threat that an incumbent party or politician feels with respect to its next election. If we assume that political parties look to past electoral results to get a sense of the threat, then we can operationalize the variable using the *margin of victory* (M), or the difference between the vote proportions of the winner and the second-place finisher.[10] All else equal, a party should feel more threatened with an electoral loss in a district it has won 55 to 45 percent than in a district that it won with 80 percent of the vote. Past electoral results will not always tell the whole story, and incumbent parties surely make use of much additional information when assessing their prospects of reelection. But the margin of victory offers one of the most simple, straightforward, and intuitive indicators of electoral competition that could possibly be generated.

Other operationalizations are also possible and reasonable. If we conceive of elections as opportunities to select good politicians rather than to punish bad ones, we might favor a dichotomous measure that separates competitive districts from noncompetitive ones, without making distinctions within the two groups. Dichotomizing M distinguishes municipalities in which one party dominates and there is little real choice from municipalities in which, *ex ante*, more than one candidate has a real opportunity to win. Beyond a certain point, increased competition does not improve the electorate's ability to empower good politicians. Districts with past election results of 52 to 48 percent, 54 to 46 percent, and 56 to 44 percent are equally competitive in this sense; they need only be distinguished from districts with election results of 80 to 20 percent or 90 to 10 percent. The threshold we choose for dichotomization is subjective, but the choice can be made reasonably and supported with robustness checks. In the multivariate analysis below, I code as competitive any election with an M less than 20 percent. But I also experiment with other thresholds and find similar results.

Finally, I use the electoral data to construct several other indicators of competition that are useful for particular tasks, or to evaluate the robustness of the central findings. Among these are measures of the PRI's vote share in a given election; the sum total of the opposition (non-PRI) vote share in a given election; indicators of party alternation in the mayor's office; the effective number of parties index (Laakso and Taagepera 1979); and other combinations of such variables. I define and use such measures as needed; in the Appendix I discuss why M is a better measure of competitiveness than any of the commonly used fractionalization indices.

Any time a researcher uses Mexican electoral data, he or she is obliged to consider the problem of electoral fraud and the havoc this might wreak on statistical analysis. This book draws on the official returns from almost fifteen thousand municipal elections that took place between 1980 and 1999. Surely, this collection includes fraudulent returns, especially from the 1980s. And of course the nature of vote fraud makes it difficult to know specifically where it has been committed. Yet I do not consider the fact of vote fraud in Mexico to be a major concern for my use of electoral data in constructing measures of electoral competitiveness. For one, most observers believe that vote fraud was much more common in the 1980s than in the 1990s; the empirical analysis here focuses primarily on the latter decade. More importantly, I believe that the occurrence of a lopsided vote—fraudulent or not—indicates a noncompetitive election. From what we know about the mechanics of vote fraud in Mexico, and giving due recognition to the ingenuity of Mexican vote-riggers, it seems that most efforts focused on artificially increasing the vote for the PRI (rather than, say, removing opposition votes, reporting results that were purely invented *de novo,* or some other method; see Molinar Horcasitas 1993). When a dominant party succeeds with such tactics and is not held to account, the level of electoral competition is obviously low. Finally, consider again the assumption that fraud will increase the reported vote for the ruling party rather than diminishing the opposition vote. This is certainly not true in all cases, but it is probably true in most. And to the extent that the assumption holds, we can still measure competition (or at least the level of support for opposition parties) by looking at the opposition vote as a percentage of the voting-age population. Calculating a measure of competition in this fashion produces results that are generally consistent with those reported here. In sum, the existence of vote fraud does not preclude the possibility of using electoral data for the analytical purposes of this book.[11]

Political Participation

It is difficult to measure political participation directly. The ideal measures would capture the quantity and quality of the myriad strategies that citizens use in everyday local politics. For example, we would be very interested to know how many people visited a municipal office each month or year to lodge a complaint. We would also like to know the frequency and size of peaceful protests that typically take place in the public square outside municipal government offices. And we would certainly be interested in the number of civic organizations per municipality, as well as their membership size, political goals, and level of engagement in political affairs.

Most of these direct measures are unavailable across a large number of cases, and it would be extremely difficult to collect such data on a systematic basis. The only available statistic that directly measures the actions of citizens is the electoral turnout rate, which is a useful indicator of participation because we know that those who vote are more likely to participate in other ways as well (Verba, Schlozman, and Brady 1995). Turnout is distinct from competitiveness. In Mexican municipal elections, which form the basis for the multivariate analysis presented here, these two variables are not highly correlated. Within the data set, higher turnout makes for slightly more competitive elections, but the coefficient calculated for each year is never stronger than 0.22. The correlation coefficient for the two composite measures used in the multivariate analysis below is 0.06, which is statistically significant but substantively small. In other words, we can be confident that the turnout measure used here as an indicator of participation is *not* actually indicating electoral competitiveness.

In addition, the literature on political participation in the United States has shown that most forms of participation are closely associated with socioeconomic status or resources. For example, Verba, Schlozman, and Brady (1995, 206) find that educated and wealthy individuals participate far more frequently than their less-educated and poorer counterparts. They also find that these differences are more important predictors of participation than are occupation, political attitudes, and party affiliation (see also Brehm and Gates 1997, 179–80). Mexico displays the same pattern. Table 4.3 shows the frequency of political activity according to the economic class and education level of respondents in two national-sample surveys (see Camp 2001; World Values Survey 2000; Inglehart et al. 2004). In both surveys, respondents were asked a series of questions that probed their level of political activity, including whether they had ever signed a protest letter or gone to a demonstration. In each case, wealthier and better-educated respondents were much more likely to report that they had done these things. According to these surveys, upper-class Mexicans are more than twice as likely as lower-class Mexicans to sign a protest letter. College-educated Mexicans are anywhere from two and a half to four times as likely to sign a letter than are their uneducated counterparts, and two to three times as likely to go to a demonstration. The data consistently show a strong relationship between the socioeconomic status and the self-reported political activity of the respondent. Another question asked in both surveys indicates that wealthier and better-educated Mexicans are also more likely to say they "would consider" signing a letter or joining a demonstration, suggesting that their potential for participation would be even higher if they were motivated by circumstances (analysis not shown; see also Fagen and Touhy 1972, 89). This is important because my theoretical expectations do not rely solely on large-scale collective action or protest movements but also on small-scale, everyday forms of participation that might not register in formal measures (survey or otherwise) of group membership, protest activity, and the like.

Thus, in addition to the turnout rate, I use municipal-level literacy and poverty rates as indicators of each municipality's propensity to participate.[12] I calculate turnout as a percentage of each municipality's adult population. Literacy and poverty rates come from the 1990 and 2000 Mexican censuses (INEGI 1990, 2000). Literacy is calculated as a simple proportion; poverty is calculated as the proportion of the economically active population earning less than the official minimum wage *(salario minimo)*. Although literacy and poverty are not direct measures of participation, they vary closely with participation. They also represent the only reasonably accurate indicators of participation that are available across the full range of Mexican municipalities. I discuss the limitations of these indicators in more detail below.

Table 4.3. Socioeconomic Status and Political Activity in Mexico

		Class (by Reported Family Income)			
Type of Activity	*Survey*	*Lower*	*Lower-Middle*	*Upper-Middle*	*Upper*
Respondent has signed a protest letter	Hewlett Foundation (1998)	12.7%	13.1%	18.3%	26.3%
	World Values Survey (2000)	14.2%	16.7%	27.6%	33.7%
Respondent has gone to a demonstration	Hewlett Foundation (1998)	10.8%	11.5%	11.1%	16.2%
	World Values Survey (2000)	2.8%	4.9%	5.3%	7.8%
		Education			
		None	*Primary*	*Secondary*	*College/ Graduate*
Respondent has signed a protest letter	Hewlett Foundation (1998)	5.4%	11.1%	15.2%	20.4%
	World Values Survey (2000)	15.5%	11.3%	15.0%	37.6%
Respondent has gone to a demonstration	Hewlett Foundation (1998)	5.3%	10.3%	12.0%	14.6%
	World Values Survey (2000)	3.6%	2.5%	3.6%	7.8%

Note: Lower class is defined as the bottom 40 percent of incomes; lower-middle is the next 30 percent; upper-middle is the next 20 percent; and upper is the top 10 percent of family incomes. Both surveys used national samples of all adult citizens, with 1,200 respondents for the Hewlett Foundation survey and 1,535 respondents for the World Values survey.

Source: 1998 Hewlett Foundation survey (reported in Camp 2001); World Values Survey 2000 (see also Inglehart et al. 2004). See also Cleary 2007, 289.

Analysis

The level of competition in Mexican municipal elections has increased dramatically over the past twenty-five years. Figure 4.1 shows the time trend in two measures of competition: the margin of victory and the proportion of the vote won by the PRI. Each point plotted on the graph represents the average score for all municipalities that held an election that year. Looking at the numbers for 1980, one can see that the average margin of victory and the average vote share for the PRI were both close to 100 percent.[13] From 1980 forward, both measures indicate a steady increase in competition, with significant jumps in 1988 and 1993. By 1999 competitiveness had progressed to the point at which the average margin of victory was just 17 percent and the average vote share for the PRI was 54 percent. But there was still wide variation, and many municipalities remained dominated by a single party, usually the PRI.

Figure 4.1. Changes in Municipal Electoral Competition, 1980–99

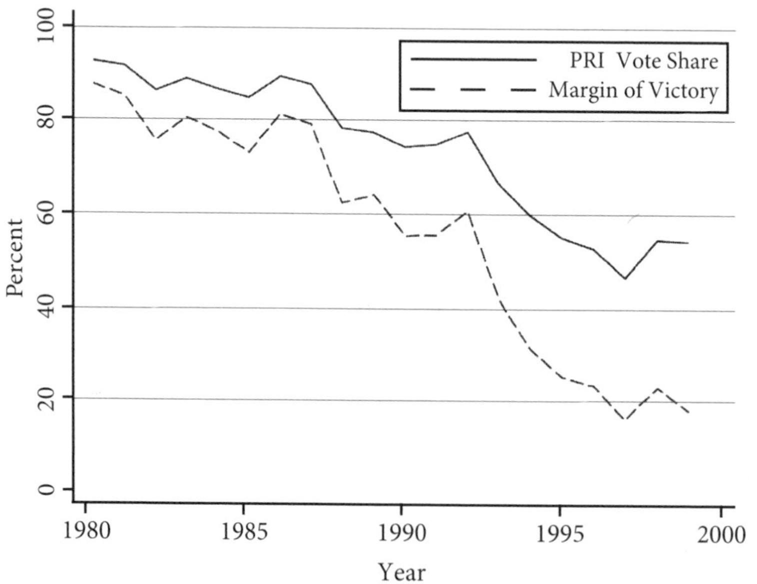

Did the rise of electoral competition cause an improvement in municipal government performance? Anecdotal evidence strongly supports such a causal hypothesis, and in chapter 2 I presented a theoretical explanation that could account for it. But even a cursory look at the data reveals that the correlation between competition and performance may not signify a causal relationship. To construct figure 4.2, I divided Mexican municipalities into two groups, depending on whether they had ever experienced party alternation in the mayor's office prior to 2000.[14] I then plotted the average water and sewerage coverage rates for these two subgroups. Looking at the data from the year 2000, we see a clear advantage for the electorally competitive group: municipalities with a history of alternation cover 14 percent more homes with sewerage and 6 percent more with potable water. This is exactly the sort of pattern that has led many scholars to posit a causal link between electoral competition and improved performance. But the data from earlier decades illustrate the fallacy. We see that competitive municipalities had a fifteen-point advantage in sewerage and a nine-point advantage in water provision in 1990, and similar advantages in 1980. In other words, the differences between competitive and noncompetitive municipalities already existed in 1980, before most municipal elections became competitive. Since the differences in service provision precede the rise of electoral competition, one is forced to question whether competition is truly a cause of improved performance.

Multivariate Model Specification

In my view, the evidence illustrated in figure 4.2 speaks compellingly against the electoral hypothesis. But for a better sense of the relationship between competition and performance, as well as simultaneous consideration of competing hypotheses, we are better served by multivariate analysis of the determinants of utility coverage rates. The specification of a multivariate model requires that we choose the most suitable modeling technique and that we include appropriate independent and control variables. It is also wise to entertain alternative measures and specifications.

Figure 4.2. Water and Sewer Coverage Rates, 1980–2000

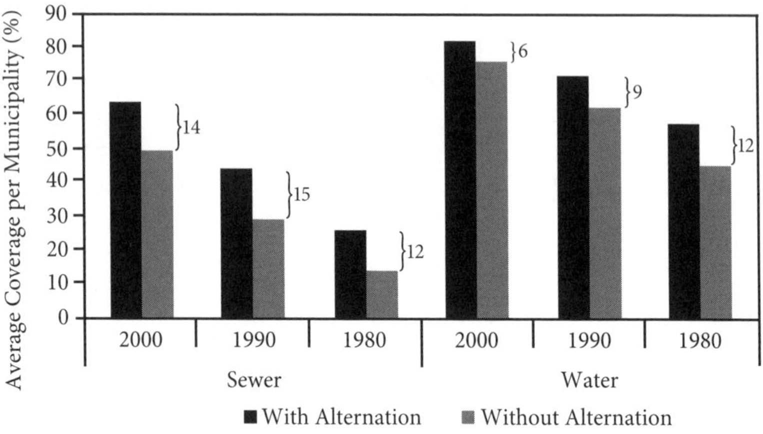

Source: INEGI (1980, 1990, 2000).

Log-Odds OLS Estimation

The dependent variables of interest are the rates of water and sewer utility provision. These variables are proportions, bound by 0 and 1, which implies that the basic ordinary least squares model (OLS) is not the best analytical tool. OLS is best employed where the dependent variable is continuous and unbounded. Further, the use of OLS on a proportional dependent variable can lead to nonsensical predicted values outside the 0–1 range. Finally, OLS assumes that the effect of the independent variables is linear. That is, the linear model would predict that if a certain change in an independent variable improved utility coverage from 20 to 30 percent in one municipality, then that same change in the independent variable would improve coverage from 90 to 100 percent in another municipality. This is an inaccurate view of how we expect rates of coverage to be influenced. A better way to think about changes in a proportional variable such as rates of provision is as a curvilinear process, in which the effect (in percentage terms) of any given causal factor tapers off as the rate approaches 100 percent. The reason is that there is less room for improvement when the initial rate of provision is already high, and no improvement is possible once the rate of provision reaches 100 percent. In a linear OLS model, a strong relationship may be obscured by the apparent lack of a relationship among cases at the high end of the dependent variable's range.

The best approach to this measurement problem is to use a logistic transformation of the dependent variable (see Greene 1997, 895).[15] This transformation "linearizes" a proportional variable, so that the variable ranges freely between positive and negative infinity.[16] OLS then becomes an appropriate estimation tool. The coefficients obtained from OLS estimation are not directly interpretable, as they represent the predicted change in the logistically transformed dependent variable for each one-unit change in the independent variable. But we can use simulations to translate the coefficients into percentage-term effects.

Heteroskedasticity is also an issue, since the variance of the error term depends (in part) on the population of each case. In the current example, this means that the variance depends on the total number of households in each municipality (this total is the denominator used to calculated the proportion of homes with access to given services). In the current data set the number of households varies by orders of magnitude, so the concern about heteroskedasticity is well founded. Greene (1997, 895) suggests that weighted least squares is a preferable remedy. In the analysis that follows, I use (unweighted) OLS but report Huber-White standard errors to correct for heteroskedasticity. In an analysis not shown, I obtained substantively similar results while weighting the regression with the inverse square root of the number of households per municipality.

The Variables in the Model

The independent variables of greatest theoretical interest include lagged values of the dependent variables, the average margin of victory over the course of the 1990s, each municipality's literacy rate in 1990, the poverty rate in 1990, and the average turnout rate in municipal elections throughout the 1990s.[17] I also include a dummy variable indicating whether 50 percent or more of the municipal population self-identify as indigenous to test the commonly stated hypothesis that indigenous communities in Mexico are marginalized by the state and unlikely to engage it in participatory terms. My own theoretical priors are mixed:

while indigenous communities are often among the most marginalized, many have a high capacity for collective action (see Hindley 1999).

The models include several additional control variables. To account for each municipality's financial capacity, I include the per capita budget, in 1995 pesos, averaged over the 1990s. I also control for (off-budget) federal transfers under the Programa Nacional de Solidaridad (PRONASOL, a.k.a. Solidarity). These funds were a significant source of federal money in the municipalities and were often used for improvements in public utilities.[18] Accordingly, I include the total amount of PRONASOL spending per capita in the municipality for the duration of the program (1989 to 1994). To measure party-specific effects, I include three dummy variables indicating whether the municipality was controlled by one of the three main parties (the PRI, PAN, and PRD) for six or more years in the 1990s. Another dummy variable indicates whether the municipal and state governments were controlled by different parties for a majority of the decade. This variable tests the conjecture that governors may attempt to disrupt the efforts of opposition mayors. This "juxtaposition" effect has been hypothesized by de Remes (1998, 1999) and has been mentioned in many case studies of local governance in Mexico (Vanderbush 1999, among others). I include the log of the total municipal population and the percentage change in population from 1990 to 2000. My theoretical priors on these factors are mixed. Urban areas are often thought to be in the vanguard of public service provision because of their concentrated populations, larger tax bases, and visibility. Yet it is also true that many large cities have experienced rapid population grown in recent years, which could adversely affect the rates of service provision. A less ambiguous demographic variable is the population density (logged population per square kilometer), which I expect to positively correlate with performance, since it should be easier to extend service to concentrated populations than to dispersed ones. Finally, I include dummy variables indicating each municipality's state (with one dummy omitted).[19]

Results

Table 4.4 presents the basic models. All six models in the table are log-odds OLS estimations; the first three estimate the rate of sewer coverage, and models 4 through 6 estimate water coverage. I begin with model 1, which includes measures of both electoral competition and participation as determinants of sewer coverage, as a simultaneous test of the two main hypotheses of interest. The model shows no significant relationship between electoral competition and service coverage: the coefficient is in the expected direction but is substantively small and statistically insignificant. The other indicators of political influence, however, all return statistically significant and substantively large coefficients. Utility coverage is higher in municipalities that are more literate, that have higher turnout in local elections, and that are less poor. Indigenous municipalities have lower rates of coverage, though the estimated effect is relatively small. Other independent variables have a moderate effect at best: all else equal, municipalities that have grown rapidly tend to have poorer coverage, and densely populated municipalities have better coverage. Higher budgets show a weak relationship with better coverage. Other political variables, including the party in power and an indicator of divided government, show no significant relationship to the dependent variable.

Clearly the most important result in model 1 is the significant relationship between sewer provision and the proxy measures of participation. To interpret the substantive impact of these coefficients, I used Clarify to estimate expected values of the dependent variable while manipulating the values on the independent variables of interest, and then I converted the expected values from the log-odds transformation back into percentage terms (see King, Tomz, and Wittenberg 2000; Tomz, Wittenberg, and King 2003).[20] The results show that turnout, literacy, and poverty have a large impact on coverage rates, even while controlling for municipal financial capacity (see figure 4.3). For example, a shift from the first- to the third-quartile score for literacy predicts a seven-point difference in sewer coverage, holding all other variables at their median values. As we would expect, predicted effects are even larger toward the more extreme cases: the predicted increase in sewer coverage as literacy moves from the tenth to the ninetieth percentile is fourteen percentage points. Turnout also has a significant impact, though the size of the effect is smaller. An interquartile change in turnout predicts just a two-point increase in coverage, and the maximum possible change attributable to turnout is about five points.

Table 4.4. Log-Odds OLS Regressions on Rates of Sewer and Water Coverage, 2000

	Sewer Coverage			*Water Coverage*		
		Split Samples			*Split Samples*	
	Full Sample	*Non-comp.*	*Compe-titive*	*Full Sample*	*Non-comp.*	*Compe-titive*
	(1)	*(2)*	*(3)*	*(4)*	*(5)*	*(6)*
Lagged Utility Score						
% access to utility	4.18***	4.31***	4.07***	3.84***	3.63***	4.00***
(1990)	(0.10)	(0.16)	(0.14)	(0.14)	(0.21)	(0.20)
Political Influence						
Margin of victory	-0.11			-0.06		
(10-year avg.)	(0.10)			(0.11)		
Literacy	1.78***	1.85***	1.84***	0.80**	0.70^	0.97**
(1990 % literate)	(0.28)	(0.36)	(0.44)	(0.25)	(0.36)	(0.35)
Turnout	0.41*	0.53*	0.55*	0.57**	0.42	0.74**
(10-year avg.)	(0.18)	(0.26)	(0.26)	(0.21)	(0.33)	(0.28)
Poverty	-0.82***	-0.82***	-0.83**	-0.11	-0.49^	0.37
(% below minimum wage)	(0.14)	(0.20)	(0.21)	(0.17)	(0.25)	(0.23)
Additional Controls						
Indigenous municipality	-0.11^	-0.10	-0.12	0.01	-0.03	0.08
(dummy)	(0.06)	(0.08)	(0.10)	(0.06)	(0.09)	(0.08)
Municipal budget	0.13	0.14	0.11	0.11	-0.03	0.17
(per cap, 000s)	(0.11)	(0.16)	(0.14)	(0.11)	(0.14)	(0.20)
PRONASOL	0.02^	0.02*	0.00	0.01	-0.01	0.02
(tot. per cap, 000s)	(0.01)	(0.01)	(0.02)	(0.01)	(0.01)	(0.02)
PAN control	-0.06		-0.07	-0.06		-0.12
(dummy)	(0.09)		(0.09)	(0.09)		(0.08)
PRD control	0.02	-0.15	0.01	-0.07	0.34	-0.10
(dummy)	(0.12)	(0.21)	(0.12)	(0.10)	(0.23)	(0.11)
PRI control	-0.04		-0.06	-0.14^		-0.09
(dummy)	(0.07)		(0.07)	(0.07)		(0.08)
Divided gov't.	-0.07	0.27	-0.07	-0.01	-0.09	0.05
(dummy)	(0.05)	(0.19)	(0.05)	(0.06)	(0.19)	(0.06)
Municipal size	0.02	0.03	0.01	-0.00	-0.08*	0.06*
(logged pop.)	(0.02)	(0.03)	(0.03)	(0.02)	(0.04)	(0.03)
Population growth	-2.32*	-3.07*	-1.66	-0.29	0.96	-2.02
(%, 1990–2000)	(0.96)	(1.37)	(1.38)	(1.15)	(1.55)	(1.64)

Population density (logged pop/km^2)	0.73*** (0.16)	0.72*** (0.22)	0.75*** (0.23)	0.74*** (0.23)	0.44 (0.30)	1.10*** (0.33)
Constant	-2.45*** (0.42)	-3.25*** (0.54)	-2.41*** (0.56)	-1.20* (0.48)	-0.03 (0.67)	-2.42* (0.63)
Valid *N*	1968	910	1058	1968	910	1058
R-squared	0.86	0.83	0.87	0.75	0.72	0.77

Note: Each model also includes dummy variables for each state (save one), coefficients not reported. The table reports Huber-White standard errors in parentheses. Statistical significance is noted with the conventional ***$p < .001$, **$p < .01$, *$p < .05$, ^ < .10.

How does the predicted effect change as turnout, literacy, and poverty vary together? Since all three variables function to indicate participation in this model, and since they typically covary, we should be interested to know their combined effect on government performance. The steeper curve in figure 4.3 simulates expected coverage rates as all three of the variables of interest move from their lowest to highest percentile within the sample (holding all other variables at their median value).[21] In this example, a shift from the twenty-fifth percentile to the seventy-fifth percentile in each of the three variables of interest would translate into a fifteen-point increase in the predicted rate of coverage, from 50 to 65 percent. All else equal, the difference between municipalities at the tenth and ninetieth percentiles of all three variables is twenty-nine percentage points. Given that rates of coverage in this sample tend slightly toward the high end of the range, these predicted differences are large.

To this point the evidence has lent no support to the electoral hypothesis. But as I outlined in chapter 3, electoral competition may improve performance indirectly, via an interactive effect with participation. Depending on how we interpret Hirschman (1970) and others who hypothesize interactive effects, we would expect either that the relationship between participation and government performance would exist *only* among competitive municipalities or that the relationship would be markedly *stronger* within this subset of municipalities. To find out, I split the sample of cases according to whether each municipality had competitive elections.[22] As one can see by comparing the coefficients in

Figure 4.3. Estimated Effect of Literacy, Turnout, and Poverty on Sewer Coverage

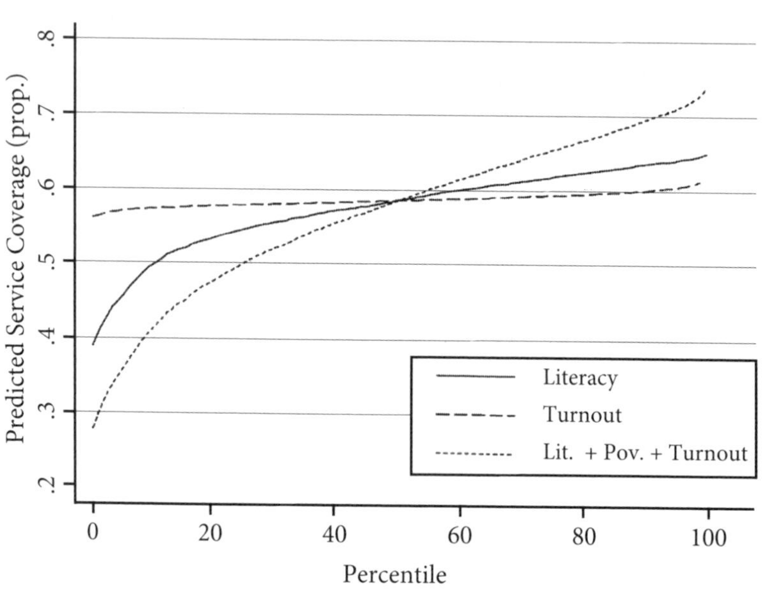

models 2 and 3, the proxy indicators of participation have the same effect in both subsets.[23] For example, the coefficient on the literacy variable is 1.85 among the noncompetitive cases and 1.84 among the competitive cases. The coefficients on the other indicators of political influence are also similar. Thus the evidence does not even support the assertion that electoral competition affects government performance indirectly, by conditioning or magnifying the effect of participation. Literacy, turnout, and poverty, which I interpret as indicators of participation, exert significant independent influence on performance, whether or not elections are competitive.

Models 4 through 6 in table 4.4 replicate the analysis of the first three models, while changing the dependent variable from sewer coverage to water coverage. The results are generally consistent with the first three models, although the magnitude of the effects is smaller. In model 4, electoral competition is not a significant predictor of coverage rates, but literacy and turnout both are both moderately strong predictors. The only control variable that has a significant influence on water coverage rates is population density.

Figure 4.4 illustrates the magnitude of the effects of turnout and literacy, drawing on three simulations of the expected values of the dependent variable. In the first, all independent variables (including the rate of water coverage in 1990) are held constant at their medians, while turnout and literacy are varied from their lowest to highest percentile scores. While the simulation shows the expected positive relationship, the size of the effect in percentage terms is quite small, primarily because the water coverage rates were already high in 1990, leaving limited room for improvement. If we predict the changes for municipalities that had lower coverage rates in 1990, we can see more substantial effects. The second and third curves in figure 4.4 represent the predicted coverage rate in 2000 for municipalities scoring at the twenty-fifth and tenth percentiles in 1990 (approximately 51 and 32 percent coverage, respectively). In these cases, as literacy and turnout increase, the predicted changes in coverage rates are more substantial. For example, the simulation predicts that a municipality with only 32 percent coverage in 1990, but with ninetieth-percentile scores on literacy and turnout, would have a coverage rate about ten points higher than a similar municipality scoring in the tenth percentile on literacy and turnout. In other words, the model predicts that literacy and turnout will have a large substantive impact on coverage rates whenever those rates were not already near 100 percent in 1990.

The results of the split-sample models (5 and 6) are also consistent with the analysis of sewer coverage, with one exception that gives a glimmer of hope to the interactive hypothesis. At first glance, it appears that the indicators of political participation have a stronger effect among electorally competitive municipalities (model 6) than among noncompetitive municipalities (model 5). The coefficients for literacy and turnout are larger in model 6 and are statistically significant at conventional levels. However, Chow tests (which tell us whether these apparent differences are themselves statistically significant) suggest that the two models are not as different as they appear (see Greene 1997, 349). The only significant difference between the two models pertains to the effect

Figure 4.4. Estimated Effect of Literacy and Turnout on Water Coverage

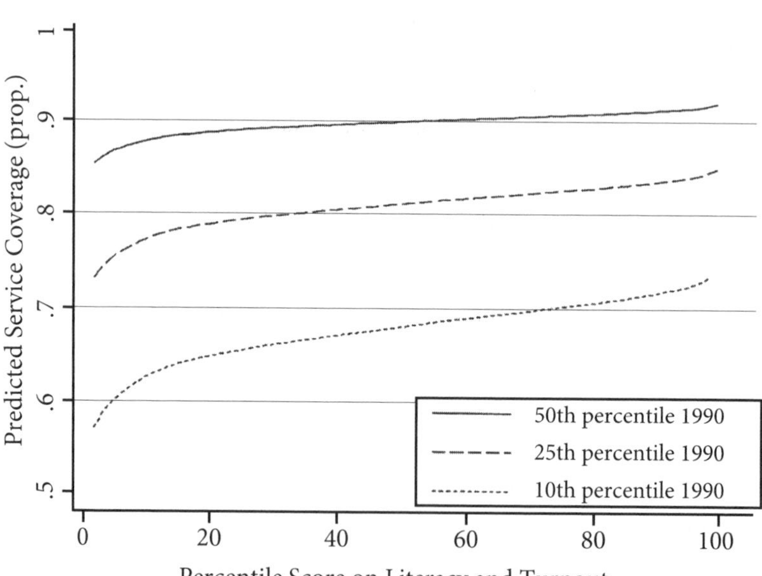

of poverty rates on water coverage.[24] Among noncompetitive municipalities, higher poverty rates predict slightly worse performance. In the competitive subset of cases, the effect of poverty is positive, though it does not achieve standard significance levels. According to a Chow test, however, the two coefficients on poverty are clearly different *from each other*. This could be interpreted to mean that citizens in poorer municipalities can still extract (relatively) good performance out of their local governments, provided that there is a modicum of electoral competition; in the absence of electoral competition, poor municipalities suffer a deficit of water provision.

If we cherry-picked this single piece of evidence, we might be able to claim support for the interactive hypothesis. However, simulations (not shown) suggest that the conditional effect is never greater than a couple of percentage points. Furthermore, the finding is not robust: recall that the differences between competitive and noncompetitive cases with respect to sewer provision were virtually nonexistent (models 2 and 3) and that there are no significant differential effects for literacy or turnout in models 5 and 6. Overall, then, the analyses of sewer and water provision generate a consistent set of findings, revealing that electoral competition is not a significant predictor of coverage rates, while turnout, literacy, and poverty are. These findings are consistent with the hypothesis that municipal government performance depends on nonelectoral participation rather than mechanisms of electoral accountability.

Making the Data Confess?

As the discussion of the split-sample estimations demonstrates, it is often possible to squeeze a desirable result out of the data, or, as some scholars put it, to "torture the data until they confess."[25] As with real torture, there is no guarantee that the eventual confession will be genuine. But the truth is that any thorough analysis of large-*N* data sets like the one used here requires a substantial amount of analysis, most of which (again, like real torture) never gets reported. I can state here that the results presented above are robust to a wide number of alternative specifications, in which I add and withdraw different control variables (including the state dummy variables) on the basis of plausible alternative conceptions of what the theoretically optimal specification might be.[26] Diagnostic and robustness checks such as these need not be reported in great detail, especially if the results are consistent with what has been presented already. In this case, however, there are a couple of points at which further diagnostic probing produces some evidence that is more favorable to the electoral hypothesis. Given the prior beliefs that many scholars hold regarding the importance of elections, a little more work is justified, particularly as it relates to our evaluation of the electoral hypothesis.

One way to probe the data further is to consider alternative measures of electoral competition. There are plausible conceptual reasons to prefer measures other than the one I used in table 4.4, and in fact I have already discussed the rationale behind several different measures, including a dummy variable indicating a minimum level of competitiveness and the well-known fractionalization indices (Laakso and Taagepera 1979; Molinar Horcasitas 1991). Earlier, I discussed the conceptual justifications for the measurement choices that I made, and I evaluated these options without casting an eye toward the results they would produce. But it is of obvious interest to know whether the substitution of some other measure would produce results more favorable to the electoral hypothesis. The analysis I present in table 4.5 provides some answers.

To construct table 4.5 I sequentially substituted twelve alternative measures of electoral competition into the base specification reported in models 1 and 4 (for sewer and water coverage, respectively) from table 4.4. The method for generating these alternative measures was brainstorming: I tried to think of any and every plausible way to operationalize competitiveness, and I include them here even though I believe some of them (particularly N and NP, two versions of a party fractionalization index; see the definitions and discussion in the Appendix) to be inappropriate measures of competitiveness. The measures include the following: three variations on M (a ten-year lag, a ten-year lag of a five-year running average, and a dummy indicating whether the average M for the 1990s was less than 20 percent); the competitiveness dummy used to split the sample in figure 4.2; a dummy indicating party alternation in the mayor's office at any time between 1980 and 1999; the total number of party alternations in the same time period; the ten-year average of the PRI's vote share; a dummy indicating whether the PRI's vote share had fallen below 55 percent at any point in the 1990s; and the ten-year average, and maximum score, for both N and NP.

Table 4.5 does not report the full regression results. Rather, I simply report the coefficient estimated for the indicator of competitiveness, and I note whether the alternative model produced divergent results on the other independent variables of interest (in comparison to the values estimated in table 4.4). As we can see from reading the table, *none* of these alternative indicators has a significant effect on rates of sewerage provision, and none significantly alters the other results of interest. However, the results for water coverage are slightly different. While most indicators show no effect, if we opt to measure competitiveness according to the PRI's vote share, or certain variations on N and NP, we can generate a statistically significant effect in the expected direction.

If one were so inclined, one could generate an argument in favor of these alternative indicators and conclude that electoral competition does, in fact, have the predicted effect on government performance.

Table 4.5. Effect of Alternative Measures of Electoral Competition

Model Number	Indicator of Competition	Sewer Coverage: Coefficient (s.e)	Sewer Coverage: Effect on Other Coefficients	Water Coverage: Coefficient (s.e)	Water Coverage: Effect on Other Coefficients
(original)	Margin of victory (10-year average)	-0.11 (0.10)	-	-0.06 (0.11)	-
(1)	Margin of victory (10-year lag)	-0.04 (0.05)	None	-0.04 (0.06)	None
(2)	Margin of victory (average, 1985–89)	-0.00 (0.06)	None	-0.02 (0.07)	None
(3)	Margin of victory (dichotomized)	-0.01 (0.03)	None	-0.02 (0.04)	None
(4)	Competitiveness (dummy for split samples)	-0.00 (0.03)	None	0.05 (0.03)	None
(5)	Alternation (dummy if any, 1980–99)	-0.00 (0.03)	None	0.05 (0.03)	None
(6)	Alternation (total no., 1980–99)	-0.01 (0.01)	None	0.01 (0.01)	None
(7)	PRI vote share (10-year average)	-0.18 (0.17)	None	-0.32^ (0.18)	None
(8)	PRI vote share (dichotomized)	0.01 (0.04)	None	0.11* (0.04)	None
(9)	Effec. no. of parties (N) (10-year average)	0.05 (0.05)	None	0.12* (0.05)	None
(10)	Eff. no. of parties (N) (max. score, 1980-99)	0.02 (0.03)	None	0.09** (0.03)	None
(11)	Effec. no. of parties (NP) (10-year average)	0.05 (0.05)	None	0.09 (0.06)	None
(12)	Effec. no. of parties (NP) (max. score, 1980–99)	0.02 (0.03)	None	0.08* (0.04)	None

Note: Each model reports only the coefficient for the listed indicator of electoral competition, substituted into models 1 and 4 of table 4.4. The table reports Huber-White standard errors in parentheses. Statistical significance is noted with the conventional $^{***}p < .001$, $^{**}p < .01$, $^{*}p < .05$, ^ < .10.

However, such an interpretation would suffer from three main weaknesses (among others). First, the findings are obviously not very robust, as the alternative indicators fail to predict any significant changes in sewer provision. Second, the measures themselves are conceptually suspect. The indicator of the PRI's vote share is a defensible measure; but the indicators based on N and NP are poor indicators of competitiveness, for reasons I elaborate in the Appendix.[27] Third, even if we accept the results at face value, the predicted effect is relatively small. According to the results of models 8, 9, 10, and 12, competitive municipalities can be expected to extend their water coverage by about three percentage points, in comparison to otherwise similar noncompetitive municipalities. Thus, even in the most favorable circumstances, we can claim only that electoral competition has a very small effect on some types of service provision. But in my view it would be unwise to invest much confidence in this result.

Discussion

I have presented multiple statistical tests of the electoral and participatory hypotheses of government responsiveness, using a variety of measures and model specifications. According to the results, electoral competition is not an important determinant of improved government performance. The data seem to show no relationship at all between competition and performance; nor does competition appear to condition the effect of other relevant causes. If we are exceedingly charitable to the electoral hypothesis, we might conclude that elections do have a small effect. But clearly they do not tell the whole story. On the other hand, turnout and literacy show a close relationship to government performance and are more influential predictors than financial and demographic control variables. Poverty rates also have a sizable effect, but on only one of two dependent variables. This evidence is consistent with the participatory hypothesis, though of course the meaning of the relationship is open to interpretation.

The indeterminacy regarding the proper interpretation of the statistical relationship between government performance and the three variables I have labeled as proxy indicators of participation warrants further consideration. Specifically, I am concerned to evaluate one alternative interpretation, according to which utility coverage rates indicate development rather than government performance, and in which literacy and poverty are related to utility coverage simply because they are also indicators of development. This interpretation has some face plausibility because scholars have documented many cases in which local communities fund public works projects themselves. A neighborhood might be asked to contribute money or labor to a project, or it might agree with a private (or semiprivate) utility company to pay a certain (presumably higher) rate for a service if the company pays for the infrastructure. Some case studies seem to suggest that utility improvements happen *in spite of* local governments, which can face incentives to prevent such development.[28] For example, Moctezuma (2001) describes the process by which "squatter" residents in the San Miguel Teotongo neighborhood of Mexico City attempted to access water and electricity in the late 1970s:[29] "Faced with the absolute lack of official regulations, norms or plans, and under conditions in which participation was not only disregarded by the government but continuously repressed, the neighbourhood's inhabitants developed their own culture of self-management. The improvement of the neighbourhood was undertaken mainly through voluntary work (called the *faena*)" (Moctezuma 2001, 119). To the extent that public utilities can be constructed and accessed without the assistance of government but rather with the financial and physical support of the community, we might view utility coverage rates as indicators of socioeconomic development rather than government performance.

In the Mexican case, Jonathan Hiskey (1999) has used public utility indicators in exactly this way. Hiskey's study attempts to understand the effects of local democracy on socioeconomic development projects, and he uses utility coverage rates as indicators of development. He finds that spending on public works, such as transfers to municipalities under the PRONASOL program, was more effective in democratic municipalities.[30] Democratic municipalities get more "bang for the buck" from public works spending because plans are developed locally and money is targeted more efficiently (Hiskey 1999). But it would be incorrect to credit municipal governments for development projects that were funded in this way, since the source of the improvement lies in the funding provided by the federal government and the leadership provided by the community group.[31]

My approach is not incompatible with Hiskey's. He conceives of improved service provision as direct evidence of development. My understanding of the process is less direct: socioeconomic development, broadly understood, increases public pressure on the state to provide services. Both approaches anticipate a link between political contestation and service provision. Still, without objecting too strongly to Hiskey's reasonable interpretation of these data, I would suggest that they are better understood as indicators of government performance.

Even where local governments do not play a productive role in the construction and maintenance of utility infrastructure, no project would be feasible without the tacit support of public officials, and most citizens believe that the local government should play a leading role. Recall that in the survey responses reported in table 4.1, citizens identified public utility services as important local problems. Local politicians and citizens commonly voice the belief that provision of these services is a responsibility of municipal governments. Clearly, the actors involved view public utilities as important responsibilities of municipal government. The situation cited above in the town of San Miguel Teotongo, in which citizens took responsibility for utility provision without any help from the local government, should not be interpreted to mean that the state is merely a secondary player in service provision. Rather, it indicates variation in local governments' responsiveness to the public interest. I designed the public utility measurement strategy precisely to explain this type of variation.

Furthermore, the case of San Miguel Teotongo is not typical. It *is* typical for citizens to feel the need to press local governments for access to services, and it is not uncommon that citizens are forced to take the initiative and even to invest their own money and labor. But politicians and citizens deploy a wide range of methods to construct and provide utility services. Systematic data on the methods they use across Mexico's 2,400 municipalities are rare. But in a representative sample taken in 1993, services were provided through a "collaboration with the community" in only 7 percent of municipalities in the case of water provision and 4 percent in the case of sewerage (García del Castillo 1999, 144).[32] Even when the citizens themselves initiate utility improvements, as in

San Miguel Teotongo, local governments still play an important role (sooner or later) by collecting fees, contributing funds, and allowing connections to existing utility infrastructure. Thus there are strong justifications for interpreting utility coverage rates as indicators of government performance.

One might also question the findings presented in this chapter because it focuses only on local government performance and partially ignores politics at the state and federal levels. In chapters 6 and 7 I will discuss the broader (and misguided) objection that local politics do not matter so much and that electoral accountability functions well at the state and federal level. Here I am concerned with a slightly different objection, which recognizes that local politics do matter but which points to the influence that state and federal governments have over local service provision as a way of objecting to the relevance of the findings presented here. This important point deserves careful consideration.

There is no question that state and federal governments play a significant role in the provision of public utilities like water, sewerage, and electricity. In fact, electricity is the direct responsibility of the (federal) Comisión Federal de Electricidad (CFE).[33] Municipalities have much more control over water and sewer projects but are still highly dependent on state and federal transfer funds. Rodríguez (1997, 130) reports that only 30 to 40 percent of municipal income came from local sources throughout most of the 1980s and that the remainder came from transfers.[34] The actual dependence on transfers is even greater because Rodríguez's calculations do not include federal and state spending on "special projects" (like PRONASOL programs) that is not channeled through municipal budgets.

Additionally, states and the federal government occasionally have concurrent jurisdiction over local public works projects, and states may take direct control of a utility when a municipality fails to administer it adequately. García del Castillo (1999, 144) estimates that the federal or state government has a formal role (through a *convenio,* or "agreement") in 18 percent of municipalities with regard for water provision and in 12 percent with regard to sewerage. Other authors imply that state and federal control in these areas is much more extensive, though their perceptions may have an urban bias because the municipalities studied most often are large cities that are most likely to witness state and federal involvement (Rodríguez and Ward 1992; Cabrero Mendoza 1996; Rodríguez 1998).

So it is clear that municipal governments are not entirely free actors. Some scholars go so far as to say that the Mexican municipality has *no* effective autonomy with respect to public utility provision or any other issue area. I believe that this characterization is exaggerated, especially for the 1990s (see the discussion in Rodríguez 1997, 115). It is most true in the case of electricity but is far less true with respect to water and sewer projects. To the extent that decisions about utility services and public works projects are made and funded outside the municipality, it is reasonable to worry about the validity of utility coverage rates as indicators of municipal government performance. In the end, however, there are several reasons for believing that the participation of state and federal governments in local affairs does not invalidate utility coverage rates as measures of municipal government performance.

First, with the partial exception of PRONASOL funds (see Molinar Horcasitas and Weldon 1994; Hiskey 1999), federal transfers are sent according to more or less objective criteria.[35] For example, funds sent under "Ramo 33" (named for the number of the line in the federal budget), a major source of federal transfers, are determined according to a formula that incorporates a municipality's population, marginalization, and needs. Furthermore, mayors have the discretion to prioritize how the money gets spent once it enters the municipal coffer. They are also responsible for negotiating with governors to have state money budgeted for public works projects in their municipalities. So, while municipalities are clearly reliant on state and federal government for finances, and in many cases for direct investment, it remains true that the municipal president is the single most important actor in securing funds, determining how they are spent, and overseeing public works projects.

State and federal interference may appear more prominent than it really is because it usually happens in large, urban municipalities. Recall that García del Castillo (1999, 144) estimates state and federal governments to be involved in water and sewer management in 18 percent and 12 percent of municipalities, respectively. The vast majority of the remaining municipalities handle water and sewer provision on their own: according to his estimations, almost 60 percent of municipalities directly manage their own water utility, and the majority of the remainder use a variety of indirect arrangements that allow them to retain some level of control, such as intermunicipal agreements, semiprivate companies, or municipal water commissions (García del Castillo 1999, 141–44).

Additionally, regardless of state and federal influence, both mayors and citizens view municipal governments as responsible for public utilities. Water and sewer coverage are quintessential local issues in much of Mexico, and local politicians are usually the focus of the public's praise and blame. As a result, they spend a significant portion of their time planning and managing public works projects.[36] I believe that mayors retain more control over these issues than many recent studies suggest and that even where they do not retain actual control they are still interested in taking credit and avoiding blame. Thus they should be seen as potentially responsive in this Mayhewian sense at least (Mayhew 1974).

Finally, note that many of the sources of state and federal influence can be accounted for through statistical controls.[37] For exactly this reason, in the multivariate analysis presented above I included controls for PRONASOL funding, the size of the municipal budget, and divided government, as well as dummy variables for every state (save one). So even if we recognize that the dependent variable is partly a function of state- and federal-level factors, the results for the variable of interest represent the best estimate of an independent effect, even controlling for these factors (as best we can). With consideration to all of these arguments, I feel confident in arguing that the possibility of state and federal influence does not render this measurement strategy inappropriate; and given the ability to control for such influences, there is no persuasive reason to believe that the results presented here are biased by them.

This chapter has generated and evaluated several testable implications for two main hypotheses of government performance: electoral competition and participation. The data do not reveal any substantive relationship between electoral competition and government performance in Mexican municipalities; thus the analysis lends no support to the accountability and selection mechanisms outlined in chapter 2. This (non)finding is largely robust to alternative specifications and alternative measures of electoral competition. In contrast, our proxy measures of participation are strongly related to government performance, thus supporting the hypothesis that local governments respond to nonelectoral means of citizen influence. This contradicts much of the literature on electoral competition in Mexico (see Hiskey 1999 and Rodríguez 1998, among others) and calls into question the tendency of many scholars to focus exclusively on elections as mechanisms of popular control and democratic governance.

While chapters 5 and 6 continue the analysis with alternative conceptualizations of government performance, I believe that the findings presented here are robust, valid, and surprising. This forces us to ask for an explanation. Why does electoral competition fail to improve government performance in Mexican municipalities, and why might participation succeed? Two answers suggest themselves.

The first possibility is that the electoral connection in Mexico labors under the strain of institutions and practices that impede mechanisms of electoral accountability. These problems include extreme centralization within the municipal government, a constitutional prohibition against reelection, and a three-year term of office (Guillén-López 1996). The latter two problems, in combination, make it exceedingly difficult for municipal presidents to gain experience or expertise in their jobs. And the last-term problem created by the no-reelection rule makes it difficult (though not impossible) to explain how Mexican politicians could ever be induced to perform well, even in theory. We might make use of progressive ambition theory or other theoretical frameworks to explain the electoral connection in an institutional setting like Mexico's (Alesina and Spear 1988; Carey 1996; Michelle Taylor 1992). But the empirical facts of the case suggest that such a theoretical shift would be fruitless—there is no point in generating an improved theory of electoral accountability when the data so clearly indicate that electoral competition is not related to responsiveness.

I do not mean to suggest here that Mexican politicians are somehow unaware of the electoral cycle or the importance of electoral victories for their parties. However, the data clearly indicate that there is a break at some point of the causal chain leading from electoral competition to responsive government. We do not need to portray Mexican politicians as callous, corrupt, and incompetent in order to make this point. In fact, my personal experience leads me to believe that many politicians in Mexico are hardworking, competent, and effective. But the fundamental institutional problem in Mexico is such that even when representatives are well intentioned their efforts can be stymied. For example, Grindle (2006) argues that the electoral cycle induces local politicians to focus on government reform and improving municipal capacity. But as I discuss in chapter 6, she also recognizes that reforms do not necessarily improve performance, and that institutional constraints make it difficult for voters to hold politicians accountable for their reform efforts (see Grindle 2006, 67). Thus, even when politicians are motivated to be responsive, institutional constraints such as the prohibition against reelection and the three-year term make sustained responsiveness quite difficult.

A second explanation for the results presented here is that electoral competition is itself an effect of some underlying political process. This prior factor might cause both electoral competition and improved performance, thus rendering spurious the apparent causal relationship that many have found between competition and performance. What might this prior factor be? The fact that municipal government performance seems most closely related to several measures of nonelectoral means of influence suggests that social and economic changes come first and political change follows. That is, both the rise of electoral competition and the improvement in government performance may be the result of prior changes in the quantity and quality of civic and political participation in Mexico. I consider this argument more closely in chapter 6. But at a minimum, these results should force us to entertain the possibility that elections are not the only, or even the most important, tool that citizens have at their disposal when they endeavor to influence the actions of their governments.

CHAPTER FIVE

Testing Hypotheses about Responsiveness

The Public Finance Approach

THE PREVIOUS CHAPTER PRESENTED SOME SURPRISING findings. With respect to the provision of public services, the available evidence suggests that the primary political source of responsive government is to be found in levels of political participation and engagement. There is very little evidence to support the view that municipal governments are rendered more responsive through mechanisms of electoral accountability; nor did we uncover significant evidence of an interactive effect. In my view, the evidence on this point is unambiguous. Yet there are several reasons to probe the matter further, including the strong priors that many scholars hold in favor of the electoral hypothesis and the inherent difficulty in supporting strong causal inferences with large-*N* correlational analyses. In this chapter, I deepen the empirical analysis by introducing an alternative approach to measuring government performance, based on municipal financial data. This approach offers a useful counterpoint to the analysis from chapter 4 because it is less vulnerable to the objections that I raised against the public utility measures. The empirical results based on municipal financial indicators are largely consistent with the findings in the previous chapter, even though the two approaches to measurement are only tangentially related. Thus I conclude that the results presented here are likely *not* the result of idiosyncrasies in the measurement of the dependent variable.

The Public Finance Approach to Measuring Government Performance

If, for whatever reason, a municipal government becomes more active in the pursuit of the public interest, we should be able to find evidence of its efforts in the municipality's financial record. Budget data for the vast majority of Mexican municipalities are available for each year since 1989, and the data include breakdowns of municipal income sources and spending patterns.[1] There may be several ways to employ these data as indicators of government performance.[2] This section focuses on one strategy that has strong intuitive and theoretical appeal. I use budget data to calculate the amount of municipal revenue that is raised locally, both as a raw total (pesos per capita) and as a percentage of the municipality's total revenue.[3]

All municipalities are able to raise their own revenue through taxes, fees, and fines (Rodríguez 1997, 127).[4] However, before the mid-1980s these revenue sources were widely mismanaged, if they were exploited at all. After the 1983 constitutional reform that granted municipal governments formal autonomy over several issue areas, municipalities reacted differently to pressures for modernization and responsiveness. The data suggest that some began to systematize the collection of local taxes, while others failed to take advantage of the potential revenue source. For example, Cabrero Mendoza and Orihuela (2000) find that large cities were more likely to take advantage of local revenue sources, possibly because cities have a larger tax base from which to draw revenue. The collection of local revenue can be seen as an attempt by the municipality to increase its capacity, modernize, and provide better services (see Grindle 2006).[5] It is a good measure of performance, not because it measures a municipality's financial capacity for utility provision, but because it signals whether the municipality has undertaken efforts to modernize its bureaucratic capacity and increase its efficiency.

So this statistic has a clear application to our main hypotheses. Electoral theories, including the accountability and selection mechanisms introduced in chapter 2, would predict that municipal governments raise more local revenue when they have competitive electoral environments. In contrast, participatory theories would predict that municipalities with higher levels of mass political activity would generate higher local revenues.

The best way to generate a measure based on local income is simply to calculate the total pesos collected locally, per capita. Adjusted for inflation, this measure should reflect a level of local income that is comparable over time and across cases. Local revenue per capita is not affected by any concomitant changes in other revenue sources or spending patterns. It may be affected by local macroeconomic conditions, but we can control for such effects by including income measures in our analysis. Further, by including a lagged value of this indicator in multivariate analysis, we can in effect estimate an equation on the change in pesos per capita from one year to the next.

An alternative measurement approach would be to calculate locally raised revenue as a percentage of total municipal income. The conventional expectation is that municipal financial reform entails (among other things) an attempt to lower the municipality's dependence on state and federal transfers. Therefore, we would expect those municipalities that are reforming, and improving their performance, to have a higher percentage of their revenue raised locally. The disadvantage of this measure is that changes in local revenue collection might be obscured by concomitant changes in state and federal spending. It is possible, for example, that electoral competition might have two effects: prompting local governments to increase their tax collections and spurring the state and/or federal government to increase transfers. If this were to happen, the relative proportion of local income to total income might remain unchanged (or could even decrease if transfers outpaced local collection), obscuring the fact that political changes did alter the behavior of political officials in ways that might be described as "more responsive." Given the potential ambiguity, in this chapter I analyze the first measure, locally raised revenue per capita. But preliminary analysis of this second measure (not reported) generally shows consistent results.

These measures, and all public finance measures, have some disadvantages. The most important potential problem is that public finance measures are indirect ways of assessing government performance. It is reasonable to suspect that the municipalities that are regularizing their tax rolls and enhancing their ability to collect local revenues are also reforming and improving efficiency in other areas of government. However, it should not be assumed that municipalities that collect and spend more money are necessarily doing a better job with the funds they have or that they are necessarily targeting their spending more effectively. In this sense, the public utility measures introduced in chapter 4 are preferable, since they are tangible indicators of performance on specific outcomes that are known to be salient in local politics. Another disadvantage of the public finance measures is the potential for an urban bias. Several scholars have noted that large, urban municipalities, which have larger and more concentrated tax bases on which to draw, are in the best position to take advantage of local revenue sources, especially the *predial,* or property tax (Cabrero Mendoza and Orihuela 2000; Rodríguez 1997). I deal with this problem in multivariate models by controlling for municipal population, but this is not a guaranteed correction for any underlying estimation bias that may exist.

The public finance approach has two main advantages over the public utility strategy presented in the previous chapter. First, the availability of annual data allows for panel analysis. A panel design increases the number of cases, allows for temporal as well as cross-sectional comparisons, and offers the potential for finer-grained inferences about sequencing and temporal effects. As we will see, the analytical leverage promised does not fully materialize because of limitations in the data. But we do learn some things about temporal dynamics that the public utility data could not demonstrate. The second advantage of the public finance approach is that it is far less susceptible to the two strongest objections raised against public utility measures: a conceptual conflation of government performance and development, and the influence of state and federal governments. Levels of development and of intragovernmental interference may indeed influence local revenue collection. But any such influence, rather than being a potential conceptual conflation that would invalidate the measure, is likely to be indirect and amenable to statistical control.

The Results

The analytical task at hand is identical to that of the previous chapter. I aim to test the same set of hypotheses about political influences on government performance, and I need to control for (roughly) the same set of political, economic, and demographic characteristics that may also be related to the dependent variable. The analysis generates findings that are largely consistent with those of the previous chapter. This should increase our confidence in the main empirical findings, as they suggest that the previous chapter's results are unlikely to stem from a quirk in the public utility measure of government performance. At the same time, the data offer suggestive hints about the possibility of an interactive effect. This will oblige us to reconsider whether electoral competition has an indirect effect on government performance by enhancing the effectiveness of political participation.

The data set I use in this chapter contains annual indicators on a variety of municipal financial statistics for each municipality in Mexico from 1989 to 2000.[6] These data were already introduced in chapter 4, where I used them to calculate total municipal budgets per capita (as a control variable in that chapter's multivariate analyses). Here too, I combine the municipal financial data with other socioeconomic and demographic data, as I explain below. To measure local revenue generation, I simply calculate the total revenue raised locally, in terms of inflation-adjusted pesos per capita.[7]

Figures 5.1 and 5.2 illustrate the time trend in local revenue and its relationship to electoral competition. In figure 5.1, I code municipalities as competitive if their average margin of victory over the previous two elections was less than 20 percent or if they have ever experienced party alternation in the mayor's office; all other cases are coded as noncompetitive. This is a time-sensitive coding scheme in which the competitiveness of each municipality is recoded for each year on the basis of the municipality's evolving electoral history. The proportion of noncompetitive municipalities is quite high in 1989 but decreases steadily over time. This explains why the average scores for the full sample and the noncompetitive subset begin at nearly the same point but then diverge over time. In figure 5.2, I offer an alternative means for categorizing municipal competitiveness. I split the sample into three categories: (1) municipalities that were consistently competitive from 1989 onwards, (2) those that became competitive at some point in the 1990s, and (3) those that remained noncompetitive throughout the entire decade.

These two graphs illustrate several interesting patterns. For one, local revenue generation has remained relatively constant across the 1990s.[8] The data appear to indicate that local revenue was increasing at the very end of the 1980s, but it is difficult to be confident of this without data from earlier years. Also, the figures reveal a significant drop in local revenue after the peso crisis of 1994 (see also Cabrero Mendoza and Orihuela 2000).[9] The crisis seems to have affected all municipalities roughly equally, yet both figures suggest that competitive municipalities recovered better in the latter half of the 1990s.

Figure 5.1. Locally Raised Revenue by Competitiveness, 1989–2000

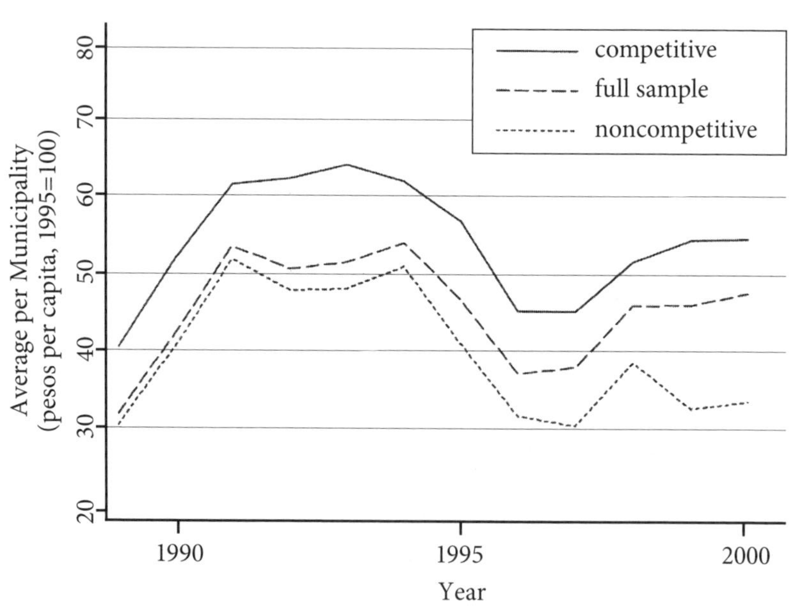

The main purpose of these graphs is to illustrate the bivariate relationship between electoral competition and government performance (here measured with local revenue) and to get a sense of any changes in this relationship over time. Both graphs display a clear pattern: municipalities with competitive elections generate more local revenue.[10] Moreover, we can see that the relationship is generally stable. Both graphs show a moderate increase in the gap between competitive and noncompetitive municipalities, but the advantage held by competitive municipalities in 1989 was already sizable, and the two time series tend to track each other closely. As with the bivariate analysis of public service provision in the previous chapter, the initial look at the evidence shows an obvious correlation of the type that leads many scholars to suggest a causal relationship.

Yet the temporal characteristics of this relationship are harder to discern. By way of comparison, in chapter 4 I was able to demonstrate that

Figure 5.2. Locally Raised Revenue by Competitiveness, 1989–2000, with Transitional Category

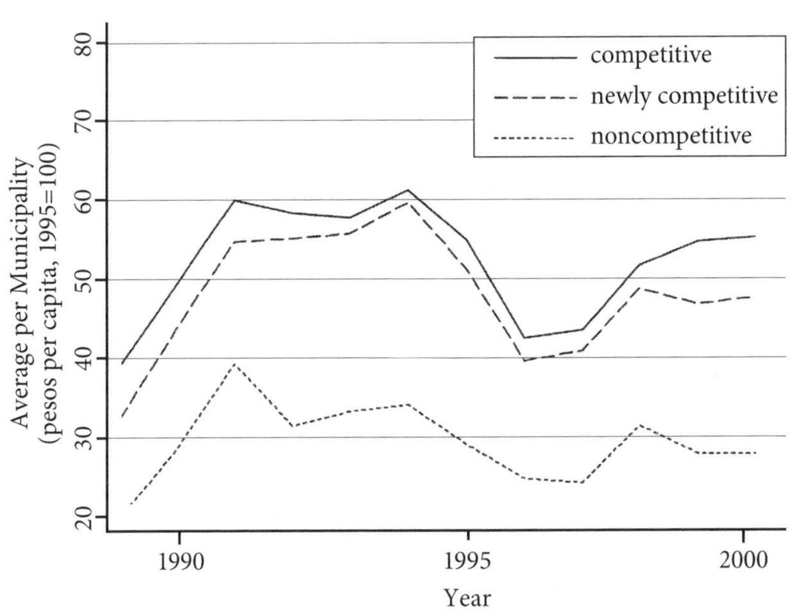

differences in service provision preceded the rise of electoral competition, suggesting that elections could not have been the cause of observed differences. Here it is harder to draw a firm conclusion because I do not have access to municipal budget data prior to 1989. However, I believe that figure 5.2 does illustrate the difficulty in establishing a causal link between competition and local revenue generation. As with figure 5.1, the competitive municipalities have a clear advantage over noncompetitive municipalities in terms of revenue generation. But the findings for the middle category do not appear to be consistent with the electoral hypothesis. Recall that this category includes all municipalities that were *not* competitive in 1989 but became competitive by the year 2000. If it were true that municipalities improved their local revenue generation in response to the appearance of electoral competition, we would expect these municipalities to resemble noncompetitive municipalities in 1989 but to come to resemble the consistently competitive municipalities over time. Figure 5.3 illustrates the predicted pattern schematically.

Figure 5.3. Hypothetical Relationship between Locally Raised Revenue and Transitional Municipalities

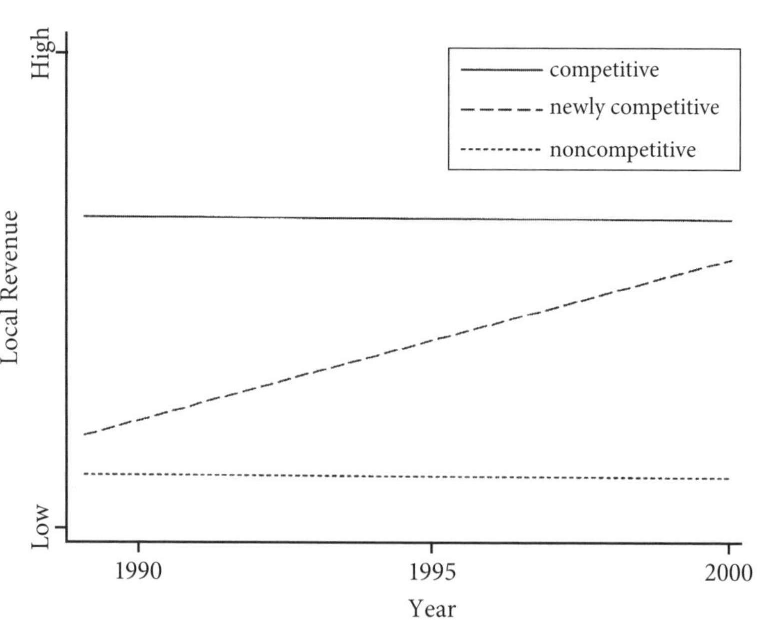

Comparing the (actual) figure 5.2 with the (hypothetical) figure 5.3, we can see that the data do not fit with this prediction. The transitional cases already resemble the competitive cases in 1989 and the early 1990s, *before* most of them became electorally competitive. And these two groups continue to track closely throughout the 1990s. In other words, the ability of these transitional cases to generate more local revenue when they remained noncompetitive suggests that their relatively high levels of local revenue should not be attributed to electoral competition. We might have more confidence in this inference if we had access to good financial data from the 1980s, but it is difficult to reconcile the facts presented in figure 5.2 with the predictions of the electoral hypothesis. A final point worth mentioning here is that, even though the data in these figures do not speak to any particular alternative explanation, they are consistent with the hypothesis that both enhanced local revenue generation *and* electoral competition are the effects of a prior factor, such as political participation, which we know to have been on the rise in the late 1970s and 1980s. I explore this hypothesis further in chapter 6.

Multivariate Analysis

To simultaneously test the main hypotheses of interest, I subject the determinants of local revenue generation to multivariate analysis. As above, the dependent variable is simply the amount of revenue generated from local sources, expressed in inflation-adjusted pesos per capita. The independent variables are similar to those introduced in chapter 4; I have modified some as appropriate for use in a panel-study analysis. The margin of victory and the turnout rate are expressed as five-year running averages and are lagged one year. The intent of the five-year running average is to reflect the general trend in competition and turnout over the past two electoral cycles. (In the next section I demonstrate that other measures generate similar results.) Other variables either take on 1990 values (when that is the only year for which an observation is available, as is the case for literacy and poverty rates) or are current-year values. I have included only one party dummy, for the PAN, because the literature singularly identifies PAN municipalities as those that were more likely to employ strategies of local revenue enhancement

(Rodríguez and Ward 1992). I include a one-year lag of the dependent variable as a regressor, and I discuss the consequences of doing so in the next section. Finally, I include dummy variables for each state (save one) and each year (save one).

As was the case in the previous chapter, multivariate analysis shows that the apparent relationship between electoral competition and government performance is not robust. Table 5.1 reports the results of GLS random-effects regression on the indicator of local revenue. Model 1 includes all cases for which data exist, or eleven annual observations on 1,817 municipalities, with just 229 case-years dropped because of missing data. The central results should be familiar by now. According to model 1, electoral competition has no significant effect on local revenue generation. Literacy and turnout rates have a sizable positive effect, while poverty rates have the expected negative association. The model also generates a few additional findings of interest. The results support the assertions of Rodríguez and Ward (1992), Rodríguez (1997), and others that local revenue generation is more feasible in larger municipalities and more likely to be the strategy of *panista* mayors. Indigenous municipalities generate more local revenue, which might give some support to two commonly held notions about indigenous communities: that they are marginalized and ignored by the central government (and are thus forced to rely on local revenue sources) and that they are tight-knit communities with strong social networks (and thus an enhanced ability to enforce local revenue collection). Municipalities held by a party other than the governor's generate less local revenue. This latter finding is contrary to expectations, but the effect is not particularly large.

Obviously, the most interesting findings in the model are related to the three proxy indicators of participation. The size of the coefficients for literacy and poverty rates are particularly large; turnout also has a moderate effect. All three effects are in the predicted direction. To get a sense of the magnitude of the coefficients, in figure 5.4 I generate a simulation in which all other variables are held at their median values and the variables of interest are set at each percentile score from the first to the ninety-ninth percentile.[11] The effect of literacy seems smaller than its coefficient might suggest, partly because literacy rates in the sample are generally quite high. On the other hand, small differences in literacy predict only small differences in local revenue. But the model predicts

Table 5.1. GLS Regression on Locally Raised Revenue, 1989–2000

	Locally Raised Revenue (Pesos per Capita)		
		Split Samples	
	Full Sample	*Noncomp.*	*Competitive*
	(1)	*(2)*	*(3)*
Lagged Revenue			
Pesos per capita	0.62***	0.55***	0.71***
(1-year lag)	(0.05)	(0.07)	(0.06)
Political Influence			
Margin of victory	-1.07	-	-
(lagged 5-year avg.)	(1.40)		
Literacy	25.83***	31.76***	20.37*
(1990 % literate)	(5.62)	(6.99)	(8.00)
Turnout	6.91**	4.49	9.39^
(lagged 5-year avg.)	(2.68)	(3.09)	(5.15)
Poverty	-20.61***	-28.41***	-9.79^
(%, 1990)	(3.61)	(4.92)	(5.27)
Additional Controls			
Indigenous municipality	3.00*	3.65*	2.64
(dummy)	(1.22)	(1.51)	(1.84)
PAN mayor	7.11***	-	4.51**
(dummy)	(1.52)		(1.50)
Divided gov't.	-1.75*	-0.42	-0.41
(dummy)	(0.83)	(2.08)	(0.98)
Municipal size	2.38***	1.51*	2.50**
(logged pop.)	(0.60)	(0.77)	(0.91)
Constant	-15.85^	-5.89	-20.15
	(8.70)	(11.13)	(13.86)
Valid *N*	19758	12393	7365
Municipalities	1817	1572	1241
Overall *R*-squared	0.58	0.52	0.70

Note: Each model also includes dummy variables for each state (save one), and for each year (save one); coefficients not reported. The table reports Huber-White standard errors in parentheses. Statistical significance is noted with the conventional $^{***}p < .001$, $^{**}p < .01$, $^{*}p < .05$, ^ < .10.

that a municipality with a literacy rate at the ninetieth percentile will generate eight more pesos per capita than a similar municipality scoring in the tenth percentile in literacy and eleven more pesos per capita than one in the fifth percentile. Given that the median municipality in the sample generates about twenty-three pesos per capita in local revenue, these differences are large. The effect of turnout is not overwhelming: at most, large swings in turnout changes estimated local revenue generation by three or four pesos per capita. The effects are larger when we vary literacy, turnout, and poverty rates in tandem. In that case, the difference between municipalities at the tenth and ninetieth percentiles is about twenty-three pesos per capita, a substantial difference.

Models 2 and 3 in table 5.1 offer a test of the interactive hypothesis, which posits that participation is more effective when it occurs in a competitive electoral environment. I split the sample according to the de-

Figure 5.4. Estimated Effect of Literacy, Turnout, and Poverty on Local Revenue

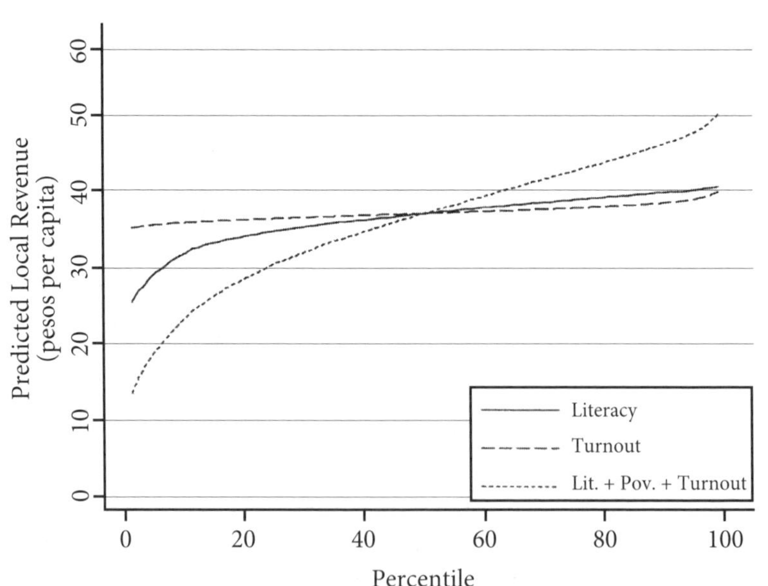

gree of electoral competition, using the same coding scheme discussed above in relation to figure 5.1.[12] The results are strikingly similar to those that I generated in the previous chapter. Overall, the effect of the variables of interest appears to be roughly the same in the two subsamples: literacy has a large positive effect in both models, turnout has a small positive effect, and poverty rates have a large negative effect. In all three of these cases, the coefficients appear to be slightly different. For example, the effect of literacy looks larger in the noncompetitive sample, and the effect of turnout appears smaller. However, Chow tests suggest that the only point at which these differences are statistically significant is with respect to poverty.[13] In municipalities that lack competitive elections, high levels of poverty translate into much lower levels of local revenue. This does not seem particularly surprising, given obvious links between poverty and local tax bases (which I discuss further below). But competitive municipalities appear to be significantly less constrained by levels of poverty, so that among competitive municipalities poor ones do not fare too much worse than wealthier ones. I noted a similar effect in chapter 4; and although neither effect is particularly strong or robust, they do seem to leave an opening for the interactive hypothesis.

Empirical Extensions

Questions about proper model specification, as well as some peculiar characteristics of the data set used here, both suggest ways in which the empirical tests might be extended and modified. In tables 5.2, 5.3, and 5.4 I offer the results of a series of such tests.

Drop State Dummies

The main model in table 5.1 (reproduced in table 5.2 as the "base model") includes dummy variables for each state (except one, as required for any estimation with a constant). I do not report the coefficients because they are not of primary theoretical interest, but I include them in the model in a crude attempt to control for idiosyncratic state-level factors that might affect levels of local revenue generation. For example, a particular governor might from time to time undertake efforts to encourage the collection of local property taxes; or a certain state might do a poor job of maintaining public records, which would make it more difficult for municipalities to keep proper accounts. I do not know that any such factors actually exist, but including state dummies seems to be a reasonable safeguard against the possibility that they do. On the other hand, one might suspect that the addition of thirty additional control variables, on not-necessarily-compelling theoretical grounds, would produce misleading or biased results.

Excluding these dummy variables generates almost no changes with regard to the variables of interest. As we can see in model 2 of table 5.2, the size of most coefficients changes only very slightly; none of the coefficients change signs. The respecification has no impact on the estimated effect of electoral competition, and the coefficients for literacy, turnout, and poverty are all moderately larger. Thus, if we were to accept model 2 as a superior specification, we would merely conclude that the relationship between participation and performance was even larger than we first estimated. This would occasion no change in our judgment on the electoral hypothesis.

The Lagged Dependent Variable

Another possible criticism of the base-model specification is that it incorrectly includes the lagged value of the dependent variable. The inclusion of such a variable may induce bias in model estimations (Greene 1997, 586–87), and the tendency of political scientists to include lagged dependent variables in their models has been criticized for this reason (Achen 2000). Consider the simple model in which Y is a function of a constant, one exogenous variable, and the lagged value of Y, and t is an index of time:[14]

$$Y_t = B_{0t} + B_1 x_{1t} + B_2 Y_{(t-1)} + e_t$$

If we have properly specified the determinants of Y_t, we can usually presume that $Y_{(t-1)}$ was generated by an analogous process:

$$Y_{(t-1)} = B_{0(t-1)} + B_1 x_{1(t-1)} + B_2 Y_{(t-2)} + e_{(t-1)}$$

If the disturbance terms in these two equations are correlated, it can be shown that the estimated coefficients in the first equation are biased.

Table 5.2. Alternate Specifications on Locally Raised Revenue, 1989–2000

	Locally Raised Revenue (Pesos per Capita)			
	Base Model (from Table 5.1)	*Drop State Dummies*	*Drop Lagged d.v.*	*Drop Top Percentile on d.v*
	(1)	*(2)*	*(3)*	*(4)*
Lagged Revenue				
Pesos per capita	0.62***	0.68***	-	0.34***
(1-year lag)	(0.05)	(0.05)		(0.04)
Political Influence				
Margin of victory	-1.07	1.25	0.55	-2.50*
(lagged 5-year avg.)	(1.40)	(1.24)	(1.97)	(1.04)
Literacy	25.83***	27.23***	70.35***	44.37***
(1990 % literate)	(5.62)	(5.22)	(11.46)	(4.52)
Turnout	6.91**	10.09***	11.75***	14.63***
(lagged 5-year avg.)	(2.68)	(2.77)	(3.55)	(2.26)
Poverty	-20.61***	-29.26***	-40.98***	-28.15***
(%, 1990)	(3.61)	(4.57)	(5.96)	(2.80)
Additional Controls				
Indigenous municipality	3.00*	0.58	6.51*	6.58***
(dummy)	(1.22)	(0.96)	(3.01)	(0.97)
PAN mayor	7.11***	7.74***	2.72*	8.03***
(dummy)	(1.52)	(1.62)	(1.36)	(1.12)
Divided gov't.	-1.75*	-0.22	-1.01	-1.39*
(dummy)	(0.83)	(0.79)	(0.82)	(0.62)
Municipal size	2.38***	2.05***	6.06***	4.58***
(logged pop.)	(0.60)	(0.54)	(1.27)	(0.46)
Constant	-15.85^	-14.42*	-60.92**	-33.33***
	(8.70)	(7.35)	(19.91)	(6.24)
Valid *N*	19758	19758	19855	19557
municipalities	1817	1817	1817	1813
Overall *R*-squared	0.58	0.56	0.32	0.60

Note: The table reports Huber-White standard errors in parentheses. Statistical significance is noted with the conventional ***$p < .001$, **$p < .01$, *$p < .05$, ^ < .10.

Because $Y_{(t-1)}$ is (in part) a function of $e_{(t-1)}$, and because $e_{(t-1)}$ and e_t are correlated, $Y_{(t-1)}$ will be correlated with e_t, which violates a standard OLS assumption and introduces bias to the estimation. Achen (2000) shows the following: (1) the coefficient on the lagged dependent variable tends to be biased upward; (2) the coefficients on the exogenous variables tend to be biased toward zero; and (3) the degree of bias is related to the strength of the correlation between e_t and $e_{(t-1)}$. Most troubling is the fact that, if the correlation in the error terms is sufficiently high, $Y_{(t-1)}$ can have this effect whether it is a true cause of Y_t or not (Achen 2000, 14).

To be clear, the potential for bias is *not* a function of a correlation between Y_t and $Y_{(t-1)}$. Rather, the bias results specifically when the error terms are correlated. While it is difficult to know with precision how closely correlated these terms are (since error terms are estimated, not observed), and while it is entirely possible that the error terms are not correlated in many practical applications, there are two reasons to believe that this may be a significant source of bias for models like the ones presented above. First, the processes that generated the data are similar over time. Whatever sources of measurement error existed in 1989 or 1990 (say, for example, that a particular state did not exercise sufficient oversight in the reporting of local budget data, or that a particular regional directorate within the statistical bureau was poorly managed), those same sources of measurement bias are likely to exist in 1998 and 1999 as well. Second, in practice most models are not perfectly specified. Misspecification in this instance is likely to omit factors that correlate over time, and thus $Y_{(t-1)}$ might correlate with the error term in the specification on Y_t. For example, it may be the case that municipalities in a certain region have "higher than expected" local revenue because representatives from the municipal governments were all trained in local revenue management at a conference sponsored by the state government or a local university. Since these factors are not modeled, their causal effect will be captured by the error term. And if they covary over time, $e_{(t-1)}$ and e_t will correlate positively. Either of these two processes can result in Y variables that are "heavily trended," meaning that the error process is correlated over time (Achen 2000).

Unfortunately, there is no easy statistical fix for this problem, for at least two reasons. First, it is usually difficult to establish in practice that this type of bias exists. Second, its existence does not necessarily imply that the lagged variable should be dropped from the equation. As with most statistical problems, I believe the best solution lies in careful theoretical thinking. In the current case there a strong theoretical justification for including the lagged variable: revenue generation is, at least in part, an additive process. Tax collectors do not begin their job anew every year; rather, they systematize their tax rolls and continuously add the capacity to identify those who owe taxes. This is especially true for the property tax, because once added to the tax rolls, a piece of real estate is likely to remain on the books in future years. Or if for whatever reason a municipality institutes a new policy to take advantage of a certain tax resource, that policy will remain in place for an extended (if not indefinite) period of time; municipalities do not typically rebuild their fee and fine structures from scratch each year. Thus the current year's local revenue generation will depend to some extent on the previous year's generation, and there are good theoretical reasons for including the lagged variable.[15]

Still, even though we do not know for certain that the inclusion of $Y_{(t-1)}$ as a regressor produces bias, it might be wise to consider the possibility that it does. This is particularly true given the negative finding on electoral competition. This is a factor that many other studies have identified as an important determinant; further, we know that if the lagged variable did introduce bias here, its function would be to *under*-estimate the coefficient on electoral competition (and other exogenous variables). Thus this finding in particular deserves closer scrutiny before we can confidently reject the electoral hypothesis.

In theory there are several ways that one might attempt to measure or account for bias here: we could generate an instrument for the lagged value, or we might attempt to control for autocorrelation in the error terms. But the simplest way to find out if the negative finding on electoral competition is due to a downward bias in the estimation is simply to remove the lagged term from the specification. To be clear, I do not believe this to be the best specification of the model; but arguably it is the most favorable toward the electoral hypothesis. And as we can see in model 3 of table 5.2, removing the lagged term has no effect on the estimated relationship between electoral competition and local revenue generation. The coefficient remains small and statistically insignificant.

On the other hand, the magnitudes of the other coefficients of interest are far larger: compared to model 1, the poverty coefficient doubles, and the literacy coefficient is almost three times as large. I do not believe that this is evidence of a downward bias in these cases; rather, by removing the lagged variable, we are in effect asking the model to estimate the total amount of local revenue rather than changes in the value from year to year. If we were to accept this model as a superior specification (as I do not), our conclusion would merely be that the proxy indicators of political participation are even more powerful predictors than we first thought, and we would remain quite confident in rejecting the electoral hypothesis.

Outliers and Influential Observations

Most municipalities generate between ten and sixty pesos per capita. But the distribution in the set of cases considered here includes an alarmingly long right-side tail: a small number of municipalities generate over one thousand pesos per capita or more, an order of magnitude higher than even the ninetieth-percentile score on this variable. There are three reasons that the data might return such results. There may be errors in either the revenue data or in population data. If a municipality's population is underreported, then local income per capita could be grossly inflated. Second, a small number of municipalities may benefit greatly from unique revenue sources that are not available to most municipalities. A third possibility is that these data are accurate and that the municipalities with extremely high levels of local revenue generation are just doing a better job. However, I find this last proposition to be extremely unlikely: the disparity in pesos per capita is far too large to be accounted for by enhanced methods of tax collection.

The first explanation seems most plausible. While I have not been able to confirm any specific errors in the population data, it is important to note that the same outliers are not generated when local revenue is calculated as a percentage of total municipal revenue. The proportional measure does not depend on population size: it is calculated simply as the amount of revenue raised locally, divided by the municipality's total operating budget. This suggests that the problem is specific to indicators based on the population estimate. But even if the second explanation I offer above is more accurate, the potential remedies to the discrepancy are the same.

The most straightforward statistical remedy (though probably not the most sophisticated) is to drop these outlying cases from the analysis.[16] Thus model 4 in table 5.2 maintains the specification of the base model but excludes all cases scoring in the top percentile on local revenue generation.[17] As we can see from reviewing the results, this modification does have a significant impact on our estimations: compared to the base model, every coefficient in the model (except one) becomes larger. The estimated effect of turnout on local revenue generation even doubles. And, at long last, we find that electoral competition is estimated to have a statistically significant effect on local revenue generation, in the expected direction.

Before we read too much into this finding, however, we should recognize at least two points. First, the rationale for excluding the top percentile of cases is not perfect—I suspect that some of these cases may be measured with error, but I do not know this to be so, and I have no theoretical reason for believing that these cases generate bias against the electoral hypothesis in particular. Second, even though we have produced a "statistically significant" coefficient, the magnitude of the effect is quite small: variation in the level of electoral competition, according to this model, would never change our prediction of local revenue generation by more than a couple of pesos per capita. At the same time, the estimated effects for the other variables of interest are much larger, predicting changes of as many as forty or fifty pesos per capita in some scenarios. In sum, I believe this finding to be very weak evidence in favor of the electoral hypothesis. The finding is not very robust, and the size of the predicted effect is very small.

Alternative Measures of Competition

As I discussed in chapter 4, I have generated a variety of indicators of electoral competition. In table 5.3, I show the results of sequentially introducing each of twelve alternative measures into the base model specification. The twelve measures are similar to those used in chapter 4: several variations of M, indicators of party alternation, the PRI's vote share, and four variations on party fractionalization indices (N and NP).

The results show that there are some measures according to which electoral competition has a significant effect on local revenue generation. In particular, while the five-year running average of M (in the base model) had no effect, we do estimate a significant effect if we use a five-year lag, or the average value of M from 1985 to 1989, as our measure of electoral competition. Similarly, we generate small (but significant) effects if we measure competition with the maximum value of N or NP.

Again, some of these results could be interpreted as providing a glimmer of hope for the electoral hypothesis. But we should not be too confident in these results, for several reasons. The main one is that there is no compelling theoretical justification for deciding that (say) the five-year lag of M is a better measure than the five-year running average. As I have argued elsewhere in the book, the fractionalization indices are particularly poor measures of electoral competition; but even if we focused on the two versions of M, we would be forced to generate a post hoc justification for preferring these measures over others. Inconsistency would quickly follow. The post hoc justification for deciding that the five-year lag of M is the best measure here would contradict the post hoc justification we would have derived in chapter 4, according to which the PRI's vote share was the best measure (see table 4.5 and the related discussion). The only way to argue that these results are robust would be to cherry-pick our indicators of electoral competition according to which one happened to produce a "significant" effect in a particular model.[18] But finally, and perhaps most compellingly, we should note that even if we throw aside all doubts about the statistical accuracy of these findings, they never translate into a predicted effect of more than about three pesos per capita. Thus, even if we grant the interpretation most favorable to the electoral hypothesis, the best we can conclude is that competition has a small effect on the margins in some cases.

Cross-Sectional Estimation

One of the main attractions of the analysis presented in this chapter is the ability to use panel data, with annual observations over the course of a decade, to learn more about the temporal aspects of changes in government performance. Annual observations for several variables of interest (like local revenue and electoral competitiveness) are useful, as can be seen in the discussion surrounding figures 5.1 and 5.2. The

Table 5.3. Effect of Alternative Measures of Electoral Competition

		Locally Raised Revenue (Pesos per Capita)	
Model Number	*Indicator of Competition*	*Coefficient (s.e.)*	*Effect on Other Coefficients*
(original)	Margin of victory (lagged 5-year average)	-1.07 (1.40)	-
(1)	Margin of victory (5-year lag)	-2.65* (1.12)	None
(2)	Margin of victory (average, 1985-89)	-4.75*** (1.45)	None
(3)	Margin of victory (dichotomized)	1.69^ (1.01)	None
(4)	Competitiveness (dummy for split samples)	1.21 (0.78)	None
(5)	Alternation (dummy if any to date)	-0.09 (0.79)	None
(6)	Alternation (total no., 1980-99)	0.07 (0.30)	None
(7)	PRI vote share (10-year average)	-5.20^ (2.67)	None
(8)	PRI vote share (dichotomized)	-0.29 (0.70)	None
(9)	Effec. no. of parties (N) (10-year average)	0.69 (0.99)	None
(10)	Effec. no. of parties (N) (max. score to date)	-1.35* (0.63)	None
(11)	Effec. no. of parties (NP) (10-year average)	-0.56 (1.32)	None
(12)	Effec. no. of parties (NP) (max. score to date)	-1.70* (0.76)	None

Note: The table reports Huber-White standard errors in parentheses. Statistical significance is noted with the conventional $^{***}p < .001$, $^{**}p < .01$, $^{*}p < .05$, ^ < .10.

multivariate analysis in table 5.1 has its advantages as well, in allowing for a comparison of local revenue generation over time. But it must also be said that the panel data are not as revealing as I had hoped with respect to temporal changes. The random-effects models presented here pick up primarily on cross-unit variation rather than within-unit variation.[19] There may be several reasons for this, including the shortness of the time series (especially in comparison to the number of units cross-sectionally) and the fact that some variables of interest (like literacy and poverty) are measured only each decade and thus appear in these models as invariant within units. It may also be the case that local revenue generation does not change over time as dramatically as I had hypothesized.

In any event, the fact that the panel results are driven primarily by cross-unit variation suggests one final check on the data: to forego the advantages of panel analysis and estimate a simpler, cross-sectional model. I think the panel models are useful and reliable, but this robustness check might be seen as a means of "getting back to basics," simply to ensure that the panel results are not an aberration or in some other way misleading. The three models listed in table 5.4 accomplish this check by modifying the variables of interest in ways that are appropriate for a cross-sectional analysis and then estimating a standard OLS model based on the more than 1,800 cases for which data exist.[20] In each model, the dependent variable is a multiyear average of locally generated pesos per capita, and the independent variables are either multiyear averages or values from the 1990 census. In model 1, I estimate the average local revenue from the latter half of the 1990s as a function of average amount from the previous five-year period, the average margin of victory from the 1990s, the 1990 literacy rate, and so on. In model 2, the dependent variable is the average of local revenue from the entire decade, with the 1989 value of the dependent variable as the lag. And in model 3, I drop the lag altogether, estimating average revenue generation from the 1990s as a function of the political variables of interest. All three models include dummies for each state (save one), whose coefficients are not reported.

The results of these models are consistent with the panel findings in that they consistently show large effects in the expected direction for

Table 5.4. OLS Cross-Sectional Specifications on Locally Raised Revenue, 1989–2000

	Locally Raised Revenue (Pesos per Capita)		
	Avg., 1995–99	*Avg., 1990–99*	*Avg., 1990–99, no lag*
	(1)	*(2)*	*(3)*
Lagged Revenue			
Pesos per capita	0.56***	0.55***	-
(lagged value[a])	(0.05)	(0.10)	
Political Influence			
Margin of victory	2.07	6.58	10.13^
(lagged 10-year avg.)	(3.27)	(4.65)	(5.64)
Literacy	19.82*	42.16***	62.10***
(1990 % literate)	(8.40)	(9.32)	(11.02)
Turnout	-3.43	15.42^	33.43**
(lagged 10-year avg.)	(7.04)	(9.20)	(12.63)
Poverty	-16.79***	-33.73***	-55.55***
(%, 1990)	(5.27)	(5.90)	(6.50)
Additional Controls			
Indigenous municipality	2.10	5.01*	8.71**
(dummy)	(1.96)	(2.29)	(3.02)
PAN control[b]	4.37	18.91***	24.95***
(dummy)	(3.18)	(4.60)	(6.46)
Divided gov't.[b]	0.48	-2.00	-2.52
(dummy)	(2.24)	(2.74)	(3.54)
Municipal size	-1.00	3.02*	6.99***
(logged pop. 1990)	(1.06)	(1.24)	(1.69)
Constant	18.82	-33.90^	-75.42**
	(17.44)	(20.02)	(28.49)
Valid *N*	1816	1806	1817
R-squared	0.80	0.68	0.46

Note: The table reports Huber-White standard errors in parentheses. Statistical significance is noted with the conventional $^{***}p < .001$, $^{**}p < .01$, $^{*}p < .05$, ^ < .10.

a. For model 1, the lagged value is the average score, 1990–94. For model 2, the lagged value is the value from 1989. In model 3 the lag is excluded.

b. As in chapter 4, in the cross-sectional models these dummies take a value of 1 if the condition held for six or more years in the 1990s.

literacy and poverty rates. The effect of turnout is not robust to all three specifications, but the weakly significant coefficient in model 2 and the large coefficient in model 3 both hint at the same relationship found previously, with higher revenue generation in municipalities with higher turnout. And importantly, we find that electoral competition has no measurable effect on local revenue generation across municipalities. Model 3 returns a weakly significant coefficient, but it runs opposite of the hypothesized direction: municipalities with larger margins (and therefore less competition) generate more local revenue. In sum, the analysis in table 5.4 gives us no cause for skepticism of earlier results and indeed supports the main findings regarding the determinants of local revenue generation.

Discussion

I doubt that any reader who has made it to this point would see a justification for further parsing of the data. The empirical findings are clear and robust: the amount of locally raised revenue generated by Mexican municipalities is strongly influenced by the municipality's level of literacy and poverty and by the turnout rate in local elections. Revenue generation does not appear to be a function of electoral competition, which has a very small effect at best. Other factors, such as the size of the municipality or the party in power, are important determinants according to these results, though they are not particularly decisive.

Yet even if I have beaten the empirical side of the question into the ground, we should still give some consideration to the link between the empirical findings and the theoretical questions at hand. I entered into the empirical investigation of this chapter, not because of a particular concern with municipal revenue-generating capacity, but rather because I believe local revenue generation is a useful indicator of government performance. Similarly, I have made use of municipal-level data on literacy, turnout, and poverty, not because I am concerned primarily with those factors, but because (as I argued in chapter 4) I believe them to be good proxy indicators of each municipality's capacity for public participation. I interpret the empirical findings presented in this chapter to be supportive of the hypothesis that local government is more responsive when its citizens have a higher capacity for this type of political participation.

In the end, the reasonableness of this interpretation will be decided by the reader on the basis of the justifications I have offered for each of the measures used here, and my explanation of the links between those measures and the concepts that I argue they identify. However, with respect to this study of local revenue generation, the use of poverty rates as a proxy for participation deserves particular scrutiny. There are good reasons for interpreting this variable as I have in this chapter and the last. However, it would be surprising if there were not also a more direct link between poverty and local revenue collection, based on the simple fact that poor municipalities are likely to have worse local tax bases from which to draw revenue. I accept that this alternative explanation for the link is reasonable; and this implies that the data (with respect to poverty) are not necessarily supportive of the participatory hypothesis.

This caveat underscores an important general characteristic of the analysis presented in this chapter: that while the findings are supportive of the participatory hypothesis they are not sufficiently precise to rule out some other potential explanations. In other words, the participatory explanation for government responsiveness is not the only possible reason that we would find literacy, turnout, and poverty rates to be so closely related with levels of locally raised revenue. I have argued at several points why I think this is the most reasonable interpretation; at a minimum, I can say that I have found a robust amount of empirical data that are consistent with the hypothesis. On the other hand, the findings with respect to the electoral hypothesis are, in my view, robust and decisive. Electoral competition cannot possibly account for more than a small fraction of the variation in local revenue generation and probably accounts for none.

One of the central arguments of this book is that mechanisms of electoral accountability are not fully functional in Mexican municipalities, in spite of the obvious and remarkable increase in electoral competition across much of the country in the 1980s and 1990s. Instead, one municipality performs better than the next because its residents are better able and more willing to employ nonelectoral strategies of political influence. Chapter 4 presented evidence in support of this claim, based on a public utility measure of government performance. My own view is that rates of utility service coverage are among the best available indicators of the performance of Mexican municipalities. But I have also acknowledged problems with these measures.

Therefore, in this chapter I have offered an additional set of empirical tests of the main hypotheses generated in chapters 2 and 3. These tests are based on an alternative strategy for measuring government performance. I introduced locally raised revenue as an (indirect) indicator of municipal government performance. This measurement strategy is not susceptible to the same objections that I raised against public utility measures in chapter 4. Local revenue generation cannot plausibly be viewed as a direct indicator of socioeconomic development, or of state and federal policies. Of course, we might expect both development and intergovernmental interference to affect the amount of locally generated revenue, and the results in table 5.1 confirm this: locally raised revenue is higher in urban, wealthy municipalities and higher in PAN-controlled municipalities. But the critical point is that local revenue stands as a conceptually distinct phenomenon, and it would be hard to make the case that local revenue levels are determined *solely* by levels of development or by state government actions.

Equally important is that local revenue is not collinear with rates of public service provision. We might expect there to be some correlation between these two factors: all else equal, a municipality that raises more local revenue will have more resources available to spend on service provision. But given the heavy reliance of municipal governments on state and federal transfers, and given the long list of factors that help determine levels of service provision, we should not worry that the similarity in the empirical results is due to a close conceptual or causal connection between service provision and local revenue. The data confirm this point: local revenue per capita correlates only moderately with rates of service provision.[21] So while both public utility and public finance indicators are useful measures of the same abstract concept (government performance), the similarity in the results obtained by using the two methods cannot be attributed to a tight statistical correlation (or causal relation) between the two factors.

Given the relative independence of the two measurement strategies, it is not likely that the results obtained with the public utility measurement strategy are idiosyncratic. Analysis of public finance data reveals similar trends, which lend considerable support to the findings from the previous chapter. Locally raised revenue increases with rates of literacy and turnout and decreases with poverty; but the competitiveness of municipal elections does not have a major impact on revenue collection. We are now even more justified, then, in questioning the validity of electoral explanations for why some municipalities have greatly improved their responsiveness to the public interest while others have languished. As I have argued previously, it is much more likely that nonelectoral means of influence are the most important political determinants of local government performance.

CHAPTER SIX

Electoral and Participatory Mechanisms in Action

THE EVIDENCE PRESENTED IN THE PREVIOUS TWO CHAPTERS contradicts several common claims about Mexican politics. It is just not possible, given the results of this analysis, to sustain the argument that the rise of electoral competition in Mexican municipalities is generally responsible for significant improvements in the quality of local government. Nor can we maintain that elections are the only effective means by which Mexican citizens can influence their governments. But the analysis of those chapters has also left many questions unanswered. The statistical findings do not provide any detailed explanation of the actual processes involved, particularly with respect to participatory mechanisms. If elections do not function as mechanisms of voter control, what goes wrong? When citizens opt for participatory strategies, how do politicians and bureaucrats react? How do modes of mass participation interact and change over time? This chapter aims to generate further evidence regarding the sources of democratic responsiveness in Mexico by looking more closely at the dynamic processes that generate competition and participation over time at the municipal and state level. In the course of doing so, the chapter will demonstrate why elections typically fail to improve responsiveness and how participation helps.

The Problem with Elections

Our everyday familiarity with election campaigns, public opinion polling, and the like make the existence of electoral accountability seem obvious and natural. But as I discussed in chapter 2, any plausible theory of electoral control is actually forced to make strong assumptions about a wide array of factors, including the amount of information voters need to have, the decision rules that govern voting behavior, the types of preferences a politician can have (i.e., they usually must have a preference for long-term continuation in office), the politician's ability to discern a mandate from election returns, and much more. In the Mexican institutional context, I identified two specific mechanisms that can explain how elections contribute to better government performance. The party-sanctioning explanation requires that parties find ways to elicit good behavior from their officeholders and that the electorate have the ability and inclination to punish parties when their representatives perform poorly (Carey 1996; Michelle Taylor 1992). The candidate selection explanation requires that parties put forth competent candidates who are genuinely committed to represent the preferences of their constituents and that the electorate have the ability to distinguish between good and bad candidates. Obviously, the negative findings reported in chapters 4 and 5 should lead us to wonder if one or more of the assumptions underlying these mechanisms are not met in Mexican municipalities. Closer inspection confirms this suspicion but also reveals that the factors weighing against electoral control in Mexico are somewhat more complicated than the discussion in chapter 2 suggested.

Voters and politicians both recognize elections as important events and often conceive of elections as opportunities for electoral control. Mexican citizens attend campaign rallies, read the electoral coverage in the newspapers, and discuss politics, just like citizens in any other democracy. Elected officials in Mexico campaign, meet with constituents, kiss babies, and make promises, just like politicians in any other democracy. Yet something, or many things, happen to make elections ineffective as instruments of voter control. The following discussion of case evidence suggests at least three possibilities. First, Mexican voters do not always strategize as mechanisms of accountability would require them to. Second, politicians often respond to electoral pressures with targeted public spending, or with other short-term efforts that help shore up electoral support, without actually improving long-term government responsiveness. Third, the institutional arrangement encourages politicians to undermine each other's social programs and reform efforts, leading to a general stagnation or stasis in government performance.

The Case of Chihuahua

Political scientists may have put more effort into understanding politics in Chihuahua than in any other Mexican state.[1] And this for good reason: one of the PRI's earliest state-level defeats anywhere in Mexico came in Chihuahua in 1992, when Francisco Barrio (of the PAN) won the governor's race.[2] The state had had a strong PAN opposition since the early 1980s, and the PAN had won the mayoral races in the two largest cities (Ciudad Juárez and Chihuahua) in 1983. After Barrio's victory, many observers began to think of the state as a bastion of PAN strength and a key state for the opposition to PRI hegemony at the national level. But the truth is that the PRI has fared well in every election after 1992, as the data in table 6.1 illustrate. The PRI recovered a majority in the state legislature in 1995 and won back the governor's office in 1998. The PRI has gone on to win every statewide election since then, with the single exception of the 2000 federal elections. So Chihuahua is an interesting case not only because of Barrio's opposition victory but also because it is the only state in which the PRI seems to have recovered almost completely from its earlier losses. In other states, such as Jalisco and Baja California, the PRI has not won any statewide or federal elections subsequent to its first major defeat.

Chihuahua's 1998 gubernatorial election particularly illustrates many of the difficulties involved in empirically establishing the existence of electoral control in the Mexican context.[3] The first important event for our purposes is the process by which Patricio Martínez earned the PRI's nomination for governor. After losing the governor's race in 1992, the state-level PRI organization was at risk of collapsing into factional fighting, as happened in the states of Baja California and Guanajuato after similar losses. In Chihuahua, however, one leader was able to unify the

Table 6.1. Results of State-wide Elections in Chihuahua, 1992–2004

Year	*Type of Election*	*Party*				*Total*
		PAN	*PRI*	*PRD*	*Others*	
1992	Governor	**51.2%**	44.3%	1.4%	3.1%	100.0% (756,292)
1994	President	28.3	**60.4**	6.2	5.1	100.0 (1,089,006)
1994	Federal deputies	27.5	**58.0**	5.7	8.8	100.0 (1,114,877)
1995	State deputies	40.1	**47.5**	6.2	6.2	100.0 (822,919)
1997	Federal deputies	41.2	**42.1**	10.3	6.3	100.0 (889,826)
1998	State deputies	41.9	**47.4**	7.3	3.5	100.0 (979,954)
1998	Governor	42.2	**50.3**	5.5	2.0	100.0 (988,199)
2000	Federal deputies	**47.1**	41.2	7.4	4.3	100.0 (1,119,844)
2000	President	**48.7**	40.9	6.8	3.6	100.0 (1,128,099)
2001	State deputies	41.4	**46.0**	5.1	7.5	100.0 (867,647)
2003	Federal deputies	37.5	**47.4**	6.2	8.9	100.0 (757,095)
2004[a]	State deputies	44.0	**53.2**	-	2.8	100.0 (988,674)
2004[a]	Governor	41.4	**56.5**	-	2.1	100.0 (993,511)

Note: This is a reproduction of table 2.4 from Cleary and Stokes (2006, 42). The winning percentage in each election is denoted in bold.

a. In 2004 state elections the six registered parties formed two coalitions, PAN-PRD-PC and PRI-PT-PVEM.

Source: Banamex (2001); Instituto Estatal Electoral de Chihuahua, "Resultados Electorales," www.ieechihuahua.org.mx/Default.aspx?mod=wrapper&name=Resultados&contenttype=W, accessed April 1, 2005.

party, and he gained predominance within the state-level party organization after the PRI won the state's midterm legislative elections in 1995.[4] This leader, Artemio Iglesias, seemed sure to be the PRI's nominee for the governor's race in 1998. However, the national-level PRI had decided in 1998 to change from party conventions to open primaries as a means of selecting candidates, and Iglesias lost the party primary to Patricio Martínez, a popular former mayor of Chihuahua City (see Langston 2003).

A second point of interest is the gubernatorial election itself, in which Martínez beat the PAN's Ramón Galindo. Galindo should have benefited from the electorate's retrospective evaluation of Francisco Barrio, a fellow *panista* and the outgoing governor, given that Barrio's approval ratings in several polls were in the 60 percent range. In a pre-electoral statewide poll designed by Yemile Mizrahi (see Mizrahi 1999), 64 percent of respondents approved of Barrio, while only 21 percent disapproved. Also, 60 percent preferred continuity to change. But the PRI's Martínez won the election with 50 percent of the vote to Galindo's 42 percent. It is hard to believe that the Chihuahuan electorate was using the 1998 gubernatorial election as a retrospective judgment of the Barrio administration. If it had been, the PAN candidate would have fared far better than he did (Mizrahi 2003).

Mizrahi (1999, 2003) advances one explanation for this apparent puzzle: maybe, contrary to conventional wisdom, the Chihuahuan electorate focused on the candidates rather than the parties. And maybe they paid attention to campaigns and forecasts about the future instead of past performance. Some of Mizrahi's evidence supports this view: 67 percent of respondents thought that the candidate was more important than the party in formulating a vote preference, while 21 percent thought the party was more important.[5] Mizrahi also reports that Martínez (the PRI candidate) worked to link his own campaign issues to the successful policies of the (*panista*) Barrio administration. The survey data and the electoral result both suggest that voters were thinking prospectively, in terms of candidates, and not retrospectively, as the party-sanctioning model would require.

Langston (2003) and Aziz Nassif (2000, 147–61) offer another explanation for Martínez's victory: the PRI's decision to use an open primary to select its candidate and the PAN's failure to do so. Without the open primary, Langston speculates that party insider Artemio Iglesias would have won the nomination. Had he been denied it, he might have defected to another party and run against the PRI.[6] But, in addition to ensuring that the nomination went to the most popular candidate (Martínez), the primary presented Iglesias with incontrovertible evidence of his own electoral weakness, making a defection less likely.[7] The use of an open primary runs counter to the party-sanctioning model, which would require parties to maintain tight control over nominations in order to use the posts to reward partisans who have performed well. Instead, we witness the PRI relinquishing power over its own nominations and using a selection method that favors popular, electable candidates over party loyalists with inside experience. Thus, if electoral competition has made state government more responsive in Chihuahua, this would seem to be due to a *candidate selection* mechanism and not to party sanctioning.

This argument presents a significant challenge to the conventional wisdom in Mexico, where opposition victories are routinely depicted as "antisystem" votes or negative retrospective judgments of the PRI. Certainly, some voters behave in this way. But the balance of the evidence presented here suggests that prospective, candidate-based mechanisms are more promising explanations of responsiveness. Direct sanctioning of candidates is obviated by term limits. And party sanctioning seems incompatible with many notable features of the electoral landscape of the mid-1990s. For example, the turn to open primaries (in Chihuahua and elsewhere) would be hard to explain from a party-sanctioning point of view, given that the open primary decreases the party's control over nominations, just when the theory would predict the judicious use of nominations as political rewards. Open primaries are consistent with a candidate selection model, however, in that the primary vote focuses on candidate electability and provides parties with valuable information about the electorate's preferences and the appeal of campaign issues.

Yet even if we accept that these selection mechanisms work, in the sense that they allow voters to empower their preferred candidates, the connection between electoral competition and democratic responsiveness is drawn only halfway. To complete the connection, we need to establish that government becomes more responsive as a result of electoral competition. In other words, we need to see that government improves when politicians are forced into a "trial by election" before earning political power. Such improvements are difficult to establish in any given case. For example, how could we know that the Chihuahuan government was better managed under Martínez than it would have been under Galindo? Of course, our inability to directly observe the counterfactual case is the central reason to turn to large-*N* analysis, as I have already done in preceding chapters (King, Keohane, and Verba 1994, 79). But more evidence can be brought to bear on this "second leg" of the electoral mechanism—the direct connection between competition and government performance.

Education Spending in Mexican States

In a recent article Douglas Hecock (2006) has established an empirical connection between electoral competition and state-level education spending in Mexico.[8] Hecock's primary interest is in testing whether exposure to the global economy produces uniformity in social policy, as some scholars have predicted. But his data are also well suited to testing hypotheses about the effects of electoral competition on government performance. Hecock hypothesizes that "the level of electoral competition will have a positive effect on education spending" because politicians in noncompetitive states "face less pressure to be responsive to their constituents," while "leaders who anticipate strong electoral challenges are likely to attempt to enact policies that will make them popular at election time" (954). He therefore includes indicators of electoral competition in his multivariate analysis of state-level educational spending (per student).

And in fact, the evidence supports the electoral hypothesis: states with higher levels of electoral competition, measured by party fractionalization in the state legislature and the margin of victory in the most recent gubernatorial election, spend significantly more per student on primary education. These results (reproduced below in table 6.2, model 1) obviously diverge from the municipal-level findings I reported in the previous two chapters. However, I believe that these contradictory findings can be reconciled. It is possible that Hecock simply finds an electoral effect at the state level, with respect to education spending, whereas I have found no such effect at the municipal level, with respect to public service provision and local revenue generation. It is also possible that the electoral competition Hecock studies during a relatively short time period (1999 to 2004) is part of a larger, more complex transformation in modes of political competition. Without education spending data from the 1980s, it is difficult to know whether the spending advantage Hecock identifies in competitive states is a result of electoral competition or whether spending differences preceded the rise of competition, as I found in the case of municipal public services (see especially figure 4.2 and the related discussion).

But the real reason to probe further on this point is not to dispute the existence of the effect; rather, I want to understand how the empirical relationship should be interpreted. Recall that my goal here is to understand whether the electoral threat leads politicians to respond *in ways that enhance democratic responsiveness.* The basic finding that competitive states spend more certainly lends some support to this argument. But further evaluation of the spending data also shows some patterns that are not entirely consistent with the spirit of the electoral hypothesis.

One way to expand on Hecock's analysis is to analyze the relationship between state-level education spending and the election cycle. Substantively, the goal is to distinguish spending that is employed for short-term electoral gain from spending that actually constitutes responsiveness to public pressures for an improved educational system. To be sure, the distinction is difficult to define clearly—often one man's pork is another man's good policy. But a closer look at the election cycle can provide some insight. If education spending is increased as a matter of public policy, it should remain relatively constant across the electoral cycle. If it is an electoral-season payoff to teachers' unions, we should expect to see increased spending during election years.

The cases in Hecock's data set are state-years. For each one, I assign a value from 1 to 6 based on the state's electoral calendar. All Mexican states have a six-year cycle, with a single six-year term for the governor and two three-year sessions for the unicameral state congress. Most states hold elections late in the year, and for those states I code the year of a gubernatorial election as year 6 and the following year as year 1. For the six states that hold elections in the first half of the calendar year, I "adjust down," coding the election year as year 1.[9] The intuition is that I want years 3 and 6 to correspond to the years in which state education

Table 6.2. Generalized Estimation Equation (GEE) on State Education Spending

			Split Models		*Split Models*	
	Base Model	*Add Electoral Cycle*	*Competitive*	*Non-Competitive*	*Alternation*	*No Alternation*
	(1)	*(2)*	*(3)*	*(4)*	*(5)*	*(6)*
Legislative competition	126.73*	138.16*	-	-	-	-
(effective no. of parties)	(60.74)	(58.24)				
Gubernatorial comp.	-956.70*	-951.62*	-	-	-	-
(margin of victory)	(447.59)	(430.03)				
FDI per capita	-0.73*	-0.77*	-1.20^	-1.31^	-0.32	-2.55**
	(0.33)	(0.32)	(0.70)	(0.71)	(0.35)	(0.74)
Maquila exports per	0.13***	0.14***	0.15***	0.09***	0.09**	-0.19***
capita	(0.03)	(0.03)	(0.04)	(0.03)	(0.03)	(0.05)
PRD legislature	-24.60	-136.51	494.91	-304.28	-625.95^	499.30
	(252.59)	(244.15)	(486.14)	(553.10)	(331.29)	(348.48)
PRD governor	237.92^	244.77*	337.81^	256.17	341.44*	-[a]
	(129.97)	(124.76)	(198.94)	(392.24)	(138.58)	
Union militancy	318.20**	297.67*	214.43	750.33***	286.40*	495.13*
(CNTE strength)	(123.55)	(122.71)	(162.52)	(207.14)	(112.81)	(221.34)
Lagged logged GDP	773.18*	664.70*	601.71	1385.24**	770.61*	1030.94^
(per capita)	(330.77)	(326.55)	(489.34)	(453.86)	(343.51)	(554.86)
Federal spending per	-0.02	-0.02	-0.03	-0.12*	-0.01	-0.08^
student	(0.03)	(0.03)	(0.06)	(0.06)	(0.04)	(0.04)
State system	753.05***	743.10***	694.71***	552.23***	829.55***	750.62***
	(146.74)	(146.43)	(195.50)	(124.67)	(155.95)	(213.50)
Election year	-	103.80**	58.70	218.17**	57.82	128.48**
(dummy)		(32.36)	(63.24)	(75.16)	(47.94)	(42.52)
Constant	-9147.55*	-7998.06*	-6809.60	-15277.97**	-8992.77*	-11771.41^
	(3685.57)	(3636.57)	(5595.79)	(4959.16)	(3837.34)	(6244.21)
Valid *N*	153	153	98	55	75	78
Pseudo *R*-squared	0.61	0.61	0.60	0.48	0.58	0.59

Note: Statistical significance is noted with the conventional $^{***}p < .001$, $^{**}p < .01$, $^{*}p < .05$, ^ < .10.

a. Dropped because of collinearity (nonalternation implies no PRD governor, by definition).

Source: Hecock (2006). Model 1 is an exact replication of Hecock's estimation (2006, 958).

spending might be responding to upcoming midterm and gubernatorial elections. For example, Chihuahua held gubernatorial elections in November 1998. This was the sixth year of Barrio's term, the year for which we might see a spike in education spending if Barrio were using such spending as a quid pro quo for electoral support. The state of Hidalgo held its gubernatorial election in February of 1999; there we would expect to see any evidence of targeted spending in the 1998 budget, and thus 1998 is coded as year 6.

For the purpose of constructing figure 6.1, I also code a dichotomous variable to represent electoral competitiveness. I code cases as competitive if the margin of victory in the most recent gubernatorial election is less than 13.5 percent, which is the mean for the sample. I separate the cases according to this variable and then plot the average level of spending for each year of the electoral cycle (the numbers are inflation-adjusted pesos per student). The figure demonstrates one fact already established by Hecock (2006): spending is generally higher in the competitive cases. But it also illustrates the relationship between spending and the electoral cycle. Among competitive cases, spending is roughly the same whether or not elections are to be held in any given year. Among noncompetitive cases, however, there is a striking electoral-cycle pattern. Spending is far higher in the third and sixth years of the electoral cycle; in these two years alone, noncompetitive states actually outspend their competitive counterparts. The size of the increase is substantial. Compared to years 2 and 5 of the electoral cycle, spending jumps 37 percent and 54 percent in years 3 and 6, respectively.

Multivariate analysis confirms the significance of the empirical relationship. I coded a dichotomous variable to indicate years 3 *or* 6 of the electoral cycle; in other words, this variable equals 1 if there is a statewide election in a given case-year. In table 6.2, model 2, I add this variable to Hecock's base model. The coefficient is positive, indicating that spending is indeed higher in the run-up to state elections. The size of the coefficient is not overwhelming, but it is substantively significant (the mean level of spending for all cases in the data set is about 1,450 pesos per student). So a first cut at the evidence gives us some reason to suspect that education spending is a device that state governments use to buy short-term electoral support rather than a longer-lasting effort to improve public policy.

Figure 6.1. State-level Education Spending over the Electoral Cycle

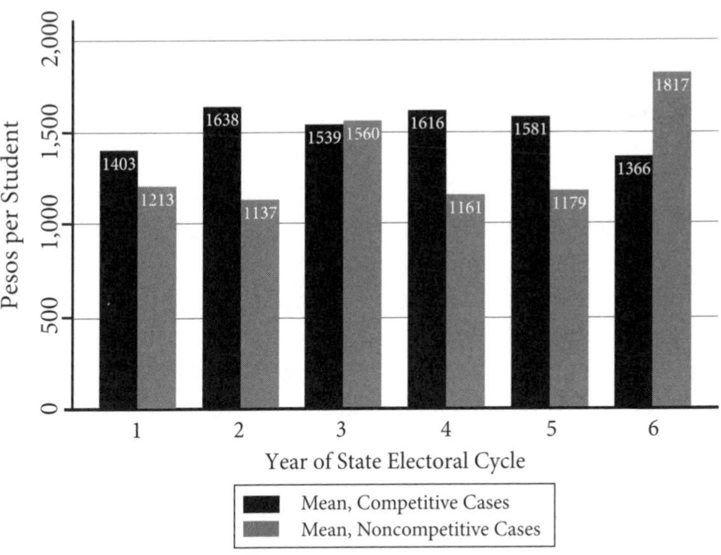

Yet the picture becomes more complicated when we consider a second extension to Hecock's analysis, which is to split the sample between competitive and noncompetitive cases, as I have done in models 3 through 6. The theoretical motivation for splitting the sample is similar to that of the previous two chapters. I want to entertain the possibility that competition has not only a direct effect on performance (represented here by education spending) but also an indirect effect by conditioning the relationship between education spending and other independent variables of interest. In models 3 and 4, the criterion for splitting the sample is the same one that I used above: dichotomizing the governor's margin of victory at the sample mean. Models 5 and 6 generate similar results with a different method of splitting the cases, based on whether the state had ever experienced party alternation in the governor's office prior to the case year.

These models generate two results that are worthy of closer inspection. The first refines the discussion of the electoral cycle effect. Comparing the coefficients for this variable in models 3 and 4 (and again in models 5 and 6), we can see that the previous finding was driven primarily by a strong electoral-cycle effect *among noncompetitive cases.* The effect among competitive states is statistically indistinguishable from zero, but the coefficient for noncompetitive states is large, positive, and statistically significant. In other words, states do appear to ramp up educational spending in the run-up to elections, but only where elections are noncompetitive. Combined with the observation that competitive states spend more on education overall, this seems to suggest that the logic of education spending differs across the two sets of cases. In competitive states, government spends more on education on a regular basis and as a matter of policy. In noncompetitive states, government wields educational spending as an electoral weapon, spending less in off-years but buying short-term support when elections are at hand.

This pattern could reasonably be interpreted as evidence of electoral accountability, since we could surmise that the risk of losing elections forces state governments (or more accurately, the governors who have an interest in the continued electoral success of their parties) to provide more, and more constant, financial support for the educational system. But the second noteworthy finding in models 3 through 6 illustrates a difficulty with this interpretation. The CNTE, or National Coordinating Committee of Workers in Education (Coordinadora Nacional de Trabajadores de la Educación), is an umbrella group composed mainly of left-leaning dissident teachers and education workers who oppose the historically tight corporatist relationship between the PRI and the "official" teachers' union, the National Union of Workers in Education (Sindicato Nacional de Trabajadores de la Educación, SNTE). Thus the strength of the CNTE in a given state is a good indicator of union militancy, as Hecock (2006) discusses. On the basis of the findings in table 6.2, model 1, Hecock argues that "the presence . . . of the relatively militant CNTE serves to place greater pressure on the government to increase education spending" and that "the presence of the CNTE along with competitive democracy has led to more dynamic union-government relations" (959).

In my view, Hecock's empirical finding (in model 1) does not clearly weigh in favor of either the electoral or the participatory hypothesis, since we know that unions commonly deploy both strategies. Unions (and especially dissenting factions like the CNTE) are just as likely to "place greater pressure on the government" via confrontational protests and strikes as by throwing around their electoral weight. But we can gain further insight into the question by looking at the differential effect of militancy in the split-sample models. If Hecock's empirical regularity were the result of an electoral accountability mechanism, we would expect the effect of union militancy to be stronger among competitive cases—after all, this is where electoral support from well-organized, mobilized groups like teachers' unions is most likely to be decisive. Surprisingly, however, we find the opposite. Comparing models 3 and 4, we see that union militancy has an incredibly large effect among the noncompetitive cases and no significant effect among competitive cases.[10] It seems unlikely that the impact of union militancy in noncompetitive cases could be attributed to a plausible electoral threat on the part of the CNTE. In fact, if these state governments respond to CNTE militancy, they are probably more worried about mass demonstrations and protests. Thus, while Hecock's data certainly offer some evidence in support of the electoral accountability hypothesis, other patterns in the data are difficult to reconcile with such an account.

Two plausible interpretations of the findings suggest themselves. The first is that union militancy in this instance is best conceived as a participatory strategy of influence rather than an electoral one. After all, Hecock's original model attributes a significant causal effect to union militancy *while controlling for the level of competition.* Further, as we have seen, this effect is strongest among noncompetitive cases, or, in other words, where electoral strategies for political influence are circumscribed. Thus, even where political options are limited, a pressing issue (like low levels of educational spending) can be successfully addressed by political actors outside the electoral arena. By itself, however, this interpretation of the data cannot easily explain the election-cycle effect. A second possibility is that the findings reflect an electoral quid pro quo between noncompetitive governments and militant labor unions. In the noncompetitive cases, governments buy union support with preelectoral budget increases wherever union militancy is strong; this would account for both of the findings of interest in models 3 and 4. In competitive cases, either the quid pro quo has broken down or it was never established, so that education spending is not strongly affected either by the election cycle or by union militancy. It remains possible in this interpretation that militant unions are able to extract some benefits from government when elections are competitive (given the positive coefficients in models 3 and 5). The benefit is not nearly as great as what their counterparts in noncompetitive cases can generate, but given that competitive states spend more as a matter of course, the net effect is substantial.

In the end, the education spending data do not speak unambiguously in favor of any single interpretation. But I can offer some conclusions with a relatively high degree of confidence. There is clearly stronger evidence of an electoral effect with respect to state-level education spending than there was with any of the municipal-level factors analyzed in chapters 4 and 5. Hecock has provided a useful starting point by establishing that competitive states spend more on education. Figure 6.1 shows that in addition competitive states assign precious resources to education without regard to the electoral calendar. Yet questions about the nature of this relationship remain. As I mentioned above, we do not know whether the spending advantage enjoyed by competitive states today predates the rise of competition in the 1980s. Further, some patterns in the data suggest that increased education spending does not necessarily result from accountability mechanisms and a desire among governors to formulate responsive policy. Rather, education spending is often used as means of shoring up political support in the run-up to an election, specifically to *avoid* accountability for poor performance in previous years.

Responsiveness and the Appearance of Responsiveness

In fact, this sort of ambiguity, according to which increased education spending might be interpreted as evidence of either electoral accountability or politicians' efforts to avoid such accountability, is a common problem in the study of elections. Consider Mayhew's (1974) classic description of U.S. congressional representatives. Arguing that congressional behavior can be best explained by assuming that individual representatives value reelection above all else, Mayhew argued that they would focus their efforts on three general types of activities: advertising, credit claiming, and position taking. For Mayhew to view these activities as evidence of electoral accountability (as he did), he would have to assume at least partial correspondence between the representatives' publicity-oriented actions and their actual legislative behavior. In other words, the "name brand" that they constructed for themselves would have to resemble their actual political positions; the constituency service for which they claimed credit would actually have to be carried out; the positions they took on policy issues would have to (at least roughly) match the votes that they cast on the House floor. Absent this type of correspondence, Mayhew's account would amount to a theory of appearances rather than an explanation of responsiveness.

As a description of congressional behavior, Mayhew's account is unquestionably accurate. We observe that congressmen do these three things on a daily basis. But the link to accountability is harder to establish, since representatives have incentives to obfuscate about their activities. They can claim credit for successes in which they played no role, avoid blame where they did play a role, advertise different images to different segments of their constituencies, and so on. If we give Mayhew's argument a cynical twist, we could fairly say that what matters to political representatives is to always *appear* responsive rather than to *be* responsive. The truth is that in most democratic political systems appearances and realities are both important to varying degrees. But much of what we know about electoral politics in Mexico suggests that politicians spend considerable effort on appearances, even to the point that true responsiveness (in the form of good policy and government output) suffers.

Consider Peter Smith's *Labyrinths of Power* (1979), a classic study of the Mexican system under the hegemonic PRI. Taking elite theory as his starting point, Smith seeks to understand the composition of the Mexican ruling class and the advancement of individuals within it.[11] Most interestingly for the current investigation, Smith offers a list of "rules of the game" that summarize the criteria according to which politicians advanced within the government (242–77). Among the important criteria were being a member of the PRI, having many well-placed friends and superiors, marrying well, showing loyalty and subservience to superiors, and avoiding the public eye. Nowhere does Smith list criteria such as efficiency, good public service, or competence. In fact, Smith writes, "It is not really necessary to acquire thorough mastery of all the details and requirements of your present office. Positions are won primarily through contacts, not merit" (267). He also suggests that politicians benefited by being purposefully inefficient, since it made even normal tasks seem like a special effort, for which the politician could request reciprocation in the future (268). Although Smith was specifically studying the top echelons of the federal government, state and local governments are often characterized in the same terms (see Fagen and Touhy 1972; Needler 1970/1982).

Much has changed since the heyday of PRI hegemony, when the only competition for positions came from within the party. The common assumption in the literature is that interparty competition has introduced a new dimension to the criteria for advancement. Since parties facing competition must worry about future elections, they are likely to become more concerned with public opinion and government responsiveness. They should therefore be more likely to advance the careers (via nominations, campaign support, and other means) of those who perform well in office. Popularity and reputation should therefore become increasingly important, while factors like family connections and subservience to the party should become less relevant.

As my recounting of recent elections in Chihuahua illustrates, there is strong evidence to indicate that this sort of shift has taken place. But popularity and reputation are not the same as performance and responsiveness. The fact is that, while politicians are clearly concerned to appear responsive, they often pursue these appearances in ways that undermine actual responsiveness. Worse, their motivation for doing so often comes from the very institutional environment that is supposed to promote electoral accountability. Rather than working toward the public interest, politicians who need to establish a good reputation among voters and party superiors often pursue projects that have a high profile but low impact. They also face incentives to personalize their policy activity, putting their own mark on new policies and canceling those of their predecessors, even when the existing programs are effective. For example, on the basis of a detailed study of thirty midsized municipalities in Mexico, Grindle (2006) concludes that "possibilities for capacity development were built upon an institutional base that rewarded change initiatives but worked against their institutionalization" and that when reform initiatives were introduced, "it was difficult to hold officials accountable for their correct functioning, a culture of service was limited by personnel changes every 3 years, and citizens did not have sufficient information to be able to insist on their rights to appropriate service." In the end, "Administrations with new priorities and new appointments in town hall would come and go, and what they left behind could not always be ensured, even if it provided a reasonable solution to the problem" (67).

Tim Campbell and Travis Katz (2004) offer a clear example of this problem from the city of Tijuana. Tijuana is a large municipality in Baja California, on the border with California and near San Diego. The city, like the state, has been a stronghold for the PAN for the past twenty years or so. Tijuana is also relatively modernized, being more urban, more industrial, and better educated than most Mexican cities.

In the mid-1990s, a series of *panista* mayors pursued innovative financial reforms and public works projects. One important reform was a project called ¡Manos a la Obra! (loosely translated, "Let's get working!"), initiated by mayor Héctor Osuna Jaime in late 1994. The Manos project funneled municipal monies to local community groups who proposed and oversaw local infrastructure improvements. Campbell and Katz note that the structure of the program was similar to PRONASOL, a widely known national-level development program. By all accounts the program was quite successful, both in terms of funding infrastructural improvements and in terms of generating public participation in the decision-making process. It was also popular and brought valuable name recognition to both the program and the mayor who spearheaded the effort. But the program proved to be short-lived because of political considerations. Campbell and Katz explain: "Héctor Osuna Jaime's term ended in December 1995, and it appeared unlikely that the Manos program would continue without the support of his successor, Guadalupe Osuna Millán. . . . For Guadalupe Osuna, the risk of continuing Manos was that it could undermine his ability to establish a political identity distinct from his predecessor. Indeed, were Manos to continue, the success would likely be attributed to Héctor, not Guadalupe, Osuna. The risk of not being recognized for continuing an innovation . . . made it unlikely that the program would continue" (95). Thus the Mayhewian logic of creating a name for oneself and gaining credit for innovation and good performance, in this case, worked against the continuing responsiveness of Tijuana's municipal government. Even more interesting is the fact that Guadalupe Osuna and Héctor Osuna are fellow *panistas.* Congruent ideologies and a common interest in furthering the fortunes of their party were apparently insufficient to maintain a functional public works program beyond the term of its original proponent. Thus, even when politicians are motivated to be responsive, the prohibition against reelection and the three-year term make sustained responsiveness quite difficult.

The Rise of Political Participation in Modern Mexico

The discussion throughout this book has pointed toward the possibility of a participatory explanation for democratic responsiveness in Mexico. But the mechanisms that might tie political participation to democratic responsiveness require further exploration. Here I offer a more detailed look at the rise of political participation in Mexican municipalities, with the aim of establishing that a participatory transformation occurred across much of Mexico, beginning in the late 1970s. This transformation was caused both by "bottom-up" mobilization at the grassroots level and by "top-down" mobilization in which political leaders, even within the PRI, attempted to stimulate local participation in politics. I will also show how this participatory transformation interacted with electoral competition and government responsiveness. While all of these factors relate to each other in complex and recursive ways over time, my central argument is that the participatory shift of the 1970s and 1980s is responsible for both the subsequent increase in electoral competition and limited improvements in government performance.

Participation in Mexican Municipalities

The Mexican regime has long confounded students of democratic politics. Today there is wide agreement that the Mexican regime was not democratic in a meaningful sense prior to the elections in 2000.[12] But the consensus about the old regime's authoritarian nature is a relatively recent development. Several classic studies, including *The Civic Culture,* treat Mexico as a democracy (Almond and Verba 1963; Gruber 1971;

Lipset 1959). In the 1970s the literature began to shift toward a recognition of the regime's authoritarian nature (Fagen and Touhy 1972; Needler 1970/1982). But as recently as 1990 it remained controversial to characterize the Mexican regime as authoritarian, as Mario Vargas Llosa showed by publicly describing the Mexican regime as the "perfect dictatorship." In retrospect we can see that the authoritarian characterization is clearly more accurate. But the reason underlying the earlier literature's ambivalence is instructive. One of the main characteristics that made the Mexican regime so hard to classify was its relatively high level of tolerance of public participation, civic organizations, and freedom of expression. In fact, it is on this very basis that Mueller (1999) cites the pre-2000 Mexican regime as evidence that democracy does not require meaningful elections. I disagree with Mueller's assertion, both in general and with respect to Mexico. But his point of view provokes interest in the recent history of participation and civic engagement in Mexican politics.

According to Mueller, Mexico is one example of a class of regimes that "might be called democracies without elections" (1999, 142). He acknowledges that elections were not competitive and were rigged by the ruling party when necessary: "Yet [in Mexico] people have been free to petition and protest and organize, and the governments can be said in a quite meaningful sense to have been responsive to the will and needs of the population. Elections [if they had been meaningful] might shade or reshape policy in one way or another, and some democrats would undoubtedly deem the result to be more just, but the essential responsiveness is already there" (142–43). Mueller is probably correct to argue that the Mexican regime under the PRI was more responsive to the public interest than most other authoritarian regimes. In fact, the regime's rare ability to incorporate the interests of disparate sectors of society and (usually) to placate demands without resorting to mass violence is what separates Mexican authoritarianism from the more repressive, less responsive, and less accommodating military dictatorships of Central and South America.[13] But the regime's responsiveness was far from routine, and Mueller's account inexplicably ignores the lack of government services, the limits on freedoms of expression and the press, the aloof culture of government functionaries, and the occasional (some would say frequent) use of small-scale violence to quell protests, decapitate independent labor movements, and intimidate dissenters. Furthermore, as studies from the time make clear, the participation that did exist under the hegemonic PRI was strikingly different from the picture of a civic, participatory, egalitarian culture that is the hallmark of democracy, as described by Almond and Verba (1963), Putnam (1993, 2000), Stokes (1995), and others.

Participation under the Hegemonic PRI

To get an idea of what participation looked like during the period of PRI hegemony, let us consider Fagen and Touhy's (1972) classic study of local politics in Jalapa, Mexico. Jalapa is the capital of the state of Veracruz, which lies along Mexico's eastern coast on the Gulf of Mexico. At the time of their study, Jalapa had a population of about ninety-five thousand and was a fairly typical central Mexican city. As Fagen and Touhy describe it, Jalapa was a polity in which the citizenry had no opportunity, electoral or otherwise, to decide who would govern them and very little influence over how they would be governed. The primary strategy that Jalapeños would use when interacting with government is reminiscent of the approach used by Almond and Verba's *subjects* or Stokes's *clients* (Almond and Verba 1963; Stokes 1995). Fagen and Touhy's activists are the stereotypical petitioners with bowed head and hat in hand: "The style of communication must be cautious. Interested parties are aware of the considerable sensitivity about status among public officials, and usually phrase their requests accordingly. The communication of deference is an important element of such transactions, especially as the socioeconomic or political distance between the petitioner and his official contact grows" (1972, 52). Occasionally, this approach would have some success. But often the petitioner was sent away with a promise at most, and the ultimate outcome of the request depended more on personalities, connections, and luck than on the merits of the request, the official's sense of duty, or the fear of losing office.

Even when citizen groups were formed to address public concerns in this type of regime, the results were inegalitarian, vague, and dependent on personal ties. As an example, Fagen and Touhy (1972) cite the use of *juntas de mejoramiento* (development councils) in Jalapa and other cities during the presidency of Adolfo Ruiz Cortines (1952–58).[14] These councils were created in response to the federal government's recognition that "state and local authorities working alone could never provide the economic opportunities and services that would be needed in the urban areas" and that development required "regularizing and increasing the participation of private citizens in community development" (75). In Jalapa, the *junta de mejoramiento* was an effective tool of local development during the 1950s, when it funded the construction of roads, drainage systems, and other public works.[15] But the junta itself was more a council of local dignitaries than a forum for public participation, and its success was based on personal ties to officials in the federal government, including President Ruiz Cortines himself. When Ruiz left office in 1958, the source of federal funds dried up, the council's most prominent members resigned, and the council became ineffective (75–77).

Furthermore, the evidence from the time indicates that Mexican citizens were aware of their low level of efficacy. A national cross-section of survey respondents in Almond and Verba's (1963) classic study shows that Mexican citizens were less likely than American, British, German, or Italian citizens to attempt to influence local government (188) and less likely to agree that any attempt at such influence would be successful (185).[16] In Fagen and Touhy's (1972) survey of Jalapeños, citizens revealed a sense of resigned impotence with regard to political affairs. Although their attitudes on life satisfaction and the fairness of government treatment were surprisingly high, they also reported little efficacy. For example, 82 percent of the respondents agreed that "almost all the decisions in Jalapa are made by a very small group of local people" (110), and 89 percent agreed with the statement that those with "a lot of influence in running the government . . . use [it] to their own advantage while forgetting the well-being of the people" (112). Additionally, only about 10 percent believed that their (hypothetical) efforts to resolve a community problem would be successful. Although one should be cautious about direct comparisons, the percentage that anticipated success in a similar question in Almond and Verba's study ranged from 51 percent (in Italy) to 78 percent (in Great Britain).[17] Finally, in a pattern that is not replicated (to my knowledge) in any established democracy, those who did in fact have contact with a government official in Jalapa had a *lower* sense of their own efficacy than the average respondent (114).

In other words, the average Mexican did not find much promise in attempting to influence governing officials—and those who actually had tried to do so were even more pessimistic.

The Participatory Transformation of the 1980s and 1990s

Has anything changed? Is participation in Mexican politics, and especially in local politics, still characterized by a quiescent citizenry, largely unable or unwilling to communicate its demands, and by an aloof, ineffective government, unlikely to respond to such demands even when they are voiced? Or have Mexican citizens begun to participate more, and has this heightened level of engagement affected the actions and policies of governing officials? I argue here that public participation in political and civic affairs has blossomed in much of Mexico over the past twenty to twenty-five years and that this new participant culture has begun to transform the way that local government interacts with, and responds to, Mexican citizens.

Evidence of a Participatory Transformation

In many ways, and in many parts of the country, participation and civic engagement remain relatively weak in Mexico, and I do not mean to overstate the extent of recent changes. But in comparison to the era of PRI hegemony, evidence of expanded participation can be seen in almost every facet of political life. Some of this evidence is clearly related to changes in the electoral arena. For example, voters have become much more active and independent. Turnout in federal elections varies, depending on the offices being contested and the national political climate. But there is a relatively clear trend toward increased turnout from the 1970s to the 1990s and beyond (Durand Ponte 2004, 196–97). Turnout in municipal elections has increased significantly in this same time period. Figure 6.2 shows the average turnout rate in municipal elections between 1980 and 1999. While the trend may not appear to be particularly steep, the change over time is significant, increasing from just over 40 percent in 1980 to about 60 percent in 1999, with a noticeable dip after 1988, the year of Carlos Salinas's suspicious presidential victory over Cuauhtémoc Cárdenas.[18] Given that vote fraud was more common in the 1980s, and that fraud usually took the form of adding votes for the

PRI (as opposed to negating opposition votes), the actual trend may be even stronger than the figure suggests.

Mexican civil society is also much more active than it was twenty to thirty years ago. Some of this activity is related to changes in the electoral arena. For example, one of the most prominent civic organizations in the country, the Civic Alliance (Alianza Cívica), originally formed in the early 1990s to monitor elections. But Mexico's civic transformation really began as early as the 1970s, preceding the rise of electoral competition by more than a decade. That decade saw the emergence of independent labor unions, peasant organizations, and business associations. Many of these groups were formed in reaction to the "regime's inability to tolerate autonomous actors and political plurality" (Olvera 2004, 412; see also Foweraker 1993; Fox and Moguel 1995, 190). After the economic crisis in 1982, civic associations proliferated among the middle and business classes (Olvera 2004, 413–14). These groups were not always long-lived or successful, but they marked a change in the way that

Figure 6.2. Turnout in Municipal Elections, 1980–99

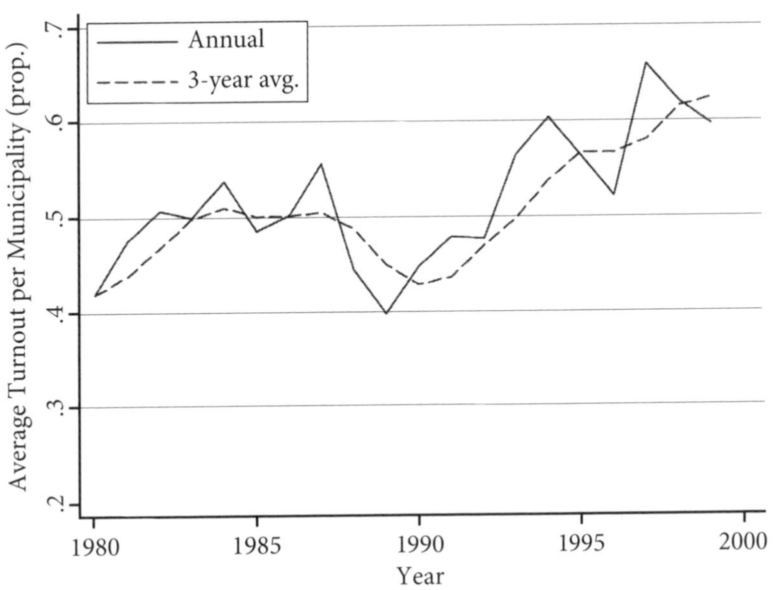

citizens organized themselves politically and interacted with the state. The civil sector has remained relatively active and independent from the state since that time.

In addition to an increase in social movements and civic organizations, a relatively new form of political participation arose in this period, especially at the local level in the 1990s. This type of participation involves direct contact with governing officials and direct participation in decision making and is often institutionalized in what I call *citizen governance groups.*[19] Citizen governance groups resemble civic organizations in some ways, but they are created by the government with the specific aim of channeling public demands and complaints to governing officials. In Mexico, these groups have many different formal functions and go by several different names, including *juntas auxiliares* (auxiliary councils), *asambleas ciudadanas* or *populares* (citizen or popular assemblies), and *comités de obra* (public works committees). In general, these working groups are formed under local laws or as a matter of policy in certain municipalities; they are not mandated by federal or state constitutions, nor do they typically enjoy any formal powers.[20] Rather, municipal officials convene citizen governance groups to collect information, consult with citizens, and disseminate information about local government projects.

Because citizen governance groups go by several different names and have a wide range of organizational structures, it is hard to generalize about their functions and goals. But a typical public works committee might function as follows. The municipal government establishes a committee within a neighborhood or *colonia* in order to set priorities for public works. Selection procedures vary, but the committee might consist of community leaders, such as teachers or doctors who live in the neighborhood. If elections are used to select the committee members, they are nonpartisan. The committee then meets with municipal officials, including the municipal president, to discuss what the neighborhood believes to be the top priority for public works projects. At the same time, the mayor provides information about the municipal budget and any extramunicipal funding that has been secured, and the committee arrives at an agreement about which public works projects should be undertaken, how much they will cost, and when they should be completed. A similar form of citizen governance group is the citizen or popular assembly. These assemblies also meet regularly, usually on a rotating basis among the municipality's main *colonias,* and the topics of discussion often involve public works, the construction and maintenance of school buildings, and other local concerns. In contrast to public works committees or auxiliary councils, these groups hold meetings that are open to the public.

These organizations vary widely in their legal standing, composition, longevity, and purpose.[21] But some things can be said with a high degree of certainty. They are more common than they used to be. They are more broadly participatory than similar organizations that existed under the hegemonic PRI (such as the *juntas de mejoramiento* described by Fagen and Touhy [1972]). And even though they are primarily institutions for public participation, they have been created from the top down, by government officials.

Finally, we should not overlook changes at the most basic level of participation—the individual level. Aside from the increased activity of independent civic organizations, social movements, and labor unions, there have been changes in the way individual citizens approach political participation. Individual Mexicans are more likely to contact governing officials, to write a letter, to make a demand, or to complain than they were in the past. I am not aware of solid longitudinal data that would help to firmly establish this point, but most country experts clearly believe this to be the case. For example, Olvera writes that while "there are no past surveys with which to compare the *Reforma* data [from a 1996 survey] . . . expanding civic participation is clearly a recent phenomenon in Mexico, occurring simultaneously with the regime's legitimacy crisis and the slow but steady process of political liberalization" (2004, 427). Enrique Cabrero Mendoza (2006) concurs, on the basis of data from a 2001 survey of innovative municipal government practices.

And here again, as with citizen governance groups, we see that government is often complicit in the creation of this type of individual-level participation (see especially Cabrero Mendoza 2006). Many mayors have instituted open office hours, often called "Citizen Wednesdays" or something similar, in which they and their *regidores* (councilors) make themselves available for a certain block of time to any citizen who wishes to visit them with a complaint, request, or suggestion (Pineda Pablos and Rodríguez Camou 2007; Vanderbush 1999). There is no preset agenda, and citizens are free to raise any issue they care to. It is difficult to know whether this style of communication is pure theater or a sincere attempt to hear from constituents. It is also likely that citizens sometimes engage public officials to ask for personal favors rather than better government services. But in any case, the institutionalization of these open meetings demonstrates that mayors are more concerned to know the public mood than they were in the past. And it is beyond dispute that local officials spend more time with their constituents than their predecessors did, either at Citizen Wednesdays meetings, public assemblies, or other less structured interactions.

Thus the participatory transformation of the 1980s and 1990s has several peculiar, even contradictory tendencies. First, some proportion of increased participation is related to electoral contestation, yet the participatory transformation also *preceded* the rise of electoral competition and is at least partially independent from the electoral arena. Second, independent civic organizations are more common and more active, but there is also a fundamental change at the individual level, which is not tied to organized civil society in a direct sense. Third, much of the transformation reveals the type of bottom-up, grassroots mobilization that commonly characterizes political participation, yet there is also a surprising level of government involvement in the creation and facilitation of local participation.

The Nature of the Participatory Transformation

While the particular manifestations of the participatory transformation are quite varied, a few common characteristics stand out. First, this transformation entails not only a quantitative increase in the amount of participation but also a fundamental qualitative shift in the nature of participation and civic engagement in Mexico. Political demand making under the hegemonic PRI was deferential and cautious (Fagen and Touhy 1972; Cornelius 1974). But over time, Mexican petitioners became "less fearful and more demanding," to the point at which "the fear of participating diminished, and an 'awakening' of the population was encouraged in order to demand collective rights and in defense of what was theirs" (Bazdresch Parada 1994, 46).[22] As Joe Foweraker writes (1993, 3), "It is not simply the accumulation of movements, nor even a changing balance of social force, that is changing the character of popular mobilization; rather, it is the political and cultural shift from making petitions and asking for benefits to making demands and insisting on rights." Juan Manuel Ramírez Sáiz concurs (2000, 16), noting that "there is an awakening and a formation of civic consciousness, in other words, of an awareness that [society] has 'the right to have rights.' For this reason, [society] is more demanding, and less tolerant towards the style of government action."

This qualitative shift is evident in every form of political participation. The act of voting has become more independent of the old hegemonic party structures, with clientelist networks and *acarreos* accounting for a diminishing proportion of the overall turnout in most elections. Labor unions, peasant organizations, and other popular groups are less likely to exist within, and to be obedient to, a corporatist hierarchy. Civic organizations are increasingly independent and assertive. When citizens meet with governing officials, either individually or as part of a citizen governance group, they are more likely to see themselves on an equal footing with the official and to treat the official as a public servant rather than a benefactor. Bazdresch Parada (1994, 48) even suggests that this transformation has changed the "democratic cultural habits" of local politicians, who have become more likely "to listen to the people, to help them shed their fear of speaking [out], [and] to accept criticisms no matter where they come from if they help to point out errors, missteps *[desviaciones],* or deficiencies."

Another common theme in the 1980s and 1990s is the increased breadth of participation. More citizens, from a wider range of socioeconomic sectors, participate now than in the past. The evidence on this is fairly clear with respect to voting, since we know that turnout rates have gone up significantly. But it is also true with respect to other forms of participation, especially new forms of local participation like citizen governance groups. Recall that the institutions themselves are not exactly new: Fagen and Touhy (1972) describe a *junta de mejoramiento* from the 1950s. But that *junta* was composed of local elites with personal connections to the president. Such citizens have always found it relatively easy to lobby or pressure local officials. The difference with new citizen governance groups is that they are more broadly representative of local populations as a whole. At the extreme are direct meetings like Citizen Wednesdays, in which all citizens have equal access to governing officials, constrained only by their ability to make time for the meetings and to clearly articulate their concerns.[23] In general terms, most scholars agree that civic participation has become more broad based in Mexico, both because of the growth of internally diverse organizations (like the Civic Alliance) and because of an expansion of civic organizations into traditionally quiescent sectors of the population (Olvera 2004). It is important to also consider the context in which this broader participation takes place. Lower classes and urban working classes in particular were often politically mobilized under the hegemonic PRI. But their participation was funneled through the system's hierarchical corporatist structure, limiting the degree to which they could autonomously assert claims or demands. The mobilization came at the cost of autonomy. It is misleading to equate this type of political mobilization, which was more common in the past, to the voluntary, civic style of participation that has become more common over time.

A third interesting characteristic of the participatory transformation is that to a surprising degree it has been nurtured by the state. This is most obvious in the cases of citizen governance groups and of open office hour policies, which are explicitly conceived and organized by local governing officials as attempts to increase participation. But state involvement in generating public participation in politics is also evident in other arenas and in earlier time periods. Alberto Olvera argues that the Mexican state began to encourage autonomous civic associations as early as the 1970s, in line with the Echeverría administration's conscious attempt "to weaken the regime's old corporatist pillars so that they would accept a relative political liberalization" (2004, 412). The PRONASOL program of Carlos Salinas also took direct aim at Mexico's clientelist hierarchy. While Salinas may simply have intended to personalize clientelism rather than eradicate it, the program's requirement that funds be distributed directly to local civic organizations was clearly intended to encourage the creation of such local groups and to keep them independent from local systems of patronage. All of these cases involved self-interested politicians whose motives may have been unrelated to the creation of an independent civil sector in Mexico, yet the examples still illustrate that state involvement was an important ingredient in the participatory transformation.

The Consequences of the Participatory Transformation

Changes in the nature of political participation in Mexico, particularly at the local level, have affected governance in several tangible ways. One obvious difference is that local governments have much better information about the types and severity of the problems that their citizens care about. Another consequence is that governments tend to be responsive to a wider range of social interests; relatedly, there seems to be more interest in political issues and a stronger (if still weak) sense of efficacy among citizens where participation is higher. Third, particularly with respect to government-led efforts, participation has become relatively routinized. Finally, the participatory transformation itself has had an effect on electoral competition. I offer evidence below to suggest that the rise of electoral competition at the local level was usually preceded by an increase in other forms of mass participation.

One well-known limitation of electoral mechanisms of accountability is that they do not provide representatives with much information about the nature of their constituents' preferences and grievances. Nonelectoral forms of participation have a clear advantage in this respect. Thus we should not be surprised to find that politicians use participation as an opportunity for information gathering and that they help to create such forms of participation where they do not already exist. For example, several municipal presidents whom I interviewed in the state of Puebla complained about the *lack* of input from the citizenry (as did several other mayors interviewed for Grindle's study of municipal performance in Mexico; see Grindle 2007, 127). For the most part, these mayors seemed to be dedicated people, who were sincerely concerned to "do a good job" *(hacer buen trabajo)* and "attend to the people's demands" *(atender la demanda social).*[24] Of course, some of them (but not all) had political careers in mind, so it is was not possible to know whether their concern with their own performance was based on career goals (and progressive ambition), a normative work ethic, a fear of confrontational protest, or some other motivation. But it was clear that the mayors all understood "doing a good job" to mean knowing something about the public mood and citizens' concerns. None of the mayors I spoke with thought that electoral campaigns were particularly useful in this type of information exchange. But they all knew the importance of having good information, and they generally seemed to believe that if the citizens did not spontaneously provide them with that information it was in their interest to go out and seek it. When I asked them how they knew what the local problems and grievances were, most of them mentioned citizen governance groups, office hour policies, and other government-initiated forms of participation as important sources of information. Local politicians use citizen governance groups to solicit, channel, and even manufacture voice.[25]

The fact that meaningful participation emanates from a broader social base than it used to also has the effect of making local governments more responsive to a wider array of citizen interests. In principle, there is nothing about participatory forms of persuasion that makes them democratic in the sense of being egalitarian. Typically, we would assume that the benefits of participation (if any) would accrue primarily to those who participate. This is true both because politicians are often able to assuage petitioners with private or semipublic goods (the mayor might promise to pave a specific street in the petitioner's neighborhood rather than promising to pave every street in town) and also because petitioners often have only particularistic concerns to begin with (truth be told, the person complaining cares only about the street in his or her own neighborhood, not about streets in general). In Mexico, nevertheless, participation has the effect of "democratizing" government responsiveness precisely because a broader segment of the citizenry has opted to use the participatory strategies of citizen influence I have been describing here. In some cases, participation also increases the perceived efficacy of those who participate. For example, when municipal officials prioritize projects in accord with the decisions made in a public works committee, the decisions appear more legitimate, and the semipublic nature of the agreement between governing officials and citizens makes government actions more transparent.

One additional consequence of Mexico's participatory transformation is more closely tied to citizen governance groups and other forms of participation in which the state is directly involved. Unlike many other forms of voice, citizen governance groups serve a *routinizing* function, making participatory influence more constant and manageable. Modes of participatory influence such as direct contact, public protest, and social movements are susceptible to the ebb and flow of mobilization cycles, which exist because of variation over time in the energy, perceived efficacy, and level of resources that participants are willing to devote to the cause. It is partly for this reason that protests and social movements often come in waves. Most commonly, these waves of protest peter out. But they also have an explosive potential, and it is notoriously difficult to know *ex ante* whether a protest or movement will fade away or escalate into a massive demonstration, a violent conflict, or another form of destabilizing and unwanted political activity (Kuran 1991).

In contrast, citizen governance groups help government officials regularize the ebb and flow of voice by providing an open outlet for it at regular intervals. Governance organizations cannot regularize voice completely: we would still expect public assemblies to be better attended, and more boisterous, when controversial local issues are on the agenda. Nevertheless, it seems likely that government officials would learn about discontent earlier, and in a less threatening manner, when they solicit information from citizen governance groups rather than learning of it for the first time via a confrontational public protest.[26] And by channeling voice into governance organizations, politicians may also gain agenda control, which they can use to help manage the cyclical nature of public expressions of grievance.

Finally, Mexico's participatory transformation has even had an effect in the electoral arena. This is doubly important, since it also explains the apparent (but spurious) relationship between competition and performance that I identified in chapter 4. Across the country, whenever we encounter a case of increased electoral competition, further investigation often shows that a quantitative and qualitative shift in mass participation has preceded, and in many cases directly caused, the changes in the electoral arena.

Paul Haber (2006) describes one such case, in the city of Durango (see also Arzaluz Solano 1995). By the early 1990s opposition victories in Mexico's larger urban municipalities were already fairly frequent. In fact Durango itself already had relatively competitive elections: the PAN won mayoral elections in 1983, and then the PRI won the next two elections in close races, winning 48 percent and 47 percent of the vote in

1986 and 1989, respectively. But the real sea change in Durango's politics came in 1992, when the Partido del Trabajo (PT, or Workers' Party) won the city's municipal elections (the PT would repeat the victory in 1995). The PT is a classic leftist party that was created from an alliance of several working-class and popular social organizations in the early 1990s. In fact, one of the driving forces behind the formation of the PT was the Popular Defense Committee of Durango (CDP, or Comité de Defensa Popular de Francisco Villa de Durango), which Haber (2006, 123–24) describes as the largest urban popular movement in all of Mexico. Thus political mobilization of the popular sector in Durango eventually led to a competitive electoral environment in that city and even helped spawn a minor party that currently competes in elections across the country.[27]

Haber traces the roots of the CDP back as far as the student movement of 1968.[28] Some members of that movement, inspired by Marxism and Maoism, came to Durango in the early 1970s with the intention of creating change by mobilizing the urban poor. These leaders were responsible for generating grassroots mobilization over several issues, including access to affordable potable water, urban land distribution (for settlement), and other issues of concern to Durango's urban poor. By 1979 the neighborhood-level organizations joined to form the CDP. From that point on the CDP became a major force in the politics of Durango, although it explicitly avoided entrance into the electoral arena. The strategic tool kit of the CDP was focused on "direct action," or face-to-face confrontation with a government official, landowner, or CTM labor leader.[29] But they would not trade votes for concessions from the government: "They made a very clear decision to resist the 'bait' of the political reforms enacted by the López Portillo administration [1976–82], which meant in practice that the CDP would not affiliate or cast votes as a bloc for a political party" (Haber 2006, 136). Instead, the CDP spent the bulk of the 1970s and 1980s mobilizing the urban poor and extracting concessions from government through protests, threats of protest, support for dissident labor union factions, and other participatory means.

This focus changed in 1986, when the leadership of the CDP decided to enter into electoral politics. Interestingly, Haber notes that one reason the leadership's position began to shift was the realization that "the conservative PAN received the majority of votes in many CDP strongholds" in the 1983 elections, which the PAN won (2006, 144). This phenomenon was actually fairly common in the 1980s. The PAN was one of the only well-established opposition parties that could actually put names on ballots, and citizens disgruntled with the PRI often cast votes for the PAN in protest, even if they did not agree with (or know about) the PAN's conservative orientation. In any event, the CDP first entered an electoral alliance with a small opposition party for the 1986 and 1989 elections and then helped to form the PT (as a national party with a strong base of support in Durango) prior to the 1992 elections (Haber 2006, 144–66). And, as mentioned above, the PT won Durango's mayoral elections in 1992 and 1995.

It is impossible to imagine that such an opposition victory would have been possible, either in 1983 or in the 1990s, without the mobilizational efforts of the CDP and its predecessor organizations. And it is important to note that electoral competition was not the original motivation of the mobilized groups. Social movements or other forms of mass mobilization typically arise in response to dissatisfaction with government policy, government responsiveness, or economic conditions; the turn to the electoral arena happens only later. This process has been observed throughout the country, particularly in many of the places where electoral competition first arose. For example, a movement based in the city of Juchitán, Oaxaca, known as the Coalition of Workers, Peasants, and Students of the Isthmus (Coalición Obrero Campesina Estudiantil del Istmo, COCEI), followed a path similar to that of the CDP in Durango. The COCEI was formed in the early 1970s and entered into the electoral arena only after significant internal debate in the early 1980s (see Rubin 1997, 1999).

In other cases, mass mobilization does not take the form of a headline-grabbing social movement but is rather less centralized, less elite driven, and more organic. In these cases, exogenous factors (like economic conditions and changes in government policies) lead to increased political mobilization among nonpartisan social groups, who eventually channel their energies toward support for existing political parties. This describes the rise of electoral support for the PAN in Chihuahua in the 1980s (see Chand 2001). According to research by Tarrés (1990), it also describes social mobilization in the middle-class neighborhood of Ciudad Satélite, outside Mexico City. Tarrés notes that electoral mobilization for the PAN occurred only after, and because of, "the development of a local parish organization and a Neighborhood Association during the first years of Satélite's history" (141). Similarly, in a study of community participation in antipoverty programs, Fox and Moguel (1995) note that the federal government began to emphasize participation in the early 1970s. Thus "this more inclusionary approach to social politics preceded the intensification of electoral competition in Mexico" (190). In all of these cases, it seems clear that increased electoral contestation did not arise randomly or as a direct response to poor government performance. Rather, masses were first mobilized for nonelectoral reasons, pursued their goals via nonelectoral strategies for some period of time, and then eventually shifted their activities into the electoral arena.

This chapter has illustrated several obstacles to electoral accountability in Mexico. Given the country's electoral institutions, voters are not able to directly punish politicians for poor performance or reward those who perform well. The evidence from Chihuahua shows that, even though in principle voters could coordinate on a strategy to reward or punish parties or to select good representatives, they do not do so with any regularity. Evidence such as the patterns of educational spending and the primacy of appearances in local politics shows that electoral pressures can easily produce perverse incentives, according to which politicians work hard to win elections but fail to improve government responsiveness in the course of doing so.

The second half of the chapter focuses on participatory politics. I argue that Mexico has undergone a qualitative shift in the style and effectiveness of mass participation. Mexican citizens are clearly more likely to adopt participatory strategies, and they are more likely to remain independent of old corporatist hierarchies while doing so. This has made participation in Mexico broader than it has been in the past. At the same time, it is important to recognize that some of this participation comes at the behest of local officials themselves; participation does not always happen purely from the bottom up. Government-induced participation does not necessarily make for more independence (though participation in citizen governance groups is clearly more free than was participation in corporatist organizations under the PRI), but it does play the important role of routinizing participation. Finally, the evidence clearly shows that the participatory transformation in Mexico preceded, and at least in some cases contributed to, the rise of electoral competition. In sum, this chapter has demonstrated that any adequate understanding of democratic responsiveness in Mexico has to consider the impact of participation on electoral competition and government performance.

CHAPTER SEVEN

Conclusion

The Sources of Democratic Responsiveness in Mexico

The Problem of Democratic Responsiveness

The introduction to this book justified the study of politics in Mexican municipalities by appealing to important and unsettled questions about the nature of democratic governance. It then proceeded to delve into the minutiae of municipal politics, offering lengthy discussions on the nature of public utility provision, party politics, citizen governance groups, and municipal financial structures. I do not regret this, since I believe that local-level political processes are interesting objects of study in their own right. But as I conclude this book, I run the risk of leaving the reader "stuck in the sewers," so to speak, with thoughts of water pipes and tax collectors, when my primary ambition is to address the broader themes of responsiveness, participation, and democratic politics. It is time to step back and look at the big picture.

This project began with a simple question: Do competitive elections make government more responsive to public preferences? There is certainly strong support for this sentiment in the literature. Studies of U.S. politics have been drawing an explicit link between elections and government responsiveness for at least fifty years.[1] The idea of electoral control also dominates the comparative literature. The comparative democracy project of scholars like Juan Linz, Arend Lijphart, Gary Cox, and G. Bingham Powell is at its core an elaborate effort to understand how electoral institutions can best be framed to maximize their efficiency at translating votes into good representation while securing minority rights and the rule of law.[2] Electoral theory has also influenced the field of democratization, which is dominated by a minimalist conception of democracy holding that the hallmark of democratization efforts (or at least the most important early step) is the installation of free and fair electoral institutions (Alvarez et al. 1996; Przeworski et al. 2000; Rogowski 1998). There are dissenters and skeptics, to be sure, who either see the diffusion of electoral institutions in nonliberal polities to be an outright harmful development (e.g., Zakaria 2003) or recognize at least that elections are far from sufficient to ensure the type of government that can comfortably be called democratic (e.g., O'Donnell 1994; Roberts 1998; Levitsky and Way 2002). Nevertheless, most scholars strongly agree that elections *are,* in fact, useful instruments of democracy in that they afford citizens some measure of control over their representatives in government. Importantly for the present investigation, this argument is frequently made with respect to Mexican elections (Rodríguez 1998; Mizrahi 1999; Coppedge 1993; Ibarra, Somuano, and Ortega 2006).

I do not doubt that elections are a positive force for democratic control in many cases, and none of the evidence presented in this book suggests that elections are uniformly impotent, let alone harmful. But I have certainly approached electoral understandings of democratic politics with a skeptical eye, for several reasons. In spite of the ease with which scholars cite and adopt them, electoral theories often have logical inconsistencies and require courageous assumptions. The formal flaws of elections as methods of preference aggregation are well known and have been for years (Black 1958; Arrow 1963; Riker 1982). Many studies adopt arguments about electoral accountability without acknowledging that these flaws exist and without carefully matching the requirements of the theory to the institutional reality of the country under study.[3] Assumptions about how much information voters and politicians have are often not met in practice. And studies of electoral accountability do not always consider the possibility that electoral pressures can have perverse effects. Empirical incongruities can be found at every turn as well. In Mexico and elsewhere, it is easy to observe cases in which objectively—and abjectly—poor performance is *not* met with electoral defeat. How can this be?

To complicate matters further, I introduced the idea of participatory influence, loosely based on Hirschman's (1970) concept of voice. Citizens typically have many participatory options at their disposal and are observed to use them in just about any political setting one can imagine. As I have used the term in this book, participation includes a broad array of political activities, from those that require large numbers, collective action, and organizational acumen to those that can be done individually, without much fanfare, and without many resources. These strategies can be deferential, cooperative, or confrontational. They can be undertaken once, perhaps in response to a particular problem, or can be used repeatedly, depending on the nature of the grievance and the resources of the actors. Most of these strategies have the advantage of communicating much more information to governing officials than can be inferred from an election return. For these reasons, some theorists suggest that participation, or what Cornelius (1974) calls "political demand making," not only can be an effective mechanism for democratic responsiveness but can even be more useful than electoral mechanisms in some settings. Accordingly, I have endeavored to investigate the possibility that variation in the amount of participatory pressure across Mexican municipalities can account for observed differences in democratic responsiveness.

Yet participatory mechanisms have their weaknesses as well, and it is important to approach them with the same critical stance that I use to study elections. This has led the investigation of the book in two useful directions. First, I developed a theoretical account that could explain how participation induces responsiveness. I focused on the ability of participation to improve the quality and quantity of information that politicians have about their constituencies, and on the social and psychological pressures that participation can place on those in official positions. The latter supposition suggests that participation will be more effective where social capital or social networks are stronger. But second, in the course of developing this explanation I exposed the difficulty of formulating a *purely* participatory explanation for government responsiveness. Many of the extant frameworks on which I built my own explanation, such as Hirschman's (1970), posit an interactive relationship between electoral and participatory strategies of influence. And even though I have departed from those frameworks to develop (and test) a participatory explanation that does not rely on an underlying or latent electoral mechanism, the intuition behind the interactive approach remains undeniably attractive. If there is any plausibility behind the idea that either electoral competition or participation can cause government to be more responsive, then it makes sense to wonder whether their interaction would also have an effect. Indeed, we might even argue that the two strategies serve complementary functions: participation provides officials with the information they need to perform well, and the electoral threat provides them an incentive to do so. If each strategy can compensate for the weakness of the other in this way, there are compelling reasons to search for evidence of this type of interactive effect.

Summary and Interpretation of the Findings

The theoretical discussion in this book has identified three potential explanations for democratic responsiveness: electoral competition, participation, and a combination of the two. Each of these explanations has its weaknesses and is open to certain objections. But I also found each of them sufficiently compelling to warrant further empirical investigation, which I undertook in chapters 4 through 6. So what does the evidence say?

Elections as Instruments of Democracy in Mexico

The most straightforward test of the electoral hypothesis that I could devise was to compare electoral competition and government performance across all Mexican municipalities for which I could find useful data. In using this approach, I temporarily set aside questions about specific mechanisms and the strategic motivations of actors and operated according to the simple premise that, no matter the logic of the explanation, if elections induce responsiveness, then levels of competitiveness and performance should correlate. The specific characteristics of the Mexican electoral transition, during which open competition began in some cases while others remained single-party dominant, were critical for making this an unambiguous empirical implication of electoral theory.

Of the two halves of this hypothesis, competitiveness was the easier to measure, given the plethora of available electoral data and the relatively tight theoretical fit between various election statistics and the concept of competitiveness. Government performance is somewhat harder to capture. To make sure that I had a good handle on this concept, I used multiple indicators, derived from two separate approaches to measurement, and I vetted each measure carefully in chapters 4 and 5. Using the public utility approach, I focused on each municipality's coverage for water and sewerage. Using public financial data, I determined that the best indicator is the amount of locally generated revenue per capita.

In spite of the frequency with which an electoral effect is posited or assumed, the data on government performance speak resoundingly against the hypothesis. Some readers might immediately focus on the econometric models reported in chapters 4 and 5, which are able to control for potential confounds and competing explanations and which have other advantages common to large-*N* analyses. But in my own view, the most powerful evidence with respect to the electoral hypothesis is presented in figure 4.2 and the related discussion. Not only does the illustration show that there is no real difference in the performance gap between competitive and noncompetitive municipalities over time; it also shows why it has been so easy for scholars to believe that a causal connection exists. In the year 2000, competitive municipalities did in fact have a significant advantage in service provision, suggesting that competition improved performance. But the figure clearly shows that this difference already existed in 1980 and 1990. Obviously, it would be impossible for electoral competition to explain variation in government performance when that variation existed prior to the rise of competition.

The econometric evidence also speaks decisively against the electoral hypothesis. As soon as appropriate controls are introduced, the apparent relationship between electoral competition and government performance disappears, suggesting that it was a spurious relationship to begin with. I believe that the evidence presented in chapters 4 and 5 is more than sufficient to demonstrate the robustness of this finding. Alternative specifications, different methods of measuring competition, and various diagnostic checks all tell the same story. To argue that the evidence lends any support at all to the electoral hypothesis, one would have to cherry-pick the few models that offer some support while ignoring the findings from better-specified models. And even then, the estimated effect of competition would remain substantively tiny. Obviously the analysis is limited to the performance of Mexican municipal governments in one particular time period, and the findings may have no bearing on the possibility of electoral accountability more generally. But at least within this domain, the conclusion is inescapable: electoral competition does not make Mexican municipal governments more responsive to the interests of their citizens.

This is a surprising finding, and it raises any number of questions. The skeptic might ask: If elections are so inconsequential, why do local-level Mexican politicians take them so seriously, working hard during campaigns, promoting their party's image at every opportunity, and trying to be, or at least appear, responsive and "in touch"? Why do voters seem so engaged with the electoral process? More generally, we might ask *why* the expected relationship does not exist. If elections really do fail to produce the outcomes expected of them, what goes wrong? The evidence presented in chapters 4 and 5 cannot provide a full answer. But in chapter 6 I was able to shed some light on these questions by focusing on specific mechanisms of electoral control and delving into the details of the municipal electoral arena in ways that are just not possible in a large-*N* correlational analysis.

One clear shortcoming of municipal elections in Mexico is that they do not always serve even the most basic function of giving voters an effective choice about who rules. Even today, elections in many municipalities remain noncompetitive, with a dominant single party and no real opportunity for alternation. Particularly among smaller and more rural municipalities, one can find many examples of authoritarian enclaves, where clientelism, intimidation, or even vote fraud restricts the effectiveness of elections. But that is not the issue at hand here. The findings in chapters 4 and 5 do not suggest that some governments perform poorly because their elections are not competitive. To the contrary, the evidence indicates that in general we should not expect performance to improve just because elections become more competitive.

The real problem for elections as instruments of democracy is what happens *after* freely competitive elections are established. For elections to be considered effective tools of democracy, they must do more than proportionally allocate government posts. They must also produce responsive behavior among the politicians they empower. This implies not only that poor performance in office gets punished but also that the replacement does better. Accountability leads to responsive government only when the electoral hammer *doesn't* drop. This will happen only when the politician perceives the electoral threat to be credible, which is to say, when the electorate has sufficient information, inclination, and ability to use the threat as a tool of control. In this sense Mexico's electoral institutions, and in particular the prohibition of reelection, are particularly incongruent with the assumptions of accountability theory. The term limit rule weakens the connection between representatives and their constituents, and other institutional rules and practices provide many incentives for individual politicians to behave in ways that do not promote the interests of their constituents.

In fact, one of the more interesting puzzles that I have attempted to describe in this book is the coexistence of electorally minded politicians at the helm of unresponsive local governments. Or, as Grindle (2007, 78) has stated the problem, there is "a strong sense of pressure to perform well, but little evidence that electoral competition resulted in better performance." Most Mexican politicians are quite aware of the exigencies of the electoral system, and in most respects they behave as we would expect and observe politicians to behave in any other electorally competitive democracy. But the incentives that the electoral environment presents to politicians, and the ways in which politicians commonly react to their strategic environment, do not produce policy or government output that could easily be classified as responsiveness. Rather, Mexican politicians often focus their efforts on pleasing party superiors rather than constituents, on sponsoring projects that maximize publicity but cost little, on shoring up their electoral base during the campaign season while neglecting the public interest during their terms, and so on. Local governments are often responsive, but it is far from clear that this responsiveness, where it exists, results from mechanisms of electoral accountability. Indeed, we often see evidence of electoral competition producing perverse incentives for politicians.

This book has not been able to identify a comprehensive list of the factors that contribute to the failure of electoral accountability in Mexico. But surely the lion's share of the problem is institutional. Municipalities in Mexico do not have the type of institutional variation that would be necessary to establish the point. But we can think theoretically about the likely effect of Mexico's current institutions, and we can consider case evidence that seems to speak to the question of institutional incentives.

Chapter 2 began this effort with a detailed theoretical discussion of the relevant political institutions and their likely effects. Clearly, the most important hurdle to electoral accountability is the term limit rule. The prohibition of reelection prevents voters from directly rewarding and punishing mayors for their performance in office. Just as importantly, it makes career-minded politicians beholden to their parties instead of their constituency. This does not necessarily preclude electoral control, but it certainly makes it more difficult. Additionally, three-year terms of office may compound the term limit problem by limiting the ability of municipal presidents to gain experience and practical expertise. Recall Peter Smith's characterization of career incentives (1979, 267), which I quoted in chapter 6: "it is not really necessary to acquire thorough mastery of all the details and requirements of your present office. Positions are won through contact, not merit," and in any event a politician should always be on the lookout for the next appointment or job. With only three years on the job, many mayors are only getting familiar with their basic duties when they begin to think about future appointments.

The institutional structures of municipal governments may also be less than ideal from a performance standpoint. One problem is *presidencialismo*. The *cabildo,* which includes the mayor and the other top administrative officials, is elected on a fused ticket, and although many municipalities now have provisions for proportional representation in the municipal councils, the opposition typically receives a token number of seats, and the mayor's party always maintains a majority on the municipal council. Since the mayor faces no real opposition from within the municipal government, he faces no (formal) incentive to compromise or build consensus. Another problem is the lack of institutional capacity. Fox and Aranda (1996) note that the trend toward decentralization in the 1990s may have had divergent effects from one municipality to the next. In municipalities that have resources, active citizens, and adequate bureaucratic structures, devolution of responsibilities to the municipal level can have positive developmental effects. But where resources and bureaucratic structures are lacking, devolution can have a negative impact. It is partly for this reason that Guillén López (1996) believes institutional reform to be more pressing than electoral reform in many municipalities.

None of this should be taken to mean that local representatives in Mexico are unaware of the electoral environment or their parties' need to win future elections. Nor do I mean to claim that these local politicians are uniformly unconcerned with good performance. But even when representatives are well intentioned, the nature of Mexico's electoral system and governing institutions stymies their efforts. Theoretically speaking, mechanisms of retrospective accountability are the most problematic with respect to institutional structure. Because of term limits, incumbents cannot be directly rewarded or punished. While many scholars simply transfer the object of accountability from the candidate to the party, we saw that in the 1998 gubernatorial election in Chihuahua the PAN lost in spite of its incumbent governor's popularity and positive reputation. Candidate selection mechanisms do not run afoul of the evidence as dramatically as the party-sanctioning mechanism does, but the balance of the evidence is mixed at best. Candidates often build the reputations that they need to attract prospectively oriented votes by pursuing publicity rather than performance, as the case of the ¡Manos a la Obra! project in Tijuana, Baja California, demonstrated. Our confidence in a selection-based explanation for democratic responsiveness should also be tempered by the empirical patterns established in chapters 4 and 5, since selection mechanisms are just as reliant on the existence of electoral competition as are accountability mechanisms.

Shifting the Emphasis to Participation

It is not difficult to understand why scholars and observers have paid such close attention to Mexican elections in recent years. In a regime whose motives, internal conflicts, and deliberative processes were opaque to most outside observers, elections often served as a window into the state of Mexico's transition toward democracy. Opposition victories in municipal contests in the 1980s were read as signs of an increasingly organized opposition and a tolerant regime. But a reversal of course in the mid-1980s led Wayne Cornelius (1986, 140) to conclude that, "from our present vantage point, it is hard to escape the conclusion that the political liberalization process in Mexico—at least as we have known it during the last 10 years—has reached a dead end." Opinions soon shifted again, as state- and federal-level opposition victories in the 1990s led many observers to speculate that true democracy was at hand. Finally, Fox's victory in 2000 was seen as unambiguous proof of democracy's arrival.

Reading these electoral tea leaves was important, no doubt. But developments outside the electoral arena have been just as momentous. A steady increase in social mobilization began in the 1970s, as is evident in the rise of social movements, autonomous civic organizations, opposition party organizations, and independent labor unions (Foweraker 1993; Collier 1992). The formation of the Corriente Democratica and Cuauhtémoc Cardenas's exit from the ruling party are evidence of exactly the type of elite split that O'Donnell and Schmitter (1986) have tied to authoritarian breakdown and democratization in other countries. Industrialization and the growth of the middle class, especially in the northern half of the country, reflect yet another potential source of political change. And the armed rebellion in the state of Chiapas, while never a serious military threat, articulated a clear challenge to the legitimacy of the single-party regime. All these factors have the potential to be significant causes of both transformations in local politics and the transition toward democracy at the national level. But all, with the possible exception of the Zapatista rebellion, have been somewhat neglected by political scientists interested in understanding the Mexican transition.

A closer look at Mexico's political transformation in recent decades reveals that social mobilization clearly preceded the rise of electoral competition and occurs independently of competition even today. I have argued in this book that the political engagement and participation engendered by this transformation is a plausible cause of observed improvements in government performance in Mexico. And in subjecting this hypothesis to empirical analysis, I have generated a large body of evidence that supports the idea. However, as has been clear throughout, the evidence with respect to the participatory hypothesis is not as tight as I would like it to be. For that reason, I think it is important to specify here what I have been able to establish, what I have not been able to establish, and the degree of confidence I can attach to each of these claims.

First, it is obvious that Mexican citizens use participatory strategies to try to influence local government all the time. Everything from letter writing to publicity seeking, direct contact with governing officials, the formation of community groups that press for action from government, and much more can be observed on a daily basis. More dramatic forms of participation, such as major street protests or local social movements, may happen with less frequency, but they are ubiquitous nonetheless (Stolle-McAllister 2005). I have personally observed citizens using these strategies virtually every time I have visited a municipal *presidencia,* as have many other scholars. So this much can be said with certainty: Mexican citizens frequently, and in some places routinely, use participatory strategies to try to influence government responsiveness.

I have also argued that participation in much of Mexico has undergone a qualitative shift that has two elements. Participation has become less deferential and obsequious. Citizens are more likely than they were in the past to view public officials as public servants rather than benefactors, and citizens confront them with demands rather than requests. Also, participation has become more autonomous. Even though it is often prompted by governing officials in public assemblies and other citizen governance groups, there is much less dependence on corporatist forms of mobilization. Recall that the PRI was always able to fill the Zocalo whenever it needed a public show of support. But that does not fit with what the comparative literature has come to view as a peculiarly democratic form of participation. Almond and Verba (1963, 21) distinguish the "participant" political culture from subject and parochial political cultures. The participant culture, which is "most congruent with . . . a democratic political structure," is distinctive in that people view themselves as citizens, rather than subjects, and so are more likely to believe that they can (and should) interact with their government in order to affect government policies and actions. Similarly,

Stokes (1995) identifies two types of participant actors in her study of Peruvian social movements. *Clients* are deferential toward authority, more accepting of hierarchical structures, and likely to view government services as a reward for loyalty or quiescence. *Radicals,* on the other hand, use the language of rights, think less hierarchically, and are more likely to view governing officials as public servants who are obligated by law and by norms to address their demands. Participation in Mexico is not always easy and it is certainly not costless. But the evidence that this book has shown and cited clearly indicates that participation in Mexico resembles this democratic ideal more than it used to.

This shift is important to recognize because it has had two significant effects on politics in Mexico. I argued in chapter 6 that increased social mobilization in Mexico eventually led to increased electoral competition in some cases. Evidence from Durango, Chihuahua, and other places showed a pattern in which citizens mobilized first with the intention to take direct, participatory action to resolve their grievances and shifted their energies into the electoral arena only later. Systematic testing of the effect of social mobilization and increased participation in the 1970s and 1980s on the rise of electoral competition in the 1980s and 1990s was beyond the scope of my investigation and impossible to conduct given the paucity of data on participation in the earlier time periods.[4] But the qualitative evidence supports the suggestion of a link. Further, if the relationship were true generally, it might account for the apparent (but spurious) relationship between electoral competition and government performance.

The second effect of increased participation in Mexico, and the effect that is most central to this book's argument, is that participation promotes improved performance in the municipalities. There can be no doubt that social mobilization has influenced government policy and political outcomes in many individual cases. Local protests prevented the federal government from building a new airport in Atenco, outside Mexico City (Stolle-McAllister 2005). Other participatory actions prevented the construction of a dam in Tetelcingo, Guerrero (Hindley 1999). A large body of literature documents similar successes, if on a smaller scale, in municipalities throughout the country (Cabrero Mendoza 2006; Rodríguez Wallenius 2006; Grindle 2007, 133–38). In these cases, the link between participation and the ultimate outcome is direct and obvious, making the counterfactual case easy to imagine. If people had not participated as they did, the airport would have been built, the dam would have been constructed, and so on. There is no ambiguity on this point. Grindle (2007) reaches the same conclusion. Even though her empirical findings are mixed regarding the impact of "civic activism," she concludes that activism "undoubtedly contributed to the delivery of . . . public works and social infrastructure" in all of the municipalities in her study. "The ongoing petitioning, lobbying, and reminders of commitments made to specific communities kept public officials from ignoring their responsibilities and promises" (142).

Yet there are also reasons to be cautious about what we can claim on behalf of the participatory hypothesis. One reason is that I have not been able to demonstrate that participation has a routine and systematic effect on responsiveness. The numerous case studies reported and cited in this book certainly attest to the plausibility of the argument. But it remains unknown how representative these cases are of the broader participatory scene. In fact, we know that major protest events are relatively rare and atypical. What do these cases tell us about the success of the more routine, day-to-day forms of participation like letter writing or direct contact with public officials? The only truly systematic evidence that I could bring to bear on this question was the inclusion of several measures of participation in the econometric models in chapters 4 and 5. The proxy indicators of participation that I used in those chapters are far from ideal, as I have already discussed. But they do have the advantage of being likely to capture small-scale and routine types of participation, rather than the more dramatic cases I have been discussing here. I used survey evidence and a pedigreed literature to argue that municipalities with higher levels of literacy, wealth, and turnout are likely to have higher potential for direct political participation. Therefore, the strong statistical relationship that I find between these factors and government performance is certainly consistent with the argument that participation causes responsiveness. But it does not prove the case beyond all reasonable doubts.

A second and broader reason to be cautious about the participatory argument is that certain characteristics inherent to participation may limit its effectiveness as an instrument of democracy. In fact, under certain conditions participation may even pervert the democratic process rather than nurturing it. The main problem is that there is no way to guarantee equality in the access to participatory opportunities, the amount of participation itself, or the seriousness and care with which government officials respond to participatory pressures. According to the arguments presented in this book, government will be responsive to the demands of those who participate if it is responsive at all. It is well known that different social groups participate unequally, within the electoral arena and without (Verba, Schlozman, and Brady 1995). So the groups that participate more often are likely to have a disproportionate effect (relative to their size) on how government responds. If we conceive of democracy as a form of government in which each citizen has an equal say (as is embodied in the principle of "one man, one vote"), this is a troubling result.

Furthermore, the potential for disproportionate influence is far greater outside the electoral arena, for the following reason. In an electoral setting, citizens are equally powerful in a formal sense. While differences in voter turnout routinely lead to a disproportionate influence in favor of wealthy, educated, and dominant groups, the problem is correctable in principle. Mandatory voting, vote mobilization, and other strategies may be used to increase turnout among traditionally disadvantaged groups. Importantly, such strategies are met with immediate formal success: if disadvantaged groups do vote, their votes are automatically included in the electoral result, and their votes automatically weigh as much as any other vote. All a citizen has to do is go to the polls.

With regard to nonelectoral forms of participation, there is no such recourse to formal equalization of voice. Whether because of social norms, anticipated campaign contributions, class solidarity, or some other reason, officials in most countries are likely to give greater consideration to a letter from the owner of a manufacturing concern than to one from an assembly line worker. And there is no formal mechanism by which the official can be forced to weigh each letter equally. Or consider the evidence I presented in chapter 6 on union strength and education spending in the Mexican states, based on Hecock's (2006) earlier analysis. I argued there that the positive relationship between CNTE strength and spending levels was evidence of a participatory effect. But is this really what we mean by democratic responsiveness? I do not think we can answer that question without knowing how the additional money is spent. If the funds are directed at students, whose educational attainment increases as a result, this would vindicate the union's participatory efforts. But if the money enriches union leaders, many would be disinclined to view their ability to extract resources as any sort of boon for democratic responsiveness.

Participation requires resources. A visit to a government office requires the financial ability to forego a day of labor; a letter to a governing official requires functional literacy. Therefore, we should expect those with political and economic resources to have disproportionate influence over government responsiveness. The potential for disproportionate influence, in turn, leaves bureaucracies open to capture by special interests, and the direct pressure placed on government agencies by nonelectoral participation can lead to inefficient and partial responsiveness rather than true interest representation (Brehm and Gates 1997, 175–80).

This is not a worry that should be taken lightly. But one effect of the participatory transformation that I described above has been to broaden participation across social sectors. The case evidence suggests that, while those with resources undoubtedly maintain an advantage, those on the lower end of the resource scale have been able to participate more frequently, and more effectively, than they have in the past. It is true that neoliberal reforms and the weakening of corporatist forms of interest representation have atomized many social groups, making participation more difficult among the poor, especially in rural areas (Kurtz 2004; Roberts 1998; Snyder 2001a). But it is also true that whatever participation exists has a more autonomous quality to it, stripped of the corporatist constraints that were intended to limit the effectiveness of participation to begin with.

Much recent scholarship has described an increasingly vibrant civil sphere in Mexico. Nongovernmental organizations are more numerous and more powerful; the press is freer; public debate is more frequent and open; labor unions and other interest group organizations have gained autonomy from the state's corporatist pillars. At the municipal level, I have argued that a new form (or at least a newly *active* form) of participation—citizen governance groups—has arisen in recent years, and several sources report that these organizations are improving government responsiveness.[5] In addition, the discussion in chapter 6 highlighted the routinizing function of citizen governance groups. If this is correct, then we should expect to observe *fewer* mass protests and conflictual types of social movements at the municipal level, even as we witness an overall increase in nonelectoral forms of participation and improved democratic performance. The evidence presented throughout this book lends some suggestive support to these conjectures.

A Nagging Suspicion about the Interaction of Competition and Participation

From the beginning, I recognized the potential for electoral competition and participation to work interactively in the production of government responsiveness. But I also took pains to construct a participatory explanation that did not rely on elections at all. Furthermore, the evidence presented in chapters 4 and 5 speaks unequivocally *against* the hypothesis. Yet I cannot shake the suspicion, in spite of evidence to the contrary, that these two mechanisms may still operate in combination, at least in some cases, to produce more responsive government in Mexico.

There are strong theoretical reasons to consider this hypothesis. Hirschman's (1970) formulation of the interaction is fluid and may not accurately capture the way the two strategies interact in Mexico. But it is revealing that his attempts to carve out a specifically voice-based explanation for responsiveness were not all successful. On closer inspection, the power that Hirschman attributed to voice was usually tied to a latent threat to use strategies of exit in the future. But the general idea of an interaction is intuitive and persuasive. Different actors may choose different strategies at the same time: public officials may need to heed participatory pressure from one group while simultaneously worrying about electoral mobilization from another. Or the same actor may use both strategies, either sequentially or at the same time.

Underlying such intuitions is the fact that elections and participation serve complementary functions. As I have stated it at other points in the book, elections give politicians the motivation to perform, and participation gives them the information they need to perform well. In other words, elections really do serve the single purpose of threatening the incumbent's (or in the Mexican case, the party's) position. But elections on their own provide little or no information about public policy preferences. Participation, on the other hand, always gives politicians specific information about the nature and intensity of grievances. Often, particularly within citizen governance groups, participation also gives citizens information about the efforts politicians have made and the constraints they may face in attempting to address a particular problem.

In fact, it is hard to consider the role that citizen governance groups play in municipal politics without viewing them as evidence of an interactive effect. It is possible that most mayors institute these participatory mechanisms purely because they feel pressure to perform well in office or because they fear that "unregulated" participation might spin out of their control. But it is also easy to imagine a mixed electoral motive for these types of reforms. In addition to providing forums for participation, citizen governance groups give public officials additional exposure to future likely voters, more information on what they can be doing now to win the voters' approval in the near future, and an opportunity to explain their actions, motivations, and preferences to their constituents. On an even more basic level, the convening of meetings and assemblies in and of itself may constitute the appearance of responsiveness, since it communicates (rightly or wrongly) to voters that the local official really does care about his or her job and constituents. The fact that citizen governance groups are created from the top down and the fact that opposition parties appear to be at the forefront of these sorts of local-level reforms both lend support to the supposition that citizen governance groups result from an electoral motive as well as a participatory impulse.

A final reason that we might continue to suspect an interactive effect, in spite of some disconfirmatory evidence, is that the two strategies seem to have a complicated and recursive relationship over time. As we have seen, social mobilization in places like Durango eventually led to the formation of opposition political parties that have competed in local elections. I also briefly mentioned the origins of Alianza Cívica, a civic organization that formed in response to the electoral openings of the late 1980s and early 1990s. The fact that one strategy often follows the other suggests that the actors who use these strategies find them wanting for the pursuit of certain goals. Evidently, for example, the CDP in Durango felt that its participatory strategies were not fully effective and that the turn to electoral competition would provide a strategic advantage. In fact, we know that the CDP's strategic decision followed directly from an internal debate on exactly this question. Similarly, groups that organize around elections, even political parties, occasionally see a need for participatory strategies, from letter-writing campaigns to mass protests. In sum, the fact that actors often use both strategies gives us reason to suspect that they are more effective when used in combination.

This book is a single-country study. But the themes I address here apply to politics far beyond the borders of Mexico. Most obviously, I hope that this book has demonstrated why democratic responsiveness is an important and interesting object of study. Democratic politics includes a long chain of causal relationships, starting with citizen's preferences and then translating those preferences into votes, votes into seats, seats into policies, and policies into tangible outcomes (Powell 2000, esp. 15). My sense is that some studies of democratic performance focus only on voting behavior and the formation of governments. This would be justified if we knew that politicians, once in office, always pursued the policies for which voters had empowered them, and with positive results. Yet of course this is not true. And the failure of some democratically elected governments to pursue good policy and provide good governance is especially troubling in unconsolidated democracies like Mexico's, where democracy may not last if it does not perform well. Thus the comparative study of democracy needs also to focus on the later stages of this causal chain, to determine whether and under what conditions democratic governments actually produce the types of outcomes that most scholars expect of them.

I hope that I have also demonstrated the importance of considering a broad range of theoretical approaches and of using empirical evidence to adjudicate among them. Specifically, this entails approaching elections with a greater degree of skepticism, as well as seeking to understand other facets of democratic practice, including social movements, voice, forms of corporatism, and other modes of interest representation. In the Mexican case, at least, my approach has produced a number of surprising findings, the most obvious being that electoral competition does not improve government performance. The Mexican case may not offer the fairest test of the general theory, since the institutional rules that hinder mechanisms of accountability in Mexico are quite rare. But as I have demonstrated, accountability theory informs the dominant view of elections in Mexico, in spite of the known institutional problems. Furthermore, not all of the problems with electoral control that I identified are specific to Mexico. In addition to the institutional rules like term limits, I discussed evidence that politicians pursued the appearance of responsiveness over the actual thing; that they sought publicity rather than good policy; that voters did not always make decisions on the basis of their evaluations of incumbent performance; and that electoral campaigns provided politicians with little information about the nature of their constituents' preferences. Surely, these factors describe democratic politics in other countries as well. I also found that Mexican citizens use a wide array of political strategies in their attempts to induce democratic responsiveness. In some cases they openly dismiss the effectiveness of elections and prefer any number of alternative participatory strategies. Surely this too describes democratic politics in other countries. Accordingly, I suggest that democratic responsiveness in general may rely more on participation and less on electoral competition than most scholars would predict.

APPENDIX

Fractionalization Indices as Measures of Electoral Competitiveness

This appendix demonstrates that in any set of elections in which the actual number of parties varies across cases, (1) fractionalization indices are not consistent indicators of electoral competitiveness, and (2) dichotomizing fractionalization indices does not produce a consistent or intuitive indicator no matter what threshold is chosen. I also compare the most commonly used index, Laakso and Taagepera's N, to alternative measures of competition.[1] Informally, I conceive of competitiveness as a sense of how safe the seat is for the winning party. More formally, we might define it as the probability that another random draw of votes would have produced a different winner. On either definition, I assume that there is some underlying distribution of voter preferences, from which any given electoral return is a single draw with a random component. As such, we know that (1) if the election were run again under the same conditions the outcome might be different but that (2) we can use the observed results to infer what the underlying distribution of preferences is likely to be. Any given statistic is a good measure of competitiveness to the extent that it captures this intuition about safeness or closeness.

To examine the properties of different measures in a systematic yet accessible way, I generated a series of twenty-five hypothetical vote distributions, which are listed in table A.1. I selected each distribution to seem plausible—I think that rough approximations of all of these distributions could be found within the electoral data set used in this book. But I also aimed for variation in the number of actual parties and the distribution of vote shares across parties. Obviously the sum total of vote shares in each case needs to be (and is) 100 percent. For simplicity, party A always wins, or at least ties, and remaining vote shares are then listed in decreasing order.

Table A.1. Alternative Measures of Competition

	Vote Distribution (Shares)				*Measures of Competition*				
Case	*Party A*	*Party B*	*Party C*	*Party D*	*N*	*N dichot-omized*	*NP*	*NP dichot-omized*	*M*
a	50	50			2.00	1	2.00	1	0
b	55	45			1.98	0	1.79	0	10
c	60	40			1.92	0	1.59	0	20
d	70	30			1.72	0	1.27	0	40
e	80	20			1.47	0	1.09	0	60
f	90	10			1.22	0	1.01	0	80
g	33	33	33		3.00	1	3.00	1	0
h	40	40	20		2.78	1	2.54	1	0
i	40	30	30		2.94	1	2.56	1	10
j	50	45	5		2.20	1	1.99	0	5
k	50	40	10		2.38	1	1.96	0	10
l	50	25	25		2.67	1	1.89	0	25
m	60	20	20		2.27	1	1.41	0	40
n	70	20	10		1.85	0	1.17	0	50
o	80	10	10		1.52	0	1.05	0	70
p	25	25	25	25	4.00	1	4.00	1	0
q	40	30	20	10	3.33	1	2.56	1	10
r	40	20	20	20	3.57	1	2.53	1	20
s	50	40	5	5	2.41	1	1.96	0	10
t	50	30	10	10	2.78	1	1.85	0	20
u	50	20	20	10	2.94	1	1.78	0	30
v	60	20	10	10	2.38	1	1.34	0	40
w	60	30	5	5	2.20	1	1.46	0	30
x	70	10	10	10	1.92	0	1.11	0	60
y	80	10	5	5	1.53	0	1.03	0	70

Note: N and NP are calculated according to formulas from Taagepera and Shugart (1989) and Molinar Horcasitas (1991). The dichotomized versions use a threshold of 2.00. M is the margin of victory measure introduced in chapter 4.

Source: Author's own calculations.

Next, for each case I calculate several statistics that might be used to indicate competitiveness. N is the familiar Effective Number of Parties Index (Laakso and Taagepera 1979), itself simply the inverse of the standard Hirschman-Herfindahl Index, and is calculated according to the formula $N = 1 / \Sigma p_i^2$. The next column dichotomizes N, using N = 2 as a cutpoint for the competitive category. The intuition here is that, even if small differences in N across cases do not always clearly relate to actual differences in competitiveness, there must be some way to use N to at least separate out the competitive cases from the noncompetitive cases. (We will see shortly that this assumption is false.) The next column reports Molinar Horcasitas's NP index, which he intends as a correction to some of the undesirable properties of N (1991). NP is calculated according to a far more complicated formula that weights the statistic against the size of the winning party (1991, 1384). Molinar argues that this produces a more intuitive indicator because it deemphasizes the influence of the winning vote share (which quickly drives N toward 1 as it increases) and because it makes the statistic less sensitive to small changes in minor party vote shares. In the next column I dichotomize NP just as I had dichotomized N, using NP = 2 as the cutpoint. Finally, I calculate the margin of victory (M), which is simply the difference between the vote shares for party A and party B.[2]

The first thing to note is that N does provide an intuitive indicator of how competitive elections are when there are two actual parties. For a virtual tie between two parties (case *a*), N = 2, and N decreases as the contest becomes more lopsided (cases *b* through *f*). It is a general property of N that when elections are tied among all parties that compete, N equals the number of actual parties (compare cases *a, g,* and *p*). For any other vote distribution, N is always less than the actual number of parties. The fact that N quickly decreases as the winning vote share gets larger is one reason that many scholars have thought it suitable as a measure of electoral competitiveness.

However, when more than two actual parties earn votes, the indicator shows several properties that are not desirable for a measure of competitiveness. One problem is that, holding constant the number of actual parties and the winning proportion, N increases as the vote shares among the losing parties are more equally distributed. Consider cases *j, k,* and *l*. In each of these cases, three parties compete and party A earns

50 percent of the votes. The N for these three cases ranges from 2.2 to almost 2.7, depending on how the remainder of the votes is distributed. But the measure marks as most competitive the case in which the two losing parties gained only 25 percent of the vote each—nowhere near what the winning party gained. In my view, case *j* is the most competitive because party B is well within striking distance of the winning party. But even if the reader wants to argue that a coalition of parties B and C in a future election would be equally formidable across these cases, it is hard to see how case *l* is more competitive than the other two. This too is a general property of N: since it is really intended as a measure of vote concentration, rather than electoral competitiveness, it assigns higher values as the nonwinning portion of the vote becomes more evenly distributed.

A second problem with N as an indicator of competitiveness is comparability across cases in which the actual number of parties differs. Consider now all cases in which party A wins 50 percent of the vote, regardless of how many parties compete. In the two-party case (*a*), the election is a virtual tie and cannot get any more competitive. In the three-party cases (*j*, *k*, and *l*), N ranges from 2.20 to 2.67, and increases as the margin of victory for party A increases. The four-party cases (*s*, *t*, and *u*) show a similar pattern, and N approaches 3 as the opposition vote becomes evenly distributed. To use N as a measure of competitiveness would indicate that case *a* (with a 50-50 distribution) was the least competitive race among these examples, while case *u* (with a 50-20-20-10 split) was the most competitive. Clearly, our intuitions about competitiveness (and the alternative measure, margin of victory) tell us exactly the opposite. Nor are these differences small: the N for case *u* is almost a full point higher than case *a*, on a scale that ranges from 1 to 4 or 5 in most actual applications.

Finally, for any reader still not convinced that N is an inconsistent measure of competitiveness, compare cases *c* and *x*.

Molinar's (1991) alternative to N might be an improvement in some respects, but it still produces counterintuitive results when comparing across cases with different numbers of actual parties. Comparing cases with the same number of actual parties, we can see that NP matches our intuitions about closeness better than N.[3] To look again at cases *j*, *k*, and *l*, note that NP decreases as the margin of victory increases. Whether the relative decrease in NP intuitively matches the degree of "decreased electoral competition" is open to interpretation, but at least the results are properly ordered. However, NP suffers from the same limitation as N when we need to compare across cases with different numbers of actual parties. Because NP (like N) has an upper bound that is equal to the actual number of parties (see cases *a*, *g*, and *p*), values for cases near the competitive end of the range tend to be influenced by the actual number of parties. Cases *a*, *g*, and *p* have vastly different scores on NP, even though all three cases are virtual ties. Similarly, the value of NP for cases *b*, *i*, *k*, *q*, and *s* ranges from 1.79 to 2.56, even though they are all basically close contests in which party A beat party B by ten points. The variation appears to be related to the potential threat of a coalition among losing parties, but the proper interpretation of these differences is not clear. (Why should cases *i* and *q*, or cases *k* and *s*, have the same scores?)

In many applications, including the current investigation, it might be sufficient to simply divide elections into two categories according to whether they are competitive. Theoretical considerations might suggest that any moderately competitive election can induce responsiveness and that we should not anticipate significant differences in responsiveness based on small perturbations in the size of M or N. According to such an argument, if we could at least separate out the cases with some minimal level of competitiveness, this would be a good start. Unfortunately, using N or NP for even this limited culling turns out to be an impossible task whenever the actual number of parties differs across cases.

If all elections were two-party contests, a cutpoint would be relatively easy to define. Looking at cases *a* through *f*, and armed with the knowledge about how close elections tend to be in whatever set of cases we are studying, we might decide that a cutpoint of 1.95, 1.9, or 1.8 would make sense. The decision would be arbitrary in a strict sense, but at least it would be consistent. If, for example, we decided that case *c* did not meet our criteria for a minimal level of competitiveness, then neither would cases *d*, *e*, or *f*.

But as soon as the actual number of parties begins to vary, identifying a consistent cutpoint becomes impossible. In table A.1, I report a dummy variable that indicates whether N is 2 or higher. On this decision rule, note that only a perfect tie is considered competitive whenever the actual number of parties is two. Note further that this decision rule is extremely permissive when the actual number of parties is higher than two: cases *m*, *v*, and *w* are counted as competitive even though party A has double or triple the vote share of its nearest competitor. The only results that qualify as noncompetitive are the extremely lopsided contests represented by cases *n*, *o*, *x*, and *y*. All other three- and four-party cases are classified as competitive. There is no way to reconcile these two characteristics of N (restrictiveness when there are two actual parties, and permissiveness when there are more than two). Considering the properties of N when the actual number of parties is two suggests that an appropriate cutpoint needs to be less than 2; but adjusting the cutpoint down makes the indicator even more permissive for cases with more than two actual parties. Using a cutpoint of 1.9 would (reasonably) allow us to consider cases *b* and *c* to be competitive but would also force us to call case *x* competitive, in spite of its 70-10-10-10 distribution.

Again, NP offers some improvement, but it is still far from ideal. The problem of an appropriate cutpoint for the set of cases with two actual parties remains: anything but a perfect tie produces an NP score of less than 2. And inconsistencies across cases with different numbers of actual parties are significant. For example, the dichotomized measure in table A.1 would have us label case *b* as noncompetitive, while case *r* is well above the threshold for competitiveness. Yet the gap between first and second place in case *r* is twice the size of the gap for case *b*. As with N, adjusting the cutpoint down provides no real solution.

I believe that the considerations detailed here are sufficient to show that fractionalization indices in general should not be used as measures of competitiveness. To be clear, my complaint here is only with this particular use of the statistic, not with the statistic itself. If the researcher is most concerned with legislative seat shares and potential coalition formation (as Taagepera and Shugart are), rather than competitiveness, then the properties of N and NP that I discuss here may be desirable. For example, suppose that the winning party desires to form a coalition to surmount a two-thirds supermajority requirement. In cases *j* and *k*, party A is limited to only one other party with whom it could bargain.

In case *l,* party A is in the advantageous position of having two bargaining partners. So in this example, the fact that N increases as the opposition vote is more evenly distributed matches our intuitions about how many effective parties there are in a system. It may also be worth pointing out that in this scenario comparison of cases *j, k,* and *l,* (or alternatively cases *s, t,* and *u*) shows N to be a preferable measure to NP. The effective number of parties index is a widely used statistic in the study of party systems and elections, for good reason. It is easy to calculate and easy to interpret, and it has many appropriate uses. However, measuring electoral competitiveness as I have defined it here is not something that N does well. Scholars are better served by other measures, including the intuitive and even-easier-to-calculate margin of victory.

NOTES

ONE What Good Are Elections in Mexico?

1. Electoral conceptions of democracy usually evoke Schumpeter's (1942/1950) formulation, though most add some qualifications: elections must be free and fair, the franchise must be sufficiently broad, and so on. Przeworski et al. (2000) and previous works by the same group of collaborators offer one of the most widely cited arguments in favor of "electoral minimalism." Munck and Verkuilen (2002) catalog several other studies with minimalist definitions and measures.

2. See, for example, the essays collected in Przeworski, Stokes, and Manin (1999).

3. The mechanical bias inherent in any process of aggregating votes has been studied in great detail by Arrow (1963), Rae (1967), Riker (1982), Taagepera and Shugart (1989), and many others. The potential for last-term shirking or other principal-agent problems has been pursued in the formal literature on accountability, including Barro (1973), Ferejohn (1986), and Myerson (1993). The thesis that elections require some sort of democratic political culture to be effective can be found in Zakaria (2003), and similar arguments can be found in several essays in Harrison and Huntington (2000); the broader argument that democracy requires a certain political culture has a long pedigree, including Almond and Verba (1963), Lipset (1960), and Inglehart (1988).

4. This last revelation is partly responsible for the recent literature on hybrid regimes and electoral authoritarianism. See O'Donnell (1994), Levitsky and Way (2002), and Diamond (2002).

5. I take the quoted term from Powell (2000).

6. Indeed, responsiveness may result from factors entirely unrelated to civic activity, such as the availability of resources or the skills and inclinations of government bureaucrats. I discuss this possibility in chapters 3, 6, and 7.

7. Strictly speaking, the PRI was created in 1946. The party known today as the PRI was first organized as the Partido Nacional Revolucionário (PNR) under president Plutarco Elías Calles in 1929. It was reorganized and renamed the Partido de la Revolución Mexicana (PRM) under President Lazaro Cárdenas in 1938 and finally received its current name under President Manuel Ávila Camacho in 1946. It is common practice to view these differently named organizations as a single, continuous political party (see Collier and Collier 1991; Craig and Cornelius 1995; Elizondo 2003).

8. The literatures are too vast to cite comprehensively. But for exemplary work that illustrates the claims made above, see the works cited in table 1.1 as well as the following: on accountability theory, see Key (1966), Fiorina (1981), and Przeworski, Stokes, and Manin (1999); for the "seats and votes" literature, Taagepera and Shugart (1989); and for democratic peace theory, Doyle (1986) and Russett (1993). Diamond (1999) offers a good summary discussion of many of these claims. Rodrik (1999) clearly recognizes that electoral competition is just one of several potential mechanisms that could explain the empirical link between democracy and wage rates. Zweifel and Navia (2000, 110) explain the empirical relationship between infant mortality and regime type by claiming that "in democracies, politicians concerned about reelection will not let their people starve." Several recent studies link electoral democracy to human rights, but often the two concepts are described as mutually constitutive or symbiotic; to the credit of this literature, it does not typically assume a direct causal link from elections to the protection of human rights and often recognizes the overlap between the two concepts (see Beetham 1999, esp. ch. 5; Hillman, Peeler, and Da Silva 2002; Griffith and Sedoc-Dahlberg 1997). Otherwise, the citations listed here hypothesize specifically about the effects of elections; were we to include claims made on behalf of "democracy" generally, the list would be even longer.

9. It might even be argued that government policy on some issues, such as those linked to difficult normative disagreements, is not objectively measurable even in principle. However, if we understand the concept of democracy strictly and seriously, then even intractable questions such as these might be resolvable by appealing to public opinion. This is the approach implicitly endorsed by much of the literature, in which the position of the median voter is the point of reference for all questions of policy responsiveness or government representativeness. See Stimson et al. (1995); Powell (2000).

10. Henceforth I will attempt to avoid the cumbersome term *nonelectoral participation* in favor of *participation,* with the understanding that this term denotes any voluntary political activity other than voting in elections. Of course voting *is* a form of participation, but my goal here is to distinguish voting from other forms of political activity (see Cornelius 1974, 1125; Verba, Schlozman, and Brady 1995, 39).

11. King, Keohane, and Verba (1994) have rightly been criticized for advising scholars to "increase their *N* " at any cost (see Brady and Collier 2004). But the subnational comparative method, properly used, increases the number of cases at a very low cost. For a good methodological discussion, see Snyder (2001b). An early endorsement of the subnational design with respect to Mexico is Menéndez-Carrión and Bustamante (1995). Several recent studies of Mexican politics have taken advantage of subnational or "intranational" comparative designs: see, among others, Hiskey (1999), Beer (2003), Fox and Aranda (1996), Hernández-Valdez (2000), Langston (2003), Snyder (2001a), and Díaz-Cayeros and Langston (2001). The method is increasingly common elsewhere as well, especially in large or federal countries. For example, Ames (2001), Setzler (2002), and Nylen (2002) all use some form of the method to study Brazil.

12. Most of the empirical work is based on this municipal-level analysis. I discuss some state-level issues in chapters 6 and 7.

13. This is a relative statement. As future chapters show, measuring government performance remains a challenge. But it is far easier to measure municipal-level performance in Mexico than it is to compare government performance across countries.

14. Of course, higher levels of government often infringe on the responsibilities and restrict the choices of municipal presidents. Intergovernmental issues are addressed in later chapters.

15. The data come from the Mexican Census, discussed in chapter 4. The percentages seem lower than the 1995 rates in figures 1.1 and 1.2 because they are averages per municipality and are not weighted for population.

16. Chapter 5 uses an alternative measure of government performance, based on the amount of revenue municipalities are able to generate from local sources. The local revenue evidence indicates a similar overall trend, with aggregate improvement over time but wide variation from one municipality to the next. Cabrero Mendoza and Martinez-Vasquez (2000, 144) summarize the shift from the late 1980s to the mid-1990s by concluding that "the expenditure shares of both state and municipal governments increased over time, but in an unsteady fashion."

17. Of course, politicians may have selfish (electoral) reasons for promoting this type of participation. I consider this possibility at various points in the book.

18. The distinction I describe here is similar to the one Stokes (1995) identified among the urban poor in Lima, Peru.

TWO Elections and Democratic Responsiveness

1. I use the term *electoral control* to refer to any instance in which elections are used as a means of empowering governments that are responsive to the public interest (Manin, Przeworski, and Stokes 1999b). I intend for this to be an umbrella term that encompasses retrospective accountability, prospective selection, and mixed mechanisms.

2. Some Mexicanists mark the student protests of 1968 as the beginning of Mexico's transition to democracy. This may be a useful starting point, but my interest here is more specifically tied to the rise of electoral competition. The current explosion of electoral competition began in the early 1980s, and this change was made possible by formal electoral reforms enacted in the late 1970s and subsequently.

3. According to Moreno (2003, 32–33), as recently as 2002 more Mexicans self-identified as PRI supporters (30 percent) than as PAN or PRD supporters (25 percent and 9 percent, respectively).

4. The conventional wisdom for many years was that Mexico was a democracy, albeit imperfect, even under the hegemonic PRI. This view has long since fallen out of favor, for good reason. (For a discussion of the view that Mexico was an "intraparty democracy," see Gruber 1971, 470.)

5. Another reform in 1988 increased the total number of deputies to five hundred, of whom two hundred are assigned by proportional representation. This is the Chamber's current configuration.

6. In general, concessions for legislative representation came earlier, and more easily, to the PRI. The party was more hesitant to accept defeat in elections to executive posts (mayor, governor, and of course president). Good general discussions include Lujambio (2000) and Méndez de Hoyos (2006).

7. It was a common strategy for the PRI to play on voters' fear of the "unknown" opposition. They portrayed opposition parties as extreme and inexperienced and often insinuated that the government would collapse if the opposition parties gained power. Magaloni (1999) suggests that this strategy was effective and that fear of the unknown is the primary reason the PRI was able to maintain its dominance in the 1980s and 1990s in spite of poor macro-

economic performance. One might guess that this strategy will be less effective in the future, but it was certainly used often in previous campaigns, including the 2000 elections.

8. The PAN claimed to have won the gubernatorial election in the state of Chihuahua in 1986, but the PRI candidate won according to official returns. As a compromise, the PRI candidate resigned (under pressure from Salinas), and an interim governor was appointed.

9. Prior to this reform, municipalities were technically nothing more than administrative units. Some scholars even argue that municipalities gained autonomous authority only in 1999, when a further constitutional modification was approved. In the article relevant to municipalities, the authority to "administer" *(administrar)* was changed to "govern" *(gobernar)*, and the qualifier was added that this "responsibility . . . will be exercised as an exclusive right" (Mexican Constitution, Article 115). Given the financial centralization of the Mexican system, the municipalities have always been somewhat beholden to the state and/or federal government. But municipalities began to act more autonomously pursuant to the 1983 reform, especially in the early 1990s. These issues are given a fuller treatment throughout the book, especially in chapter 5.

10. Executive branches dominate in all jurisdictional levels in Mexico. Like governors and the federal president, municipal presidents have few institutional checks on their power within the municipal government structure, though there can be power struggles between a mayor and his or her governor, especially when they belong to different parties.

11. See Fox (1994b); Gil Villegas (1996). For similar arguments in a broader Latin American context, see T. Campbell (2003), Nickson (1995), and Rehren Bargetto (1992).

12. Since 1964, the Mexican lower house has had a combination of single-member districts and proportional-representation (PR) seats. The total number of seats, as well as the number of each type of seat, has changed many times over the past forty years (see Lujambio 2000, 33–41). Currently, the congress has five hundred seats, three hundred of which are assigned to single-member districts and two hundred of which are awarded according to PR. Many states enacted similar reforms in the mid-1970s, adding a number of PR seats to the unicameral state legislatures (Lujambio 2000, 46–54).

13. See also Mizrahi (2003, 111).

14. Formal treatments of accountability tend to share this candidate-centered approach, perhaps because clear predictions of (group-based) party behavior are difficult to sustain (see Austen-Smith and Banks 1989; Myerson 1993; Harrington 1993; Fearon 1999).

15. See, for example, Sniderman, Brody, and Tetlock (1991, ch. 9). For a Mexican example, see Domínguez and McCann (1996).

16. Ackerman (2004, esp. 448–49) offers a set of critiques that overlap with these, and he also points out several additional problems with the idea of electoral accountability.

17. *Outcomes* can refer either to policies (like a minimum-wage law) or to the effects of policies (like the resultant unemployment rate). Selection mechanisms rely on expectations about outcomes, since outcomes have not been realized at the moment of electoral choice.

18. More recent work, such as Hansen (1998), has challenged A. Campbell et al.'s (1960) conclusion even within a policy-based perspective.

19. Obviously Riker's use of the term *populist* is different from contemporary usage in Latin America.

20. Some authors make a distinction between *vote maximizing*, in which a candidate values each additional vote, and *minimax* behavior, in which a candidate tries to maximize the probability that he will get a minimum winning plurality of the vote (Mayhew 1974, 46–47; see also Myerson 1993).

21. "Más vale lo malo conocido que lo bueno por conocer."

22. For recent empirical studies that report evidence of last-term shirking in the U.S. Congress, see Rothenberg and Sanders (2000) and Tien (2001).

23. In many cases, the legislative branch (at all levels of the federal system) has become more powerful in recent years (Beer 2003). Like much of the description contained in this section, the statement above is most accurate with respect to political reality during the 1980s and 1990s.

24. The survey is the 2001 Encuesta Nacional de Cultura Política. See Secretería de Gobernación (2002).

25. The institutional features I discuss here are uniform across Mexico, with two exceptions. The Federal District of Mexico City has an elected government, but it is neither a state nor a municipality, and its institutional structure is unique within Mexico. In the state of Oaxaca, several hundred municipalities govern themselves according to *usos y costumbres* (roughly translatable as "customary rule"), which differs significantly from the typical municipal system. Empirical analyses in later chapters exclude both the Federal District and Oaxaca's customary-rule municipalities.

26. The federal president and state governors serve six-year terms. Mayors, federal legislators, and state legislators serve three-year terms.

27. Carey (1996) offers the same speculation with regard to term-limited legislators in Costa Rica. He finds that they do indeed spend a great deal of energy promoting their party's interests while in office, since their future po-

litical appointments depend on their party's fortunes in the subsequent presidential election.

28. On the other hand, below I discuss counterevidence suggesting that party loyalty is not an important factor for most voters.

29. It is not clear whether these were open-ended or multiple-choice questions.

30. This national survey was conducted by the newspaper *Reforma* and is reported in Klesner (2001, 109).

31. These surveys were collected for a collaborative project with Susan C. Stokes and are reported in detail in Cleary and Stokes (2006). Although the research design called for a focus on four states instead of a national sample, we found that the pooled sample roughly matches the Mexican profile according to distributions on age, education, and social class. However, because of the inclusion of Baja California, the sample overrepresents PAN supporters. I feel comfortable using these data illustratively, but they should not be weighed too heavily.

32. The findings do not vary significantly according to which party the respondents identified as being "most important" in the locality.

33. In chapter 6 I discuss similar (and even stronger) findings reported by Yemile Mizrahi, based on a survey collected in Chihuahua state in 1998 (see Mizrahi 1999).

THREE Political Participation and Democratic Responsiveness

1. See Schumpeter (1942/1950). Pateman (1970), Putnam (2000), and others argue that this conception *originated* with Schumpeter, before whose work the participatory conception of democracy was more prevalent.

2. See Pharr and Putnam (2000), Putnam (2000), and Verba, Schlozman, and Brady (1995, esp. 529–32).

3. As in previous chapters, I will henceforth drop the cumbersome term *nonelectoral participation,* with the understanding that participation indicates political activity other than voting.

4. By *practical,* I mean that these are problems common to the world's existing electoral systems, though it would be possible in principle to devise electoral institutions that avoided them.

5. The literature to which I refer is obviously too broad and varied to cite comprehensively. Putnam (1993) and Verba, Schlozman, and Brady (1995) are two well-known studies that show different forms of participation to have positive effects.

6. Strictly speaking, the exit mechanism would require the nonincumbent competitor to actually perform better than the incumbent he or she was replacing. But even if this is not always the case, Lott and Reed (1989) show that in the long run the quality of incumbent politicians could be improved through a sorting mechanism, according to which poor performers were continually replaced, while good ones were continually reelected. The sorting mechanism would not be compatible with strict term limits.

7. This definition is consistent with Hirschman's own (see Hirschman 1970, 4). However, my understanding of exit and voice in a political context is slightly different from Hirschman's in that I understand the two strategies to be available (in principle) to all citizens. In his discussion of voice and exit in the political context, Hirschman implies that voice is an option only for party militants.

8. The "smoke detector" terminology is clearly meant to signal an amendment to the "police patrol" and "fire alarm" models of congressional oversight, introduced in McCubbins and Schwartz (1984).

9. This mechanism is compatible with Hirschman's (1970, 73–74) conjecture on the same point, cited above.

10. These "other ends" might be faithful service to the constituency, or they might involve rent seeking.

11. Stokes's story does not end there: the women's group were not satisfied with the offer of building materials and demanded that the ministry construct the building as well. Stokes does not report the ultimate outcome.

12. The other example is British Hong Kong. For further discussion of Mueller's thesis, see chapter 6.

13. I originally based these conjectures on interviews with several current and former municipal presidents from around Puebla that I conducted in June and July of 2002. These themes also recurred during three interviews I conducted with municipal officials in different towns in the state of Oaxaca in April 2008.

14. The mayor spoke in the plural because he was referring to his municipal cabinet.

15. Admittedly, however, the citizen's influence probably would not be as great as that of a known party member or supporter who lodged the identical complaint.

16. "Decline" in this example could be interpreted as an increase in the party's distance from the median voter or from its own median voter, or as a failure to accept reformist policies in the face of evidence that they would be successful (politically or economically).

17. If this expectation is true, we can expect voice to generate responsiveness even in liberal authoritarian systems that are relatively tolerant of public protest and dissent, even as they prohibit or manipulate elections. The Mexican regime of the 1980s and 1990s represents one such system.

18. I substantiate this claim in chapter 6.

FOUR Testing Hypotheses: The Public Services Approach

1. This does not mean that these hypotheses are generally and invariably true; rather, they are hypotheses that seem plausible, and that therefore might be tested, in a wide array of locations and levels of government.

2. Or more technically, "conditional on the existence of" a competitive electoral environment.

3. On my count there were 2,419 municipalities in Mexico circa the year 1999. The exact number varies slightly over time as municipalities are created anew or (less frequently) incorporated into neighboring municipalities. (For example, as of 2008 INEGI and other agencies report 2,436 *municipios.*) The data set is available from the author; all of the data can also be directly collected (or verified) from public sources. See Banamex (2001); de Remes (2000a); INEGI 1990, 2000); Secretaría de Desarrollo Social (1994). INEGI publishes census data in book format and also makes it easily accessible online. For many years the data were accessible through a system known as SIMBAD (Sistema Municipal de Bases de Datos), which could be found through the main INEGI Web site. This is how I accessed the data on multiple occasions in the early 2000s. SIMBAD is no longer operational, but the data are still accessible through the Web site, at www.inegi.org.mx.

4. Municipal presidents are roughly equivalent to U.S. mayors and are often referred to as mayors in this book. The Mexican *municipio,* however, is typically a county-sized area. Mexican municipalities are contiguous and comprehensive, covering all Mexican territory (except the federal district).

5. The questions are as follows: "Changing the subject, I would like to ask you, what in your opinion is the biggest problem in Chihuahua [Puebla]?" and "What is the principal problem of your district, neighborhood, or locality?" (Mizrahi 1999, 2000).

6. The four states in the former survey were Baja California, Chihuahua, Michoacán, and Puebla. We collected four hundred responses in each state.

7. Furthermore, even if we accepted the measure as accurate, analysis would be made difficult by the findings of Villarreal (2002), who shows that crime rates (specifically, homicide) are positively correlated to electoral competition. He suggests that interparty competition *causes* increased crime—surely not the effect intended by proponents of free and fair elections.

8. In previous versions of this research I also analyzed provision of electricity. I omit analysis of this variable here because electrification of homes (as opposed to "public lighting" of streets and parks) is the responsibility of the Federal Electricity Commission and because rates of provision are already close to 100 percent in 1990, leaving little statistical leverage for measuring improvements.

9. The *Conteo* is a "quick-count" that uses a hybrid technique combining raw data collection and statistical estimation. INEGI conducts these counts at the midpoint between census takings (1995, 2005, and so on). Several country specialists with whom I have raised the issue believe that these data are of poorer quality than census data, and I do not use them here.

10. Cox (1988) criticizes the use of M in studies of voter turnout, but his objection does not apply to the way I employ M here. Cox's main methodological objection is specific to cases in which turnout is the dependent variable (the problem is that the total effective vote is used to calculate both the independent and dependent variable). Furthermore, the problem is most serious when districts are of equal size, which greatly increases the chance of a spurious finding. Neither of these conditions holds in the present investigation: turnout (or any other variable in which "total votes cast" is part of the calculation) is not used here as a dependent variable; and the case units (municipalities) vary widely in terms of population size and total votes cast.

11. In fact, it seems likely that any fraud-based bias in the data would have the primary effect of *decreasing* the estimated effect of turnout, since the most common type of bias would be artificially high reported turnout in some poorly performing municipalities.

12. In principle it would be possible to use literacy and poverty rates to form a single index of "socioeconomic resources" or "propensity to participate." I favor the approach used here, in which the two variables are kept separate; but preliminary experimentation with an indexed version, including estimation based on factor analysis, generated results consistent with those shown below.

13. The actual numbers for 1980 are an average margin of 82.8 percent and a PRI vote share of 90.4 percent. Incredibly, the *median* margin of victory in 1980 is 1.0, indicating that one party (invariably the PRI) won 100 percent of the vote in over half of that year's elections.

14. We could obtain similar results with any of the competitiveness measures introduced in this chapter.

15. The model is $\ln (p_i / (1 - p_i)) = \beta_0 + \beta_1 x_i + \ldots + \beta_k x_i + \varepsilon_i$, where p is the proportional variable of interest and β_0 is the intercept term. The estimation consists of calculating $\ln (p_i / (1 - p_i))$ and then using OLS on this transformed variable. Where p equals 0 or 1, I first recode the value as 0.001 and 0.999, respectively.

16. Another plausible approach would be to model the difference in utility coverage between 1990 and 2000 rather than the rate of coverage in 2000 (while controlling for the 1990 rate). I do not believe that this model has any particular advantage, and may actually introduce new specification problems. For one, it would still be necessary to control for the 1990 level of coverage, meaning that the lagged rate would, in effect, appear on both sides of the equation. (In a slightly different context, Cox (1988) explains why this is problematic.) Additionally, the boundedness of the proportional variables would necessitate that we use the difference in log-odds ratios, rather than the straight percentage difference between the two years. This adds yet another layer of abstraction between the concept that we care about and the indicator used to represent it. For these reasons I am not confident that such a specification would be preferable; but I also note that substitution of the difference in coverage (in log-odds terms) on the left-hand side of the equation produces results comparable to those offered here (analysis not shown).

17. Achen (2000) shows that inclusion of a lagged dependent variable is often unjustified and can bias the coefficients for other independent variables. In this case the lag should be included because the rate of service provision in 2000 is the result of an additive process starting with the 1990 rate of provision.

18. While it is possible in principle to identify how much money went specifically to water and sewer projects, practical limitations have prevented me from doing so. Over five hundred thousand spending grants would have to be coded on the basis of the title and description of each grant.

19. I believe that inclusion of these dummies is appropriate to account for potential causal factors specific to each state. Analysis of the coefficients on these variables does not reveal any interpretable pattern across states. Removal of these variables from the model does affect the magnitude of some of the coefficients of interest; but in no case does the coefficient for competition approach statistical significance.

20. To convert the log-odds expected values into percentage terms, I reverse the log-odds equation and calculate $p = \exp(\hat{y}) / (1 + \exp(\hat{y}))$.

21. To illustrate the effects consistently, I reversed the percentile scores for poverty, so that the lowest percentile is equivalent to the highest level of poverty and vice versa. This makes it easier to illustrate the combined effect of poverty, literacy, and turnout.

22. For the split-sample analysis I counted a municipality as competitive if its average margin of victory for the 1990s was less than 20 percent or if it ever had party alternation in the mayor's office prior to 2000. The results presented in table 4.5 are robust to alternative methods for splitting the sample. The results are also consistent when I model conditional effects with interaction terms (interacting the margin of victory with the other measures of political influence). Computationally, the split-sample and interaction-term approaches are very similar; I prefer the split-sample approach because I find it easier to explain and interpret.

23. In models 2 and 3, I account for electoral competitiveness by splitting the sample, so I drop the competitiveness variable from the model. In model 2, the PAN and PRI dummies (and three state dummies) are dropped from the model because of perfect collinearity.

24. The coefficients for literacy and turnout in the two models are statistically indistinguishable, as are the joint effects of any combination of the four indicators of political influence.

25. I do not know the origin of this saying, but I first heard it attributed to Michael Dawson.

26. For example, I have altered the construction of the party variables; weighed the turnout variable to account for higher turnout in elections that are concurrent with state and federal elections; restricted the model to towns with populations greater than twenty thousand; and much else. Results are not always identical, but the main findings reported here are highly robust. To my knowledge no reasonable alternative specification, other than those discussed here, suggests a significant effect for electoral competition.

27. For those readers disinclined to refer to the Appendix, consider this simple illustration: suppose electoral results of 60-40 in municipality A, and 70-10-10-10 in municipality B. Most readers would agree that elections in municipality A are more competitive. Yet according to the standard fractionalization index, these municipalities are equally competitive, as they both generate an N of 1.92.

28. Utility provision can be a net drag on municipal finances if the cost of running the service exceeds the income generated in fees. In such cases, municipalities hesitate to expand coverage because it would drain more money from the municipal coffers (Rodríguez 1997; Díaz Cayeros and McClure 2000, 197).

29. *Squatters* might not be the best term for these settlers. Moctezuma reports that the residents purchased their land from a development company with ties to a local party official and were unaware that the sale was fraudulent, leaving them without legal title.

30. Hiskey uses the term *competitive electoral environment* where I use the term *democratic,* but we mean the same thing. Hiskey codes municipalities as competitive if they have had at least one party alternation in the mayor's office *and* an average vote share for the PRI of less than 65 percent over the 1989–95 period (Hiskey 1999, 146–47).

31. PRONASOL disbursements are commonly described as federal funds that were awarded directly to community groups, implying that state and local governments were left entirely "out of the loop." However, Victoria Rodríguez cautions that "almost all Solidarity [PRONASOL] programs were funded by both federal and state governments [based on matching funds arrangements], thus giving state government an important say in the allocation of these resources" (Rodríguez 1997, 102).

32. García del Castillo's data come from a survey of municipal treasurers taken in 1993 under a collaborative project between researchers at the Centro de Investigación y Docencia Económicas (CIDE) and INEGI. The author does not specify what type of "collaboration" is involved, but the most common forms of community collaboration are financial and labor contributions. Direct provision by the municipalities was by far the modal form of provision (58 percent for water, 48 percent for drainage), and agreements *(convenios)* with the state government were the second most common form of provision (more on this point below). Even contracting to a semiprivate or private corporation was relatively rare.

33. Municipalities are charged with *alumbrado publico,* or public lighting (see table 4.1). This refers to lighting of public parks and streets and not to the electrification of individual homes.

34. Similarly, Díaz-Cayeros and McClure (2000, 194) estimate that on average transfers account for 64 percent of municipal revenue and that local sources constitute the remaining 36 percent.

35. This might seem to be a huge exception. However, Rodríguez (1997, 102) reports that PRONASOL never accounted for more than 15 percent of federal investment spending in the states.

36. Author's interviews, Puebla, summer 2002. It is not clear, either from my interviews or from the secondary literature on this point, whether the source of this pressure to secure funding is related to a concern for the party's electoral future or a desire to respond to participatory pressures. But as I argued in chapter 3, mayors are just as likely to mention the latter motivation as they are the former.

37. With regard to estimation, state-level involvement actually raises two distinct problems: state influence as a causal factor in utility coverage rates, and state influence as a source of dependence across observations. This paragraph focuses on the first problem, but the second is also important to consider. If a state government with a finite budget funnels funds toward a particular municipality, then other municipalities will suffer financially as a consequence. Thus the funding available to each municipality, and potentially the resultant coverage rate, are not truly independent across municipalities within the same state. However, I do not believe that this will produce any significant bias in the results reported here. State-level influence is only a small part of the utility-provision process. Further, within-state dependence is explicitly modeled to the extent that it is reflected in municipal budget data (which includes most state-level financial transfers). If there are unmodeled sources of within-state dependence, they will affect only the efficiency of the estimates rather than the size of the coefficients. In analysis not shown, I repeated the main estimations with cluster-corrected standard errors (rather than "robust" Huber-White standard errors) and obtained comparable results.

FIVE Testing Hypotheses: The Public Finance Approach

1. I have also located an INEGI publication that reports similar data for several hundred municipalities for the years 1979–88, but an apparent problem of comparability to the later data series has thus far prevented me from combining the two data sources (see INEGI 1991).

2. To my knowledge, the only other study to relate municipal budget performance directly to electoral competition is a recent article by Ibarra, Somuano, and Ortega (2006). In contrast to the research reported here, these authors find a positive relationship between electoral competition and municipal financial capacity. The difference might be explained by the facts that Ibarra et al. use a different indicator for financial capacity (local revenue as a percentage of operating expenses, rather than local revenue per capita); that these authors focus on a sample of 142 municipalities; or that the specification of their causal model is different from mine.

3. The other plausible approach would be to analyze the proportion of the municipal budget devoted to operating expenses and public works investment (the two main spending categories reported by INEGI). However, it is difficult to derive clear empirical implications based on these statistics. For

example, one might think that a municipality aiming to improve its performance would increase its operating expenses for items such as computers, improved communications equipment, and a more professional staff. But spending on personnel is ambiguous: the municipality might be professionalizing its staff, or it might be hiring supporters as a form of patronage. Similarly, increased public works spending could be evidence of improved performance or of spending that was either wasteful (as in a public works boondoggle) or partisan (as in spending targeted at political supporters). In both cases, we might know that more money was being directed to a given budget line, but we could not infer that the money was being well spent. Given these ambiguities, I favor the local revenue approach presented here.

4. INEGI categorizes locally generated revenue according to four budget line items: *impuestos* (taxes), *derechos* (fees), *productos* (revenues from sale or lease of municipal assets), and *aprovechamientos* (fines and other sources). Locally raised revenue is simply the sum of these four line items. See Rodríguez (1997, 126–36).

5. It is important to recognize that transfers remain enormously important, even in municipalities with significant local revenue sources. The median municipality in the current sample counts on local sources for just over 11 percent of its total revenue; fewer than 1 percent of Mexican municipalities derive a majority of their revenue from local sources.

6. I have excluded all municipalities in the state of Oaxaca from this analysis. The majority (418 of 570) would have been excluded in any event, as they are governed by *usos y costumbres* arrangements. Among the remaining cases, there is an unusually large amount of missing data, resulting in as few as one or two valid observations for some municipalities.

7. I use the consumer price index inflation multiplier reported by the International Monetary Fund (2000), with 1995 as the base year.

8. Stationarity is difficult to discern here, because there are only eleven time points in the data. Visual inspection of figures 5.1 and 5.2 does not reveal any obvious trend. A Dickey-Fuller test for a unit root (which would indicate nonstationarity) offers weak evidence ($p = 0.09$) in favor of stationarity in the full-sample series illustrated in figure 5.1 (see Gujarati 1995, 719).

9. Local revenue as a percent of total revenue also fell after 1994, indicating that local revenue sources were more sensitive to this economic crisis than were federal transfers.

10. The interquartile range for all cases is forty-four pesos per capita, with a median of twenty-three and a mean of forty-five. Thus the differences illustrated in figures 5.1 and 5.2 are substantial, though not overwhelming.

11. As with previous simulations, I reverse the percentile score for the poverty rate so that all three effects of interest are running in the same direction.

12. Note that this method of splitting the sample recategorizes each municipality in each year; and thus the same municipality may appear in both samples for different years. Thus the number of cases (municipalities) listed for models 2 and 3 sum to a number higher than the total number in the sample. Note also that the PAN dummy is dropped from model 2 because of perfect collinearity: no cases exist in which the PAN holds the mayor's office *and* the municipality is coded as noncompetitive.

13. The F test of equivalence for the coefficients on poverty in models 2 and 3 suggests that we can reject the possibility of equivalence with 99 percent confidence ($p = 0.01$). Chow tests also suggest that the joint effect of the three variables is not significantly different in the two models.

14. The following discussion draws extensively and directly from Greene (1997) and Achen (2000).

15. I offered an analogous argument for the inclusion of the lagged dependent variable in the analysis in chapter 4, though I did not go into as much detail.

16. I have also studied two other possible remedies for the problem of influential outliers. First, I transformed the dependent variable into the natural log of local revenues per capita; this is often done to a variable with a large skew because it reduces the relative distance of the outliers from the more modal values, making them less likely to be "influential points." Second, I calculated df-beta statistics (Belsley, Kuh, and Welsch 1980) and dropped cases that were potentially influential according to this measure. In all cases, the results were consistent with other findings presented here: electoral competition is estimated to have either no effect or a very small one; literacy, turnout, and poverty consistently have larger effects, similar to those shown in the base model of table 5.1.

17. In effect this removes any case with more than 298 pesos per capita in local revenue generation. Changing the cutoff point to the ninety-eighth, ninety-seventh, or even ninety-fifth percentile does not affect the results shown here.

18. I trust that it need not be demonstrated here, but I use the postmodern scare quotes around the word *significant* because we know that an occasional finding with a p value of less than 0.05 is bound to happen by chance. Anyone who doubts this should generate twenty random variables in any standard statistical software program and regress them on each other.

19. Model 1 in table 5.1 explains 94 percent of the cross-unit variation but only 5 percent of the within-unit variation. Worse, fixed-effects estimations produce poor-fitting models in which no variable other than the lagged dependent variable obtains a significant coefficient and in which the proportion of the variance explained by the model is vanishingly small.

20. As with the previous models, Oaxacan municipalities are excluded from the analysis, and a few more are dropped because of missing data.

21. In 1990, for example, local revenue per capita correlated at 0.27 with water and 0.39 with sewerage.

SIX Electoral and Participatory Mechanisms in Action

1. Monographs about the state are too numerous to cite exhaustively. Good analyses of recent political history in Chihuahua include Aziz Nassif (2000), Langston (2003), Mizrahi (1999), Rodríguez and Ward (1992), Chand (2001), and numerous other books and articles by these same authors.

2. Some scholars believe that Barrio also won the 1986 race but was denied the office through electoral fraud. The first recognized victory for an opposition party in a governor's race was Ernesto Ruffo's win in Baja California, 1989.

3. This paragraph relies heavily on Langston (2003).

4. Recall that the Mexican federal system has three tiers: national, state, and municipal. Each of Mexico's thirty-one states has a legislature. Elections for municipal and state offices are held every three years (but for the governor only every six years), according to each state's electoral calendar, which typically does *not* coincide with the federal electoral calendar.

5. See also table 2.1.

6. Such a move would not have been without precedent, given Cuauhtémoc Cárdenas's split from the PRI in 1988, which has been imitated numerous times in state elections. Cárdenas left the PRI after being denied the presidential nomination for the 1988 election, and he ran under an opposition banner whose supporters eventually formed the PRD.

7. Interestingly, Langston (2003) reports that the PRI's national leadership had polling information telling them that Martínez could win not only the primary but also the general election.

8. I thank Doug Hecock for sharing his data set, which I analyze further in this section.

9. The six states in this category are Baja California, Baja California Sur, Guerrero, Hidalgo, Quintana Roo, and Yucatán.

10. In models 5 and 6 the estimated difference is much smaller, and the effect among competitive cases is statistically significant. But as in models 3 and 4, the coefficient for union militancy is significantly larger among noncompetitive cases.

11. Elite theory, generally, is the study of elite interaction in politics and society and is typically based on the belief that (1) all political systems have a ruling class (a.k.a. Robert Michels's "iron law of oligarchy") and that (2) studying the way these elite groups form and operate is the best way to gain insight into political and social events (Putnam 1976).

12. At the earliest, a few scholars might identify 1994 or 1997 as the real turning point, on the basis of the relative fairness of the federal elections in those years.

13. Of course, the massacre of several hundred protesting students at the Plaza de Tlatelolco in 1968 is one of many illustrations of the violent potential of the Mexican regime. Nevertheless, the Mexican regime was probably less violent toward its citizens than were most Latin American military dictatorships of the day.

14. The full formal name of these organizations was *juntas de mejoramiento moral, cívico, y material.* Similar organizations have existed to a greater or lesser degree throughout modern Mexican history, though they were often dormant or ineffective.

15. Fagen and Touhy (1972, 76) estimate that the junta's budget, derived from federal transfers, was substantially larger than the municipality's budget.

16. With the exception that Italian respondents reported slightly lower rates of anticipated success than Mexicans.

17. The percentage for Mexico is 52 percent, indicating either that Jalapa is not representative of most Mexican cities in this respect or that the two questions are of limited comparability. Still, a reported efficacy score of 10 percent is very low by just about any standard. See Almond and Verba (1963, 185).

18. The graph plots the average turnout rate for each year (limited to states that held local elections in that year), as well as a three-year running average (which amounts to the average turnout rate for all cases, based on their most recent election). A simple OLS regression of the year of the election on the turnout rate reveals a statistically significant predicted effect of about a 1 percent increase in turnout per year. It is also important to note that in-

creased turnout is not simply a function of increased competitiveness: I show in chapter 4 that the two indicators are only mildly correlated. Municipalities in Oaxaca that converted to *usos y costumbres* in the 1990s are excluded from these calculations.

19. Similar groups have been studied in other Latin American countries. In particular, scholars have focused a good deal of effort on *participatory budgeting* in Brazil (Avritzer 2002; Baiocchi 2003; Wampler and Avritzer 2004). Some Mexican citizen governance groups clearly follow the Brazilian model.

20. Grindle (2007, 91–93) reports that state and federal laws require the establishment of "municipal development committees" (*comités de desarrollo municipal,* or CDMs), which have functions similar to those that I ascribe to citizen governance groups here. But my emphasis is on the plethora of less formal groups that municipal presidents sometimes convene or establish to exchange information and consultation with citizens. Grindle reports that only a portion of the municipalities in her sample actually convened CDMs and that some who did also used the CDM to convene further meetings and organizations of the type I describe here.

21. To my knowledge, no systematic survey of the existence and uses of citizen governance groups has ever been undertaken in Mexico. But case studies of local governance routinely discuss them, local politicians I interviewed referenced them frequently, and some recent publications have begun to document their range and frequency. For example, Cabrero Mendoza et al. (2001) record basic information on a few dozen such organizations, and Rodríguez (1997, 124–26) discusses their importance. Rodríguez Wallenius (2006) describes three different groups, and Pineda Pablos and Rodríguez Camou (2007) document their existence in several cities in the state of Sonora.

22. I found this sentence difficult to translate. The original is "También disminuyó el temor a participar, y alentó un 'despertar' de la población para exigir derechos de beneficio colectivo y en defensa de lo que consideran suyo."

23. It remains possible that governing officials are still less receptive to complaints from poorer citizens, but at least in a formal sense the ability to participate is much more equal than in the past.

24. From author's interviews of two municipal presidents, state of Puebla, June 2002. Several other mayors used similar language when describing their goals and/or their perceptions of their responsibilities.

25. From the author's interviews of about ten sitting or former municipal presidents in the state of Puebla, June and July 2002.

26. The underlying logic of this argument is similar to Brehm and Gates's (1997) "smoke alarm" theory, described in chapter 3.

27. By no means is the PT a major party; it currently holds eleven seats in the federal congress (out of five hundred), five senate seats, and a handful of state- and local-level offices. Still, by most criteria it is the fifth or sixth largest party in the country.

28. This paragraph draws heavily from Haber (2006, ch. 4). Arzaluz Solano (1995) cites several studies that concur with Haber in identifying the origins of the CDP in Durango with the aftermath of the 1968 student movement.

29. Haber (2006, 133–34). The CTM is the Confederation of Mexican Workers (Confederación de Trabajadores de México), a PRI-affiliated confederation of labor unions and one of the central pillars of Mexican corporatism under the PRI.

SEVEN Conclusion

1. Among many others, see Downs (1957), A. Campbell et al. (1960), Key (1966), Barro (1973), Mayhew (1974), Fenno (1978), Fiorina (1981), and Ferejohn (1986).

2. See Linz and Valenzuela (1994), Lijphart (1992, 1994, 1999), Cox (1997), and Powell (2000).

3. On the Mexican case, see Balinski and Ramírez González (1999), who show that the 1997 federal electoral law has logical loopholes such that all of its provisions cannot simultaneously be met.

4. Other studies have attributed the rise of electoral competition in the municipalities to socioeconomic factors such as wealth, education, or inequality (Hernández-Valdez 2000). A complication of the process in Mexico is that after 1988 a large number of the newly competitive municipalities were relatively poor and rural towns that were contested between the PRI and the PRD, a finding that would conform to an elite-split explanation. Settling this issue is beyond the scope of the research presented here. But in the end each of these explanations may contribute to a fuller understanding of the rise of electoral competition in Mexican municipalities.

5. These sources include my own interviews with municipal officials in the state of Puebla and other accounts of such groups in Ackerman (2004), Hiskey (1999), T. Campbell and Katz (2004), Chand (2001), Rodríguez Wallenius (2006), and Selee and Santín del Río (2006), among others.

APPENDIX

1. See Laakso and Taagepera (1979). For other discussions of the limitations of N, see Taagepera and Shugart (1989) and Molinar Horcasitas (1991).

2. In the statistical analysis throughout the book I calculate M as a difference of proportions, bound by 0 and 1. Here I report it in percentage terms simply for ease of presentation.

3. On the other hand, notice the discrepancy in NP between cases *g* and *h*. Both cases are virtual ties, but the values of NP are significantly different.

WORKS CITED

Achen, Christopher H. 2000. "Why Lagged Dependent Variables Can Suppress the Explanatory Power of Other Independent Variables." Paper presented at the annual meeting of the Political Methodology Section of the American Political Science Association, Los Angeles, July 20–22.

Achen, Christopher H., and Larry M. Bartels. 2004. "Musical Chairs: Pocketbook Voting and the Limits of Democratic Accountability." Unpublished manuscript, Princeton University.

Ackerman, John. 2004. "Co-governance for Accountability: Beyond 'Exit' and 'Voice.'" *World Development* 32 (March): 447–63.

Alesina, Alberto, and Stephen E. Spear. 1988. "An Overlapping Generations Model of Electoral Competition." *Journal of Public Economics* 37:359–79.

Almond, Gabriel A., and Sidney Verba. 1963. *The Civic Culture: Political Attitudes and Democracy in Five Nations.* Princeton: Princeton University Press.

Alvarez, Mike, et al. 1996. "Classifying Political Regimes." *Studies in Comparative International Development* 31 (Summer): 3–36.

Ames, Barry. 1987. *Political Survival: Politicians and Public Policy in Latin America.* Berkeley: University of California Press.

———. 2001. *The Deadlock of Democracy in Brazil.* Ann Arbor: University of Michigan Press.

Arrow, Kenneth. 1963. *Social Choice and Individual Values.* 2nd ed. New Haven: Yale University Press.

Arzaluz Solano, Socorro. 1995. "Del movimiento urbano al gobierno local: El caso de la gestión del Partido del Trabajo en el municipio de Durango." In *La tarea de gobernar: Gobiernos locales y demandas ciudadanas,* edited by Alicia Ziccardi, 199–236. Mexico City: Instituto de Investigaciones Social, UNAM.

Austen-Smith, David, and Jeffrey S. Banks. 1989. "Electoral Accountability and Incumbency." In *Models of Strategic Choice in Politics,* edited by Peter Ordeshook, 121–48. Ann Arbor: University of Michigan Press.

Avritzer, Leonardo. 2002. *Democracy and the Public Space in Latin America.* Princeton: Princeton University Press.

Aziz Nassif, Alberto. 2000. *Los ciclos de la democracia: Gobierno y elecciones en Chihuahua.* Mexico City: CIESAS and Porrua.

Baiocchi, Gianpaolo. 2003. "Emergent Public Spheres: Talking Politics in Participatory Governance." *American Sociological Review* 68, no. 1:52–74.

Balinski, Michel, and Victoriano Ramírez González. 1999. "Mexico's 1997 Apportionment Defies Its Electoral Law." *Electoral Studies* 18, no. 1:117–24.

Banamex. 2001. *México electoral: Estadísticas federales y locales, 1970–2000.* CD-ROM. Mexico City: Banamex.

Barro, R. 1973. "The Control of Politicians: An Economic Model." *Public Choice* 14:19–42.

Baum, Matthew A., and David A. Lake. 2001. "The Invisible Hand of Democracy: Political Control and the Provision of Public Services." *Comparative Political Studies* 34 (August): 587–621.

Bazdresch Parada, Miguel. 1994. "Gestión municipal y cambio politico." In *En busca de la democracia municipal: La participación ciudadana en el gobierno local mexicano,* edited by Mauricio Merino, 25–59. Mexico City: El Colegio de Mexico.

Beer, Caroline. 2001. "Assessing the Consequences of Electoral Democracy: Subnational Legislative Change in Mexico." *Comparative Politics* 33, no. 4:421–40.

———. 2003. *Electoral Competition and Institutional Change in Mexico.* Notre Dame: University of Notre Dame Press.

Beer, Caroline, and Neil Mitchell. 2001. "Democracy and Human Rights: Elections or Social Capital?" Paper presented at the annual meeting of the Midwest Political Science Association, Chicago, April.

Beetham, David. 1999. *Democracy and Human Rights.* Cambridge: Polity Press.

Belsley, David A., Edwin Kuh, and Roy E. Welsch. 1980. *Regression Diagnostics: Identifying Influential Data and Sources of Collinearity.* New York: John Wiley.

Black, Duncan. 1958. *The Theory of Committees and Elections.* Cambridge: Cambridge University Press.

Boix, Carles, and Daniel N. Posner. 1998. "Social Capital: Explaining Its Origins and Effects on Government Performance." *British Journal of Political Science* 28, no. 4:686–93.

Booth, John A. 1995. "Introduction. Elections and Democracy in Central America: A Framework for Analysis." In *Elections and Democracy in Central America, Revisited,* edited by Mitchell A. Seligson and John A. Booth. Chapel Hill: University of North Carolina Press.

Brady, Henry E., and David Collier, eds. 2004. *Rethinking Social Inquiry: Diverse Tools, Shared Standards.* Lanham, MD: Rowman and Littlefield.

Brehm, John, and Scott Gates. 1997. *Working, Shirking, and Sabotage: Bureaucratic Response to a Democratic Public.* Ann Arbor: University of Michigan Press.

Brown, David S., and Wendy Hunter. 1999. "Democracy and Social Spending in Latin America, 1980–1992." *American Political Science Review* 93, no. 4:779–90.

Bruhn, Kathleen. 1997. *Taking on Goliath: The Emergence of a New Left Party and the Struggle for Democracy in Mexico.* University Park: Pennsylvania State University Press.

Cabrero Mendoza, Enrique. 1996. *Los dilemas de la modernización municipal: Estudios sobre la gestión hacendaria en municipios urbanos de México.* Mexico City: CIDE.

———. 2006. "Participación y deliberación en la acción pública local: La experiencia municipal." In *Democracia y ciudadanía: Participación ciudadana y deliberación pública en gobiernos locales mexicanos,* edited by Andrew D. Selee and Leticia Santín del Río. Washington, DC: Woodrow Wilson International Center for Scholars.

Cabrero Mendoza, Enrique, Rodolfo García del Castillo, Gilberto García Vazquez, and Luis Gómez Castro, eds. 2001. *Prácticas municipales exitosas.* Mexico City: CIDE.

Cabrero Mendoza, Enrique, and Jorge Martinez-Vazquez. 2000. "Assignment of Spending Responsibilities and Service Delivery." In *Achievements and Challenges of Fiscal Decentralization: Lessons from Mexico,* edited by Marcelo Giugale and Steven B. Webb, 139–76. Washington, DC: World Bank.

Cabrero Mendoza, Enrique, and Gabriela Nava Campos, eds. 1999. *Gerencia pública municipal: Conceptos básicos y estudios de caso.* Mexico City: CIDE.

Cabrero Mendoza, Enrique, and Isela Orihuela. 2000. "Expansión financiera y gestión hacendaria en municipios de México (1978–1997)." CIDE Documento de Trabajo, División de Administración Pública, no. 87, Mexico City.

Camp, Roderic Ai, ed. 2001. *Citizen Views of Democracy in Latin America.* Pittsburgh: University of Pittsburgh Press.

Campbell, Angus, et al. 1960. *The American Voter.* New York: John Wiley.

Campbell, Tim. 2003. *The Quiet Revolution: Decentralization and the Rise of Political Participation in Latin American Cities.* Pittsburgh: University of Pittsburgh Press.

Campbell, Tim, and Travis Katz. 2004. "The Politics of Participation in Tijuana, Mexico: Inventing a New Style of Governance." In *Leadership and Innovation in Subnational Government: Case Studies from Latin America,* edited by Tim Campbell and Harald Fuhr, 69–97. Washington, DC: World Bank.

Carey, John M. 1996. *Term Limits and Legislative Representation.* Cambridge: Cambridge University Press.

Carothers, Thomas. 1995. "Recent U.S. Experience with Democracy Promotion." *IDS Bulletin* 26 (April): 62–69.

———. 2002. "The End of the Transition Paradigm." *Journal of Democracy* 13, no. 1:5–21.

Chand, Vikram K. 2001. *Mexico's Political Awakening.* Notre Dame: University of Notre Dame Press.

Cleary, Matthew R. 2000. "Democracy and Indigenous Rebellion in Latin America." *Comparative Political Studies* 33, no. 9:1123–53.

———. 2003. "Competencia electoral, influencia ciudadana y desempeño del gobierno en los municipios mexicanos." *Política y Gobierno* 10, no. 1:183–217.

———. 2004. "Electoral Competition and Democracy in Mexico." PhD diss., University of Chicago.

———. 2007. "Electoral Competition, Participation, and Government Responsiveness in Mexico." *American Journal of Political Science* 51, no. 2:283–99.

Cleary, Matthew R., and Susan C. Stokes. 2006. *Democracy and the Culture of Skepticism: Political Trust in Argentina and Mexico.* New York: Russell Sage Foundation.

Collier, Ruth Berins. 1992. *The Contradictory Alliance: State-Labor Relations and Regime Change in Mexico.* Berkeley: International and Area Studies, University of California at Berkeley.

Collier, Ruth Berins, and David Collier. 1991. *Shaping the Political Arena.* Princeton: Princeton University Press.

Coppedge, Michael. 1993. "Parties and Society in Mexico and Venezuela: Why Competition Matters." *Comparative Politics* 25, no. 3:253–74.

Cornelius, Wayne A. 1974. "Urbanization and Political Demand Making: Political Participation among the Migrant Poor in Latin American Cities." *American Political Science Review* 68 (September): 1125–46.

———. 1986. "Political Liberalization and the 1985 Elections in Mexico." In *Elections and Democratization in Latin America, 1980–1985,* edited by

Paul W. Drake and Eduardo Silva, 115–42. San Diego: Center for Iberian and Latin American Studies, University of California, San Diego.

———. 1999. "Subnational Politics and Democratization: Tensions between Center and Periphery in the Mexican Political System." In *Subnational Politics and Democratization in Mexico,* edited by Wayne A. Cornelius, Todd A. Eisenstadt, and Jane Hindley, 3–16. San Diego: Center for U.S.-Mexican Studies, University of California, San Diego.

Cox, Gary W. 1988. "Closeness and Turnout: A Methodological Note." *Journal of Politics* 50, no. 3:768–75.

———. 1997. *Making Votes Count: Strategic Coordination in the World's Electoral Systems.* New York: Cambridge University Press.

Craig, Ann L., and Wayne A. Cornelius. 1995. "Houses Divided: Parties and Political Reform in Mexico." In *Building Democratic Institutions: Party Systems in Latin America,* edited by Scott Mainwaring and Timothy R. Scully, 249–97. Stanford: Stanford University Press.

Dahl, Robert A. 1956. *A Preface to Democratic Theory.* Chicago: University of Chicago Press.

———. 1971. *Polyarchy: Participation and Opposition.* New Haven: Yale University Press.

de Remes, Alain. 1998. "The Causes of Juxtaposition: A Theoretical Framework for the Study [of] Municipal and State Elections in Mexico." CIDE Documento de Trabajo, División de Estudios Políticos, no. 96, Mexico City.

———. 1999. "Gobiernos yuxtapuestos en México: Hacia un marco analítico para el estudio de las elecciones municipales." *Política y Gobierno* 6, no. 1:225–53.

———. 2000a. *Banco de datos electorales a nivel municipal, 1980–1999.* CD-ROM. Mexico City: CIDE.

———. 2000b. "Juxtaposition in Mexican Municipal Electoral Contests: The Silent Cohabitation." CIDE Documento de Trabajo, División de Estudios Políticos, no. 127, Mexico City.

Diamond, Larry. 1999. *Developing Democracy: Toward Consolidation.* Baltimore: Johns Hopkins University Press.

———. 2002. "Elections without Democracy: Thinking about Hybrid Regimes." *Journal of Democracy* 13, no. 2:21–35.

Díaz-Cayeros, Alberto, and Joy Langston. 2001. "The Consequences of Competition: Gubernatorial Nominations in Mexico, 1994–2000." Unpublished manuscript.

Díaz-Cayeros, Alberto, and Charles E. McClure Jr. 2000. "Tax Assignment." In *Achievements and Challenges of Fiscal Decentralization: Lessons from*

Mexico, edited by Marcelo Giugale and Steven B. Webb, 177–99. Washington, DC: World Bank.

Domínguez, Jorge I., and Chappell Lawson, eds. 2004. *Mexico's Pivotal Democratic Election: Candidates, Voters, and the Presidential Campaign of 2000.* Stanford: Stanford University Press.

Domínguez, Jorge I., and James A. McCann. 1996. *Democratizing Mexico: Public Opinion and Electoral Choices.* Baltimore: Johns Hopkins University Press.

Downs, Anthony. 1957. *An Economic Theory of Democracy.* New York: Harper and Row.

Doyle, Michael. 1986. "Liberalism and World Politics." *American Political Science Review* 80, no. 4:1151–69.

Durand Ponte, Víctor Manuel. 2004. *Ciudadanía y cultura política: México, 1993–2001.* Mexico City: Sigle Veintiuno Editores.

Eisenstadt, Todd A. 2004. *Courting Democracy in Mexico: Party Strategies and Electoral Institutions.* Cambridge: Cambridge University Press.

Elizondo, Carlos. 2003. "After the Second of July: Challenges and Opportunities for the Fox Administration." In *Mexico's Politics and Society in Transition*, edited by Joseph S. Tulchin and Andrew D. Selee, 29–53. Boulder, CO: Lynne Rienner.

Fagen, Richard R., and William S. Touhy. 1972. *Politics and Privilege in a Mexican City.* Stanford: Stanford University Press.

Fearon, James D. 1999. "Electoral Accountability and the Control of Politicians: Selecting Good Types versus Sanctioning Poor Performance." In *Democracy, Accountability, and Representation*, edited by Adam Przeworski, Susan Stokes, and Bernard Manin, 55–97. Cambridge: Cambridge University Press.

Fenno, Richard F. 1978. *Home Style: House Members in Their Districts.* Boston: Little, Brown.

Ferejohn, John. 1986. "Incumbent Performance and Electoral Control." *Public Choice* 50:5–25.

Fiorina, Morris P. 1981. *Retrospective Voting in American National Elections.* New Haven: Yale University Press.

Foweraker, Joe. 1993. *Popular Mobilization in Mexico: The Teachers' Movement, 1977–1987.* Cambridge: Cambridge University Press.

Foweraker, Joe, and Ann L. Craig, eds. 1990. *Popular Movements and Political Change in Mexico.* Boulder, CO: Lynne Rienner.

Fox, Jonathan. 1994a. "The Difficult Transition from Clientelism to Citizenship: Lessons from Mexico." *World Politics* 46:151–84.

———. 1994b. "Latin America's Emerging Local Politics." *Journal of Democracy* 5, no. 2 (April): 103–16.

———. 2007. *Accountability Politics: Power and Voice in Rural Mexico.* Oxford: Oxford University Press.

Fox, Jonathan, and Josefina Aranda. 1996. *Decentralization and Rural Development in Mexico: Community Participation in Oaxaca's Municipal Funds Program.* San Diego: Center for U.S.-Mexican Studies, University of California, San Diego.

Fox, Jonathan, and Julio Moguel. 1995. "Pluralism and Anti-poverty Policy: Mexico's National Solidarity Program and Left Opposition Municipal Governments." In *Opposition Government in Mexico,* edited by Victoria E. Rodríguez and Peter M. Ward, 189–204. Albuquerque: University of New Mexico Press.

García del Castillo, Rodolfo. 1999. *Los municipios en México: Los retos ante el futuro.* Mexico City: CIDE and Miguel Ángel Porrúa.

———. 2003. "La política de servicios municipals en México: Casos y tendencias recientes." In *Políticas públicas municipals: Una agenda en construcción,* edited by Enrique Cabrero Mendoza, 231–64. Mexico City: CIDE and Miguel Ángel Porrúa.

Garrido, Luis Javier. 1993. *La ruptura: La Corriente Democrática del PRI.* Mexico City: Grijalbo.

Gil Villegas, Francisco. 1996. "Descentralización y democracia: Una perspectiva teórica." In *Descentralización y democracia en México,* edited by Blanca Torres. Mexico City: El Colegio de Mexico.

Greene, William H. 1997. *Econometric Analysis.* 3rd ed. Upper Saddle River, NJ: Prentice Hall.

Griffith, Ivelaw L., and Betty N. Sedoc-Dahlberg, eds. 1997. *Democracy and Human Rights in the Caribbean.* Boulder, CO: Westview Press.

Grindle, Merilee S. 2006. "Modernising Town Hall: Capacity Building with a Political Twist." *Public Administration and Development* 26:55–69.

———. 2007. *Going Local: Decentralization, Democratization, and the Promise of Good Governance.* Princeton: Princeton University Press.

Gruber, Wilfried. 1971. "Career Patterns of Mexico's Political Elite." *Western Political Quarterly* 24, no. 3:467–82.

Guidry, John A., and Mark Q. Sawyer. 2003. "Contentious Pluralism: The Public Sphere and Democracy." *Perspectives on Politics* 1, no. 2:273–89.

Guillén-López, Tonatiuh. 1994. "Ayuntamientos y pluralidad política en los municipios fronterizos del norte de México." In *La autoridad municipal y su compromiso con la democracia,* edited by Centro Nacional de Desarrollo Municipal, 217–27. Mexico City: CEDEMUN.

———. 1995. "Presentación." In *El municipio y el desarrollo social de la frontera norte,* edited by Tonatiuh Guillén-López and Gerardo Manuel Ordóñez Barba, 7–11. Mexico: El Colegio de la Frontera Norte.

———. 1996. *Gobiernos municipales en México: Entre la modernización y la tradición política.* Mexico City: Miguel Angel Porrua.

Gujarati, Damodar N. 1995. *Basic Econometrics.* 3rd ed. New York: McGraw-Hill.

Haber, Paul Lawrence. 2006. *Power from Experience: Urban Popular Movements in Late Twentieth-Century Mexico.* University Park: Pennsylvania State University Press.

Hamilton, Alexander, James Madison, and John Jay. 1787–88/1992. *The Federalist Papers.* Cutchogue, NY: Buccaneer Books.

Hansen, John Mark. 1998. "Individuals, Institutions, and Public Preferences over Public Finance." *American Political Science Review* 92, no. 3:513–31.

Harrington, Joseph E. 1993. "Economic Policy, Economic Performance, and Elections." *American Economic Review* 83, no. 1:27–42.

Harrison, Lawrence E., and Samuel P. Huntington, eds. 2000. *Culture Matters: How Values Shape Human Progress.* New York: Basic Books.

Hecock, R. Douglas. 2006. "Electoral Competition, Globalization, and Subnational Education Spending in Mexico, 1999–2004." *American Journal of Political Science* 50 (October): 950–61.

Hernández-Valdez, Alfonso. 2000. "Las causas estructurales de la democracia local en México, 1989–1998." *Política y Gobierno* 7, no. 1:101–44.

Hillman, Richard S., John A. Peeler, and Elsa Cardozo Da Silva, eds. 2002. *Democracy and Human Rights in Latin America.* Westport, CT: Praeger.

Hindley, Jane. 1999. "Indigenous Mobilization, Development, and Democratization in Guerrero: The Nahua People vs. the Tetelcingo Dam." In *Subnational Politics and Democratization in Mexico,* edited by Wayne A. Cornelius, Todd A. Eisenstadt, and Jane Hindley, 207–38. San Diego: Center for U.S.-Mexican Studies, University of California, San Diego.

Hirschman, Albert O. 1970. *Exit, Voice, and Loyalty: Responses to Decline in Firms, Organizations, and States.* Cambridge, MA: Harvard University Press.

Hiskey, Jonathan T. 1999. "Does Democracy Matter? Electoral Competition and Local Development in Mexico." PhD diss., University of Pittsburgh.

Ibarra, Juan Fernando, Maria Fernanda Somuano, and Reynaldo Yunuen Ortega. 2006. "La competencia electoral y su impacto en el desempeño hacendario de los municipios en México." *Foro Internacional* 46, no. 3:465–92.

INEGI. 1980. *X censo general de población y vivienda.* Aguascalientes and Mexico City: INEGI.

———. 1990. *XI censo general de población y vivienda.* Aguascalientes and Mexico City: INEGI.

———. 1991. *Finanzas públicas estatales y municipales de México, 1979–1988.* Aguascalientes, Mexico: INEGI.

———. 2000. *XII censo general de población y vivienda.* Aguascalientes and Mexico City: INEGI.

Inglehart, Ronald. 1988. "The Renaissance of Political Culture." *American Political Science Review* 82, no. 4:1203–30.

Inglehart, Ronald, Miguel Basáñez, Jaime Díez-Medrano, Loek Halman, and Ruud Luijkx, eds. 2004. *Human Beliefs and Values: A Cross-Cultural Sourcebook Based on the 1999–2002 Values Surveys.* Mexico City: Sigle XXI Editores.

International Monetary Fund. 2000. *International Financial Statistics.* CD-ROM. Washington, DC: International Monetary Fund.

Kalandadze, Jekaterina. 2006. "(In)efficient Revolutions: Obstacles to Democratization in the Hybrid Regimes of Georgia and Ukraine." Unpublished manuscript, Syracuse University Department of Political Science.

Key, V. O., Jr. 1966. *The Responsible Electorate: Rationality in Presidential Voting, 1936–1960.* Cambridge, MA: Harvard University Press.

King, Gary, Robert O. Keohane, and Sidney Verba. 1994. *Designing Social Inquiry: Scientific Inference in Qualitative Research.* Princeton: Princeton University Press.

King, Gary, Michael Tomz, and Jason Wittenberg. 2000. "Making the Most of Statistical Analyses: Improving Interpretation and Presentation." *American Journal of Political Science* 44, no. 2:347–61.

Kitschelt, Herbert, Zdenka Mansfeldova, Radoslaw Markowski, and Gábor Tóka. 1999. *Post-communist Party Systems: Competition, Representation, and Interparty Cooperation.* Cambridge: Cambridge University Press.

Klesner, Joseph L. 2001. "The End of Mexico's One-Party Regime." *PS: Political Science and Politics* 34, no. 1:107–14.

Kuran, Timur. 1991. "Now Out of Never: The Element of Surprise in the East European Revolution of 1989." *World Politics* 44:7–48.

Kurtz, Marcus J. 2004. *Free Market Democracy and the Chilean and Mexican Countryside.* Cambridge: Cambridge University Press.

Laakso, Markku, and Rein Taagepera. 1979. "'Effective' Number of Parties: A Measure with Applications to West Europe." *Comparative Political Studies* 12 (April): 3–27.

Langston, Joy. 2003. "Rising from the Ashes? Reorganizing and Unifying the PRI's State Party Organizations after Electoral Defeat." *Comparative Political Studies* 36, no. 3:293–318.

Laso de la Vega, Jorge. 1987. *La Corriente Democrática: Hablan los protagonistas.* Mexico City: Editorial Posada.

Levitsky, Steve, and Lucian Way. 2002. "The Rise of Competitive Authoritarianism." *Journal of Democracy* 13, no. 2:51–65.

Lijphart, Arend, ed. 1992. *Parliamentary versus Presidential Government.* New York: Oxford University Press.

———. 1994. *Electoral Systems and Party Systems: A Study of Twenty-seven Democracies, 1945–1990.* New York: Oxford University Press.

———. 1999. *Patterns of Democracy: Government Forms and Performance in Thirty-six Countries.* New Haven: Yale University Press.

Linz, Juan J., and Arturo Valenzuela. 1994. *The Failure of Presidential Democracy.* Baltimore: Johns Hopkins University Press.

Lipset, Seymour Martin. 1959. "Some Social Requisites of Democracy: Economic Development and Political Legitimacy." *American Political Science Review* 53:69–105.

———. 1960. *Political Man: The Social Bases of Politics.* Baltimore: Johns Hopkins University Press.

Lott, John R., Jr., and W. Robert Reed. 1989. "Shirking and Sorting in a Political Market with Finite-Lived Politicians." *Public Choice* 61, no. 1:75–96.

Lujambio, Alonso. 1995. *Federalismo y congreso en el cambio político de México.* Mexico City: UNAM.

———. 2000. *El poder compartido: Un ensayo sobre la democratización mexicana.* Mexico City: Oceano.

Magaloni, Beatriz. 1999. "Is the PRI Fading? Economic Performance, Electoral Accountability, and Voting Behavior in the 1994 and 1997 Elections." In *Toward Mexico's Democratization: Parties, Campaigns, Elections, and Public Opinión,* edited by Jorge I. Domínguez and Alejandro Poiré, 203–36. New York: Routledge.

Manin, Bernard, Adam Przeworski, and Susan C. Stokes. 1999a. "Elections and Representation." In *Democracy, Accountability, and Representation,* edited by Adam Przeworski, Susan Stokes, and Bernard Manin, 29–54. Cambridge: Cambridge University Press.

Manin, Bernard, Adam Przeworski, and Susan C. Stokes. 1999b. "Introduction." In *Democracy, Accountability, and Representation,* edited by Adam Przeworski, Susan Stokes, and Bernard Manin, 1–26. Cambridge: Cambridge University Press.

Mayhew, David R. 1974. *The Electoral Connection.* New Haven: Yale University Press.

McCubbins, Matthew D., and Thomas Schwartz. 1984. "Congressional Oversight Overlooked: Police Patrols versus Fire Alarms." *American Journal of Political Science* 28, no. 1:165–79.

McKelvey, Richard D. 1975. "Policy Related Voting and Electoral Equilibrium." *Econometrica* 43, no. 5/6:815–44.

Méndez de Hoyos, Irma. 2006. *Transición a la democracia en México: Competencia partidista y reformas electorales, 1977–2003.* Mexico City: FLACSO and Fontamara.

Menéndez-Carrión, Amparo, and Fernando Bustamante. 1995. "Purposes and Methods of Intraregional Comparison." In *Latin America in Comparative Perspective: New Approaches to Methods and Analysis,* edited by Peter H. Smith, 59–80. Boulder, CO: Westview Press.

Mizrahi, Yemile. 1999. "Los determinantes del voto en Chihuahua: Evaluación del gobierno, identidad partidista, y candidatos." CIDE Documento de Trabajo, División de Estudios Políticos, no. 106, Mexico City.

———. 2000. "Las elecciones en puebla: La continuidad de la dominación Priísta." CIDE Documento de Trabajo, División de Estudios Políticos, no. 112, Mexico City.

———. 2003. *From Martyrdom to Power: The Partido Acción Nacional in Mexico.* Notre Dame: University of Notre Dame Press.

Moctezuma, Pedro. 2001. "Community-Based Organization and Participatory Planning in South-East Mexico City." *Environment and Urbanization* 13, no. 2:117–33.

Molinar Horcasitas, Juan. 1991. "Counting the Number of Parties: An Alternative Index." *American Political Science Review* 85, no. 4:1383–91.

———. 1993. *El tiempo de la legitimidad.* 2nd ed. Mexico City: Cal y Arena.

Molinar Horcasitas, Juan, and Weldon, Jeffrey A. 1994. "Electoral Determinants and Consequences of National Solidarity." In *Transforming State-Society Relations in Mexico: The National Solidarity Strategy,* edited by Wayne A. Cornelius, Ann L. Craig, and Jonathan Fox, 123–41. San Diego: Center for U.S.-Mexican Studies, University of California, San Diego.

Moreno, Alejandro. 2003. *El votante mexicano: Democracia, actitudes políticas y conducta electoral.* Mexico City: Fondo de Cultura Económica.

Mueller, John. 1992. "Democracy and Ralph's Pretty Good Grocery: Elections, Equality, and the Minimal Human Being." *American Journal of Political Science* 36, no. 4:983–1003.

———. 1999. *Capitalism, Democracy, and Ralph's Pretty Good Grocery.* Princeton: Princeton University Press.

Munck, Gerardo, and Jay Verkuilen. 2002. "Conceptualizing and Measuring Democracy: Evaluating Alternative Indices." *Comparative Political Studies* 35, no. 1:5–34.

Myerson, Roger B. 1993. "Incentives to Cultivate Favored Minorities under Alternative Electoral Systems." *American Political Science Review* 87, no. 4:856–69.

Nacif, Benito. 1996. "Political Careers, Political Ambitions and Career Goals." CIDE Documento de Trabajo, División de Estudios Políticos, no. 51, Mexico City.

Needler, Martin C. 1970/1982. *Mexican Politics: The Containment of Conflict.* New York: Praeger.

Nickson, R. Andrew. 1995. *Local Government in Latin America.* Boulder, CO: Lynne Rienner.

Noll, Roger G., and Andrew Zimbalist. 1997. *Sports, Jobs, and Taxes: The Economic Impact of Sports Teams and Stadiums.* Washington, DC: Brookings Institution Press.

Nylen, William R. 2002. "Testing the Empowerment Thesis: The Participatory Budget in Belo Horizonte and Betim, Brazil." *Comparative Politics* 34, no. 2:127–46.

O'Donnell, Guillermo. 1994. "Delegative Democracy." *Journal of Democracy* 5, no. 1:55–69.

O'Donnell, Guillermo, and Philippe Schmitter. 1986. *Transitions from Authoritarian Rule: Tentative Conclusions about Uncertain Democracies.* Baltimore: Johns Hopkins University Press.

Olson, Mancur. 1965. *The Logic of Collective Action.* Cambridge, MA: Harvard University Press.

Olvera, Alberto J. 2004. "Civil Society in Mexico at Century's End." In *Dilemmas of Political Change in Mexico,* edited by Kevin Middlebrook, 403–39. London: Institute of Latin American Studies and Center for U.S.-Mexican Studies.

Pateman, Carole. 1970. *Participation and Democratic Theory.* New York: Cambridge University Press.

Pharr, Susan J., and Robert D. Putnam, eds. 2000. *Disaffected Democracies: What's Troubling the Trilateral Countries?* Princeton: Princeton University Press.

Pineda Pablos, Nicolás, and Eliseo Rodríguez Camou. 2007. *De las buenas intenciones a las cuentas claras: Planeación, desempeño, y rendición de cuentas en seis municipios de Sonora.* Hermosillo, Mexico: El Colegio de Sonora.

Plott, Charles. 1967. "A Notion of Equilibrium and Its Possibility under Majority Rule." *American Economic Review* 57:787–806.

Powell, G. Bingham, Jr. 2000. *Elections as Instruments of Democracy: Majoritarian and Proportional Visions.* New Haven: Yale University Press.

Przeworski, Adam, and Fernando Limongi. 1993. "Political Regimes and Economic Growth." *Journal of Economic Perspectives* 7, no. 3:51–69.

Przeworski, Adam, Susan C. Stokes, and Bernard Manin, eds. 1999. *Democracy, Accountability, and Representation.* Cambridge: Cambridge University Press.

Przeworski, Adam, et al. 2000. *Democracy and Development: Political Institutions and Well-Being in the World, 1950–1990.* Cambridge: Cambridge University Press.

Putnam, Robert D. 1976. *The Comparative Study of Political Elites.* Englewood Cliffs, NJ: Prentice Hall.

———. 1993. *Making Democracy Work: Civic Traditions in Modern Italy.* Princeton: Princeton University Press.

———. 2000. *Bowling Alone: The Collapse and Revival of American Community.* New York: Simon and Schuster.

Rae, Douglas W. 1967. *The Political Consequences of Electoral Laws.* New Haven: Yale University Press.

Ramírez Sáiz, Juan Manuel, ed. 1998. *¿Cómo gobiernan Guadalajara? Demandas ciudadanas y respuestes de los ayuntamientos.* Mexico City: Instituto de Investigaciones Sociales, UNAM.

———. 2000. "Introducción." In *Cambio político y participación ciudadana en México: Actores, movimientos y organizaciones,* edited by Juan Manuel Ramírez Sáiz and Jorge Regalado Santillán, 9–23. Mexico City: Centro de Estudios de Política Comparada.

Rehren Bargetto, Alfredo. 1992. "El gobierno local en la ciencia política." *Política* (Santiago, Chile), no. 29:87–108.

Riker, William H. 1962. *The Theory of Political Coalitions.* New Haven: Yale University Press.

———. 1982. *Liberalism against Populism: A Confrontation between the Theory of Democracy and the Theory of Social Choice.* Prospect Heights, IL: Waveland Press.

Roberts, Kenneth M. 1998. *Deepening Democracy? The Modern Left and Social Movements in Chile and Peru.* Stanford: Stanford University Press.

Rodríguez, Victoria E. 1997. *Decentralization in Mexico: From Reforma Municipal to Solidaridad to Nuevo Federalismo.* Boulder, CO: Westview Press.

———. 1998. "Opening the Electoral Space in Mexico: The Rise of the Opposition at the State and Local Levels." In *Urban Elections in Democratic Latin America* Henry, edited by A. Dietz and Gil Shidlo, 163–97. Wilmington, DE: SR Books.

Rodríguez, Victoria E., and Peter M. Ward. 1992. *Policymaking, Politics, and Urban Governance in Chihuahua: The Experience of Recent PANista Governments.* Austin, TX: Lyndon B. Johnson School of Public Affairs.

Rodríguez Wallenius, Carlos. 2006. "Experiencias municipals de participación y deliberación en México: Hacia la construcción de una democracia territorial de proximidad." In *Democracia y ciudadanía: Participatión ciudadana y deliberación pública en gobiernos locales mexicanos,* edited by Selee and Santín del Río, 181–90. Washington, DC: Woodrow Wilson International Center for Scholars.

Rodrik, Dani. 1999. "Democracies Pay Higher Wages." *Quarterly Journal of Economics* 114 (August): 707–38.

Rogowski, Ronald. 1998. "Democracy, Capital, Skill, and Country Size: Effects of Asset Mobility and Regime Monopoly on the Odds of Democratic Rule." In *The Origins of Liberty,* edited by Paul W. Drake and Matthew D. McCubbins. Princeton: Princeton University Press.

Rosenstone, Steven J., and John Mark Hansen. 1993. *Mobilization, Participation, and Democracy in America.* New York: Macmillan.

Rothenberg, Lawrence S., and Mitchell S. Sanders. 2000. "Severing the Electoral Connection: Shirking in the Contemporary Congress." *American Journal of Political Science* 44, no. 2:316–25.

Rubin, Jeffrey W. 1997. *Decentering the Regime: Ethnicity, Radicalism, and Democracy in Juchitán, Mexico.* Durham: Duke University Press.

———. 1999. "Zapotec and Mexican: Ethnicity, Militancy, and Democratization in Juchitán, Oaxaca." In *Subnational Politics and Democratization in Mexico,* edited by Wayne A. Cornelius, Todd A. Eisenstadt, and Jane Hindley, 175–206. San Diego: Center for U.S.-Mexican Studies, University of California, San Diego.

Russett, Bruce. 1993. *Grasping the Democratic Peace: Principles for a Post-Cold War World.* Princeton: Princeton University Press.

Schumpeter, Joseph A. 1942/1950. *Capitalism, Socialism, and Democracy.* New York: Harper and Row.

Secretaría de Desarrollo Social. 1994. *Hechos en solidaridad.* CD-ROM. Mexico City: SEDESOL.

Secretería de Gobernación. 2002. *Encuesta nacional de cultura política y prácticas ciudadanas 2001.* Mexico City: Poder Ejecutivo Federal, Ciudad de México.

Selee, Andrew D., and Leticia Santín del Río, eds. 2006. *Democracia y ciudadanía: Participatión ciudadana y deliberación pública en gobiernos locales mexicanos.* Washington, DC: Woodrow Wilson International Center for Scholars.

Setzler, Mark H. 2002. "Democratizing Urban Brazil: Voters, Reformers, and the Pursuit of Political Accountability." PhD diss., University of Texas at Austin.

Smith, Peter H. 1979. *Labyrinths of Power: Political Recruitment in Twentieth-Century Mexico.* Princeton: Princeton University Press.

Smulovitz, Catalina, and Enrique Peruzzotti. 2000. "Societal Accountability in Latin America." *Journal of Democracy* 11 (October): 147–58.

Sniderman, Paul M., Richard A. Brody, and Philip E. Tetlock. 1991. *Reasoning and Choice: Explorations in Political Psychology.* New York: Cambridge University Press.

Snyder, Richard. 2001a. *Politics after Neoliberalism: Reregulation in Mexico.* New York: Cambridge University Press.

———. 2001b. "Scaling Down: The Subnational Comparative Method." *Studies in Comparative International Development* 36, no. 1:93–110.

Stimson, James A., Michael B. Mackuen, and Robert S. Erikson. 1995. "Dynamic Representation." *American Political Science Review* 89, no. 3:543–65.

Stokes, Susan C. 1995. *Cultures in Conflict: Social Movements and the State in Peru.* Berkeley: University of California Press.

———. 2001. *Mandates and Democracy: Neoliberalism by Surprise in Latin America.* Cambridge: Cambridge University Press.

Stolle-McAllister, John. 2005. *Mexican Social Movements and the Transition to Democracy.* Jefferson, NC: McFarland.

Taagepera, Rein, and Matthew Soberg Shugart. 1989. *Seats and Votes: The Effects and Determinants of Electoral Systems.* New Haven: Yale University Press.

Tarrés, María Luisa. 1990. "Middle-Class Associations and Electoral Opposition." In *Popular Movements and Political Change in Mexico,* edited by Joe Foweraker and Ann L. Craig, 137–49. Boulder, CO: Lynne Rienner.

Tarrow, Sidney. 1994. *Power in Movement: Social Movements, Collective Action, and Politics.* Cambridge: Cambridge University Press.

Taylor, Michael C. 1997. "Constitutional Crisis: How Reforms to the Legislature Have Doomed Mexico." *Mexican Studies/Estudios Mexicanos* 13, no. 2:299–324.

Taylor, Michelle M. 1992. "Formal versus Informal Incentive Structures and Legislator Behavior: Evidence from Costa Rica." *Journal of Politics* 54 (November): 1055–73.

Tien, Charles. 2001. "Representation, Voluntary Retirement, and Shirking in the Last Term." *Public Choice* 106, no. 1:117–30.

Tomz, Michael, Jason Wittenberg, and Gary King. 2003. "Clarify: Software for Interpreting and Presenting Statistical Results." Unpublished manuscript, http://gking.harvard.edu/clarify.

Tsai, Lily L. 2007. "Solidary Groups, Informal Accountability, and Local Public Goods Provision in Rural China." *American Political Science Review* 101, no. 2:355–72.

Tulchin, Joseph S., and Andrew D. Selee. 2003. "Introduction." In *Mexico's Politics and Society in Transition,* edited by Joseph S. Tulchin and Andrew D. Selee. Boulder, CO: Lynne Rienner.

Ugalde, Luis Carlos. 2000. *The Mexican Congress: Old Player, New Power.* Washington, DC: Center for Strategic and International Studies Press.

Van Cott, Donna Lee. 2005. *From Movements to Parties in Latin America: The Evolution of Ethnic Politics.* Cambridge: Cambridge University Press.

Vanderbush, Walt. 1999. "Assessing Democracy in Puebla: The Opposition Takes Charge of Municipal Government." *Journal of Interamerican Studies and World Affairs* 41 (Summer): 1–27.

Verba, Sidney, and Norman H. Nie. 1972. *Participation in America: Political Democracy and Social Equality.* New York: Harper and Row.

Verba, Sidney, Kay Lehman Schlozman, and Henry E. Brady. 1995. *Voice and Equality: Civic Voluntarism in American Politics.* Cambridge, MA: Harvard University Press.

Villarreal, Andres. 2002. "Political Competition and Violence in Mexico: Hierarchical Social Control in Local Patronage Structures." *American Sociological Review* 67 no. 4:477–98.

Wampler, Brian, and Leonardo Avritzer. 2004. "Participatory Publics: Civil Society and New Institutions in Democratic Brazil." *Comparative Politics* 36, no. 3:291–312.

World Bank. 1999. *World Development Indicators.* CD-ROM. Washington, DC: World Bank.

World Values Survey 2000 Official Data File, v. 7. 2000. World Values Survey Association. Aggregate File Producer, ASEP/JDS, Madrid. www.worldvaluessurvey.org.

Zakaria, Fareed. 2003. *The Future of Freedom: Illiberal Democracy at Home and Abroad.* New York: W.W. Norton.

Ziccardi, Alicia, ed. 1995. *La tarea de gobernar: Gobiernos locales y demandas ciudadanas.* Mexico City, Mexico: Instituto de Investigaciones Social, UNAM.

Zweifel, Thomas D. and Patricio Navia. 2000. "Democracy, Dictatorship, and Infant Mortality." *Journal of Democracy* 11 (April): 99–114.

INDEX

Matthew R. Cleary

is assistant professor of political science in the Maxwell School of Citizenship and Public Affairs, Syracuse University.
He is coauthor of *Democracy and the Culture of Skepticism: Political Trust in Argentina and Mexico.*